T0278616

Praise for *Saved By*

"The incredible story of Celina Karp Biniaz, a child of the Shoah who was a witness to the greatest Nazi horrors. It took many miracles for Celina to survive Płaszów the most notorious concentration camp in Poland where Amon Goth, 'the most evil SS Nazi murderer', was the commander. During her brief stay in Auschwitz, when she was only 13 years old, she confronted Dr. Josef Mengle, 'the angel of death.' She was one of the youngest children saved by Schindler and his wife. This book is a precious gift about an amazing woman, who still teaches us how to remain human, despite all the evil in our time. As she always says in her talks, 'Don't hate, try to see the good in people. Nobody is better than anyone else.'"
—Harold Kasimow, George A. Drake Professor of Religious Studies Emeritus Grinnell College, Grinnell, Iowa

"It is hard to fathom that this story was almost never told. Celina Biniaz's eyes have seen the darkest of evil, the deepest of generosity, the greatest of courage, and the most inspiring of miracles. *Saved By Schindler* is a relevant, timely reminder of the need to stand up against injustice, no matter the risks."
—Debbie Bornstein Holinstat, *NY Times* bestselling author, *Survivors Club: The True Story of a Very Young Prisoner of Auschwitz*

"Bill Friedricks has done a superb job writing this very readable biography of Celina Karp Biniaz who after her 8th year lived through the most horrendous childhood imaginable but was able to mature into a well-educated, compassionate woman and caring teacher to all she has encountered."
—Robbie Winick, President Emeritus, Iowa Jewish Historical Society

"Deeply researched and well written, *Saved By Schindler* details the horrors of the Holocaust, but maybe more important, it captures survivor Celina Biniaz's dogged determination to rise above this past and carve out a well-lived, impactful life."

—David Wolnerman, last known Holocaust survivor in Des Moines, Iowa

"Long reluctant to share her story, Celina Biniaz now gives generously of her memories and wisdom. As the U.S. Holocaust survivor population dips below 50,000, this new biography of an eyewitness to Nazi genocide is precious indeed."

—Elinor Brecher, Author, *Schindler's Legacy: True Stories of the List Survivors*

SAVED BY SCHINDLER

THE LIFE OF
CELINA KARP BINIAZ

WILLIAM B. FRIEDRICKS

ICE CUBE PRESS, LLC
NORTH LIBERTY, IOWA, USA

To the Iowa Jewish Historical Society

Contents

Photographs appear following pages 84 & 158

ACKNOWLEDGMENTS

THE FIRST TIME I HEARD Celina Karp Biniaz speak was in September 2017. A Holocaust survivor and one of the last living members of "Schindler's List," the eighty-six-year-old told her powerful and poignant story, highlighting the roles of three people—businessman Oskar Schindler, nun Mater Leontine, and filmmaker Steven Spielberg—who transformed her life forever. Celina's presentation was captivating, and I was also struck by her poise and sense of humor. The venue was noticeably cold because of a malfunctioning air conditioning system and after she was introduced, Celina broke the ice, so to speak, by asking, "Can you hear me, because my teeth are chattering?" With that she immediately connected with all of us in the audience.

Following the program, I emailed Sandi Yoder, the director of the Iowa Jewish Historical Society (IJHS), the sponsor of the event, and told her how impressed I was with Celina. Sandi and I had known each other for years and worked together on a couple of previous programs. I had also placed and supervised several Simpson College student interns at the IJHS.

Roughly two years later, Sandi invited me to another IJHS program and asked if I could stay afterward to talk about a possible book on Celina. The late David Gradwohl, a professor emeritus of anthropology at Iowa State University and one of the founding members of the IJHS, originally suggested the organization produce a slim book on Celina, featuring some biographical background and highlights from her presentations and poetry. But by the time Sandi and I met, the idea had evolved into a full biography. She asked me to undertake it, and I readily agreed.

The IJHS generously facilitated the work from the outset, paying for a year's leave of absence for me from Simpson College so I could focus on the book. This was made possible through an IJHS fund established by

Robbie Winick's children in honor of her eighty-fifth birthday. Robbie soon directed that the fund be used in support of the Celina biography and then went out to secure additional contributions. Donors included Lou and Marilyn Hurwitz, Gail and Stanley Richards, Steven Winick and Machelle Burkstrand, Ellen Winick and Gary Mitchiner, Laura and Martin Lipshutz, Alan Zuckert, Charna Axelrod, Sophie Barich, Leslie Buckman, Karen Engman, Sara and John Kanive, Michael and Jamie Lipshutz, Charles Mitchiner, Emma Mitchiner, Brad Robinow, Mark Robinow, Lauren Rothman, Heidi Sauber, Lisa Stein, Ben and Joyce Swartz, Jacob Winick, Leslie Winick, Naomi Winick, and Marvin Winick. Thank you to all.

From that point on, the organization's board and staff provided constant encouragement and assistance. Sandi and Sarah Carlson, the IJHS's curator, were especially helpful in tracking down resources and getting me contact information for a number of people. One person they put me in touch with was Brigitte Reynolds, a native German speaker. I'm particularly indebted to Brigitte for translating some key material into English.

Shortly after I started the project, the COVID-19 pandemic hit, which affected my work in significant ways. Maybe the most important, I had scheduled a visit to Southern California to meet Celina for the first time in March of 2020 but had to cancel the trip. That meant that all my interviews with Celina were done by telephone, or later, Zoom. Celina was especially kind and patient in putting up with my numerous phone calls, questions, emails, and requests for documents and photographs. Her son, Rob Biniaz, was a big help scanning and sending me those images.

I really wanted to meet Celina in person and finally got the chance in the summer of 2021. That July, my wife Jackie and I had the opportunity to visit Celina and her husband Bini during a trip to Southern California. Celina prepared a delicious lunch for us, and we enjoyed a delightful afternoon with them at their Camarillo home.

The pandemic also made research more challenging because libraries were closed, and archives were shut down. Likewise, lockdowns and social

ACKNOWLEDGMENTS   xi

distancing meant that most of the other interviews I did were by telephone. This book would not have been possible without the many who shared their pasts and connections to Celina with me. A list of these people, as well as those who opened their personal papers or corresponded with me is included at the end of the book.

Jayne Perilstein of the Shoah Foundation put up with a slew of email questions and provided generous help, as did Steven Vitto of the United States Holocaust Memorial Museum. I also wish to extend special thanks to Daryn Eller, an archivist at the USC Shoah Foundation and Martha McClintock, a senior sales associate at Getty Images, for their help in obtaining photographs.

Friend and editor extraordinaire Holly Carver read the manuscript at a particularly crucial time and provided much-appreciated encouragement and suggestions. I am also grateful to Steve Semken at Ice Cube Press. He showed immediate interest in the project and carefully shepherded the manuscript through the publication process.

Finally, and most importantly, I want to thank Jackie. As always, she was supportive and understanding, which proved especially significant as we navigated the pandemic together. And as she has done with all my previous work, she read and reread various drafts, offering valuable comments and advice on the entire project. I'm certain she made this a much better book. Thank you for everything, Jackie.

SAVED BY SCHINDLER

INTRODUCTION

CELINA KARP BINIAZ WAS just a little girl when the Nazis invaded her Polish homeland in 1939. She, her family, and the rest of the Jews in the city of Kraków faced immediate persecution and were eventually forced from their homes into a ghetto. The nightmare only got worse. When the ghetto was liquidated, she and her parents were ordered to a slave labor camp; later she and her mother were sent to Auschwitz, as Celina found herself in the throes of the Holocaust. Her overarching memories are of great suffering and fear: the bitter cold winters in threadbare clothing; the perpetual pangs of hunger; and the constant, all-consuming terror. But she survived.[1]

Now ninety-one years old, Celina speaks frequently about her experience, regularly opening her presentations with the simple, straightforward statement: "I am a Holocaust survivor, and every survival story is unique. What makes mine unique is that I was fortunate enough to be on 'Schindler's List.'"[2]

The so-called "list" was actually several lists, and it referred to a compilation of nearly eleven hundred names of Jewish prisoners designated to work at businessman Oskar Schindler's new armament factory in Brünnlitz, Czechoslovakia. Inclusion on the list was essentially a passport to safety and kept the *Schindlerjuden* (Schindler Jews) from being sent to the Nazi death camps.

Celina was one of the youngest members on the list and is one of its last remaining survivors, but the incredible story of the list and Oskar Schindler was largely unknown and untold until 1982. It finally surfaced that year with the publication of author Thomas Keneally's best-selling historical novel, *Schindler's Ark* (released in the United States under the title *Schindler's List*). Celina happened upon a review of Keneally's book shortly after it came out in the fall. She could not believe it: "I practically jumped out of my chair. There was my life in print, and I found it extremely accurate."[3]

Just over a decade later, in 1993, renowned director and producer Steven Spielberg made the story much more widely known with his epic black-and-white film adaptation of the book, *Schindler's List.* Some *Schindlerjuden,* like Moshe Taubé, decided against seeing the film. He explained to the *New York Times* that he feared its realism would be too much to take: "Every frame in this movie is my personal history, and to relive it would take tremendous stamina, a special fortitude that I do not have." Celina had similar concerns but attended its Los Angeles premiere. She found the "whole movie unbelievably true," but the realism made it "incredibly painful and shocking."[4]

The film went on to become an "historic phenomenon," wrote the *Los Angeles Times.* It was both a critical and box office success, winning seven Academy Awards, including best picture and best director for Spielberg, while grossing over $320 million worldwide. Culturally, it shined a light on the Holocaust, vastly increasing the public's knowledge and understanding of one of the darkest moments of the recent past. Film critic Gene Siskel wrote, "What Spielberg has done in this Holocaust story is simply and forcefully place us there."[5]

Historians weighed in as well. Holocaust scholar Deborah Lipstadt said: "Is it the best depiction of the Holocaust in film? I don't know. But did it reach a tremendous number of people who would otherwise not have been reached? Did it bring the story to countless people who no other filmmaker would have been able to reach? There is no question. So, in terms of impact, it certainly deserves its iconic status." While historian David Crowe, author of the exceptional biography, *Oskar Schindler: The Untold Account of His Life, Wartime Activities and the True Story Behind the List,* noted: "Up until 1990, it was hard to find a textbook about the Holocaust." But "once the museum [the United States Holocaust Memorial Museum] opened and Spielberg's film came out the same year, there was an explosion in this country in terms of interest in the Holocaust."[6]

Schindlerjude Rena Ferber Finder understood the film's power: "After the movie came out, more people wanted to learn [about the Holocaust]." And for survivors who had rarely talked of their experiences, she added, "It seemed like the wall of silence fell down."[7]

Finder was among those who had begun sharing their stories before the film was released, but like most survivors, she had found it impossible to talk about the experience for years because "it would be too painful to discuss publicly, and…nobody wanted to hear such horrible things." Leon Leyson, another *Schindlerjude,* seldom brought up his past after coming to the United States because "it was too hard to explain, and there didn't seem to be a vocabulary to communicate what I had gone through." Instead, he explained, "My parents and I focused on getting settled and finding work."[8]

And so it was with Celina. She and her parents arrived in Iowa in 1947, and they were soon asked about their past. When her parents opened up about it, they found that people were not interested in their story, and so they stopped talking about it. Celina faced similar reactions and chose to keep quiet about it as well. Why dredge up these awful memories and discuss them when no one, she thought, could possibly understand them?

Rather, Celina concentrated on the present and future and eagerly pursued the American dream. She finished high school, graduated Phi Beta Kappa from Grinnell College (fifty-five miles east of Des Moines) and went on to get a master's degree from Teacher's College, Columbia University, in New York. She then married Amir "Bini" Biniaz, a dental student, and the couple bought a home in the Long Island hamlet of Wantagh. They had two children, and Celina happily stayed home to raise them as the couple was soon enjoying the fruits of economic prosperity of the 1950s. Life was good, as the Biniazes quickly integrated into the community with other like-minded, upwardly mobile families. Roughly a decade later, Celina went back to work, finding her calling in teaching elementary school, which she did for twenty-five years.

But throughout her time on Long Island, Celina kept the horrific memories of her past bottled up, hidden beneath the veneer of her picture-perfect suburban life. "My community did not know anything about my Holocaust experience because I never talked about it." And her silence continued when the couple retired and moved to the Southern California city of Camarillo in 1993.[9]

Spielberg's *Schindler's List* ultimately changed this and broke down Celina's "wall of silence." Its brutal depictions of the Holocaust coupled with the great interest the film garnered made Celina rethink her reluctance to discuss this part of her past. It was so realistic, she later remarked, "I could actually say…if you want to know more about what I went through, go and watch *Schindler's List*."[10]

With the movie providing background and context, Celina began to believe people could understand and appreciate her story. Shortly after the film's release, she took the first tentative steps to discussing her Holocaust past, agreeing to some interview requests. A decade would pass before she was convinced to talk publicly about these painful years, but once she started, she began speaking regularly at schools, colleges and universities, synagogues and churches, and community groups in Southern California and around the country.

Oskar Schindler had given her a second chance at life, and she seized the opportunity. Years later, Steven Spielberg had given her a second chance to tell her story, and she remains grateful to share it.[11]

ONE

BEFORE THE WAR

EARLY IN THE SUMMER of 1939, Celina Karp's aunt, Gucia Wittenberg, bought the youngster a white German Spitz puppy that the eight-year-old named Leda. Celina delighted in her new, playful pet, and the gift seemed to open yet another chapter in her "wonderful childhood." She and her parents, Ignacy and Felicja, lived in Kraków, a cosmopolitan city that had once served as Poland's capital and remained an important cultural, artistic, and intellectual hub of the eastern European nation. The Karps were among its fifty-six thousand Jews, who made up nearly 25 percent of its population, and although the family certainly knew antisemitism, Felicja recalled that they enjoyed "a beautiful life," delighting in the city's various amenities with their many friends.[1]

Over the centuries, Poland had, in fact, become the center of European Jewry. On the eve of World War II, 3.3 million Jews lived there, accounting for nearly 10 percent of the nation's population. It was "the second largest Jewish community in the world...and the origin of the largest Jewish community in the world, the American." Jews had had a long and complicated history in Poland, first inhabiting the land a thousand years earlier. Here competing sentiments of toleration and discrimination had always informed their lives. Years of protection from Polish princes and kings brought Jews to Poland, but in the late eighteenth and early nineteenth centuries, Poland was broken up, partitioned by Russia, Prussia, and Austria. Russia ended up controlling most of the former Poland and gradually restricted Jewish life over the decades until rising antisemitism led to a series of pogroms in the late nineteenth century. Nearly two million Jews fled the region following the violence, many coming to the

United States. But when an independent Poland was reestablished after World War I, it remained a thriving center of Jewish life over the next twenty years.[2]

It was here in Poland that Celina and her family made their way, savoring a comfortable life. While Celina's idyllic upbringing took place in Kraków, the family story began in Radomsko, a smaller city eighty-five miles to the northwest, where her parents were born and raised.

Her father, Izak Szyja (generally known as Ignacy or Ignac and later Irvin or Ike), was the sixth of seven children born to Leon and Cyrtla Karp in early 1903. At the time, the city was under Russian control and called Noworadomsk. Its population stood at roughly twelve thousand; four of ten residents were Jewish.[3]

Ignacy's parents were conservative Jews, and his father was active in local Zionist organizations, which called for the recreation of a Jewish state in Palestine. The family celebrated all the Jewish holidays, but as Ignacy remembered, most Jews in Poland did. Even though the city had a large and vibrant Jewish community and the Karps were assimilated, the family faced antisemitism. Ignacy's father Leon was a construction engineer, yet he had been unable to get a formal university degree because of a strict quota system designed to keep Jews at such institutions to a minimum. Instead, he learned on the job, apprenticing for a Russian engineer. He eventually took a position with a Jewish-owned company. The firm and Leon were held in high regard, and despite being Jewish, most of their work was for Czarist Russia, building railroad lines through occupied Poland. Later, when Poland regained its independence in 1918, Leon was hired by the new government and did some work on the Warsaw-Vienna Railroad Station—Warsaw's main railway terminal. In the early 1920s, however, he was laid off because the government decided it no longer would employ Jews. After that, he worked almost exclusively in Radomsko.[4]

Before being fired by Polish officials, Leon spent most of his time away from home on jobs, and Cyrtla was left to raise the children by herself. But she died of pneumonia in 1910, when Ignacy was just seven years old, and

Leon quickly remarried to ensure there was someone to watch the children and care for the home. This eventually led Ignacy's oldest brother David, eight years his senior, to leave the family and Poland and head to the United States. The teenager did not want to be at home under a stepmother's eye, and he too wished to avoid his upcoming mandatory service in the Russian military. He also thought he would have better prospects in America.[5]

Unlike most European immigrants at the time who entered the United States through Ellis Island in New York City, David arrived in Galveston, Texas, as part of an effort designed to divert Jewish immigrants away from the eastern metropolis. Many poor Jewish immigrants had already arrived in the city, overwhelming Jewish charity services there and creating a fear that a rising tide of anti-immigration sentiments might lead to legislation closing the country's door to further Jewish immigration.[6]

To relieve pressure on the city's Jewish charitable organizations and quell antisemitic feelings in New York, the Galveston Movement was born. It was the brainchild of New York banker and philanthropist Jacob Schiff and operated from 1907 to 1914, bringing ten thousand Jews into the country through the southern Texas city instead of Ellis Island. Young, healthy, Eastern European Jews interested in moving to the United States were assisted by the Jewish Territorial Organization, which helped them get to Bremen, Germany, and then provided them with lodging in the city before they boarded ships for Galveston. Upon their arrival in the United States, the immigrants received help from the Jewish Immigrant Information Bureau. The organization furnished them temporary housing and food before giving them money and putting them on trains to other communities in Texas and throughout the Midwest where jobs had been arranged.[7]

Whether through a brochure or word of mouth, David learned of the program, liked what it offered, and signed on. He made his way to Bremerhaven in 1913, where he boarded the *SS Chemnitz*, joining other Jews on their way to Galveston. David was initially sent to another Texas city, where he worked briefly before receiving word from an old friend from

Radomsko who had immigrated to the United States earlier and lived in Des Moines, Iowa. The friend explained that the economy was good in the Iowa capital and suggested David head north to the city. He did, coming to Des Moines later that year where he found work as a clothing presser. He stayed in Des Moines and went on to become a highly successful businessman. From there, he would eventually play a vital role in the lives of Celina and her parents.[8]

But that was decades down the road. In the meantime, David's younger brother Ignacy had gone to a heder, a private Jewish elementary school, where he learned Hebrew and the tenets of Judaism. He then went to a public school solely for Jewish students before attending the public gymnasium (a senior secondary school that prepared students for study at a university). From there, Ignacy hoped to go on to a university to become an engineer. Years later, Ignacy remembered the antisemitism of the period: "Poland was 90 percent Roman Catholic, and Jews were hated. We had to be the very best students if we wanted good grades." He was therefore disappointed but not surprised when his road to the university was blocked by a July 1920 decree stating that leaders in universities across the nation could "limit the number of entering Jewish students as they saw fit." Even though the Polish parliament did not vote on the issue and later stated that such action by university officials had "no official sanction," Ignacy did not believe he would be accepted into the university and therefore dropped out of the gymnasium.[9]

Instead, he went to an ORT (a Russian acronym that translates as The Society for Trades and Agricultural Labor, which was originally established in Russia in the 1880s to provide vocational and professional training for Jews). The school was in Częstochowa, a city twenty-five miles southwest of Radomsko. After completing the two-year program there, he hoped to attend a school in Warsaw that had been accepting Jews and become an engineer. But that institution soon restricted admission to Jews as well, and Ignacy quit school and joined his father in Warsaw. There he found a position as a clerk in a retail shop and studied accounting at night. After finishing the coursework, he and his father returned to Radomsko, and Ignacy took a position at an import-export company, the first of several jobs he held over the next few years doing bookkeeping and then accounting.[10]

It was through this first job back in his hometown that Ignacy met his wife-to-be, Feiga Raza (generally known as Felicja or Fela and later Phyllis) Wittenberg. Felicja had been born in Radomsko in 1905 to Shmuel and Zysla Wittenberg, the fifth of six children. Her father owned and ran a grocery business, which had been in his family for years. It had begun as a wholesale operation but expanded to be a retail grocery as well. Felicja's parents ran the store together, sometimes assisted by her older sister, Dvora. Their house was adjacent to the store, and Felicja recalled: "My father was very proud of his large home and had chosen every brick for it."[11]

The Wittenbergs were observant Jews and highly respected in the city's large Jewish community. Felicja's father attended an orthodox synagogue every Friday, while her mother went to a more progressive one on Saturday. Some of Felicja's most distinct memories of her childhood focused on the family's weekly celebration of the Sabbath. "Friday nights were special. Father always brought people back home from the synagogue to share our traditional Friday night dinner. Mother lit the candles, and the table was filled with fish, meat, and wine [which Zysla had made]."[12]

Although Felicja was aware of antisemitism, she led a much more insular life than Ignacy had and did not have as much contact with the outside world. "Judaism had been the bedrock of her existence; it was embedded in her everyday life," recalled Scott Temple, who married a great-niece of Ignacy's. Felicja had grown up in a Jewish neighborhood, gone to Jewish elementary schools, and most of her friends were Jewish. After graduating, she studied accounting at a business school before beginning a job at a Jewish bank in Radomsko. This experience led her to conclude that "Jews and non-Jews got along fairly well."[13]

Shortly after starting at the bank, nineteen-year-old Felicja met Ignacy through her father in 1924. Shmuel had become acquainted with the twenty-one-year-old because he bought products from the import-export firm where Ignacy worked. It turned out Ignacy and Felicja had grown up on the same street and attended one of the same schools, but since Ignacy was a couple of years older, he and Felicja had not known each other.[14]

The two soon started dating, but the budding relationship worried Felicja's parents because they feared that Ignacy "was not Jewish enough" for their daughter. Shmuel was especially concerned but realized how much his daughter cared for Ignacy and after consulting his rabbi, he decided against intervening. After a lengthy, five-year courtship, the two finally wed in 1929. The small ceremony took place in Częstochowa because the two families knew a lot of people, and Felicja explained, "if we'd married in Radomsko, we would have had to invite five hundred to the service."[15]

Following the wedding, the couple moved to Kraków because Felicja required an appendectomy and her doctor recommended she have surgery there. The newlyweds also thought the larger city would offer greater opportunities. Kraków's housing market was tight, but the couple got lucky and found a lovely apartment on the second floor of a four-story building at 22 Krupnicza Street. Their apartment was part of a three-building complex with their living room and kitchen overlooking an interior courtyard, while the bedroom faced a backyard garden. It was located a few blocks from the historic Old Town district. The mixed, middle-class neighborhood was just west of such landmarks as Main Market Square, the largest medieval town square in Europe, and the beautiful Planty Park, a series of greenbelts and gardens built in place of the city's medieval walls in the early nineteenth century. Two miles south of their apartment was Kazimierz, the traditional Jewish section of the city.[16]

Ignacy found a bookkeeping position while Felicja was still in the hospital recovering from her surgery, but once she was released, she found a job as well, overseeing the bookkeeping department for a wholesale winery. The company imported Hungarian wine in bulk, which it then bottled and distributed. It also produced and sold its own Polish mead.[17]

The couple's accounting skills would prove especially important, helping them navigate the deep depression that engulfed much of the world by

1930, including Poland. Even though the country's gross domestic product fell 20 percent and unemployment rose to over 40 percent before a mid-decade recovery began, the Karps were largely shielded from the economic hardships many faced, continuing to earn a good living throughout the decade. In fact, the couple had the wherewithal to hire a full-time, live-in maid/cook, and would do so until World War II. On weekends, Felicja fondly remembered, she and Ignacy enjoyed many of the pleasures the city had to offer. "We made lots of friends and saw them Friday, Saturday, and Sunday. We went to the cafes for coffee and tea, listened to music, and went to the movies." She and Ignacy also enjoyed dancing and occasionally attended operas staged by Jewish actors in the Kazimierz district.[18]

Two years later, on May 28, 1931, Felicja gave birth to Celina (called Celinka or Linka while a youngster), the couple's only child, and she quit her job to stay at home with the baby. The apartment had only one bedroom, so Celina's crib and later her bed were in her parents' room. The maid, meanwhile, slept on a cot in the kitchen. Later in the decade, there was another addition to the household. One of Felicja's sisters, Gucia Wittenberg, an artist, took a job as a graphic designer in Kraków and moved in as well, sleeping in the apartment's main room, a combination living room and dining room.[19]

Celina grew up in a family that was "very assimilated" in its dress and habits. Only Polish was spoken in the home, and while her parents remained rooted in their beliefs and celebrated high Jewish holidays, Celina had no memory of "ever going to a temple or synagogue." But the Karps maintained the tradition from Felicja's childhood of holding a special Sabbath dinner every Friday evening, and Celina always enjoyed going to the fish market with her mother to get items for the meal.[20]

Because the apartment building was only about one-quarter Jewish, most of Celina's friends were gentiles. The children spent a lot of time in each other's homes, and Celina especially liked being around when her playmates' mothers were preparing food or baked goods because Felicja did not spend much time in the kitchen, and Celina "wanted her to be a cooking mother." Nonetheless, she was close to her mother who stayed at home fulltime until her daughter turned three years old before returning to her job at the winery.[21]

It was then that Celina began attending a private, progressive Froebel preschool/ kindergarten, and the Karps hired a governess to care for their daughter when she was not in school. The governess often took the child to the nearby Planty Park and to her ballet lessons. When she turned six in 1937, Celina started first grade at her local public school, named for the famous Polish poet Adam Mickiewicz. Besides a regular educational curriculum, genteel manners were emphasized. The cleanliness of students' hands were checked when they walked in the door, and they were taught to show respect for their elders, especially officials of the Catholic Church. Celina's governess stressed such proper comportment as well, going so far as to require the youngster to wear her white gloves while playing in the sand at the park.[22]

Celina loved school, especially reading, and Johanna Spyri's *Heidi* books were some of her early favorites. Books quickly became her most requested gift, and she accumulated a small library. Outgoing, Celina made many friends at the school and on weekends, she routinely spent time with them at the park or enjoying movies at the Bagatela Theater, just down the street from her apartment. Like many other children in much of the world, Celina had gone to see Walt Disney's *Snow White and the Seven Dwarfs* in 1939. By happenstance, Rena Ferber (now Finder), another Jewish child in Kraków at the time who also became a member of "Schindler's List," saw the same animated feature—likely at the same theater—shortly before the war broke out.[23]

Young, assimilated, and well-integrated into the community, Celina grew up without feeling the sting of antisemitism and recalled "not even being aware I was Jewish or different." Mietek Pemper, a German-born Polish Jew who was a prisoner at Płaszów—a Nazi slave labor camp in a southern suburb of Kraków—became Commandant Amon Göth's secretary, and eventually typed "Schindler's List," explained that it was the rural

Jews who spoke mostly Yiddish and poor Polish who became easy targets of antisemitism. "The Poles felt insulted when country Jews didn't speak good Polish, and they often made fun of them." But much like Celina, Pemper spoke perfect Polish and did not encounter much prejudice.[24]

However, Pemper understood that Polish antisemitism went well beyond the language issue. It was deeply embedded in the state's culture and dominant religion. The hostility toward Jews, he noted, "was the glue holding together a new kind of Polish nationalism," and "the fires of [this] prejudice were fanned especially by the Catholic Church." Celina's initial encounter with such prejudice, in fact, was at the hands of the Catholic Church when a priest came into her first-grade classroom to teach a catechism class. She was told to leave the room and required to stand in the hallway for the duration of the course. She went home that afternoon puzzled and upset by the episode. Her mother explained why she had been so treated, and Celina much later saw the occasion as her "first experience of feeling like the other."[25]

These occasions were rare, and even when they occurred, Celina quickly forgot about them and returned to the many carefree joys of childhood. One of those pleasures was going on business calls with her parents.

After working in his bookkeeping job for a while, her father took a job at an accounting firm, which often sent him to see clients throughout the city. Celina accompanied him on some of these calls, but she was especially intrigued by their visits to the Agfa (a German competitor of Eastman Kodak) camera shop. Another one of his accounting clients was the Hogo shirt manufacturing company, where Ignacy was eventually hired as a manager.[26]

Felicja, meanwhile, also took her daughter on customer calls while at the winery. These were often to nightclubs and restaurants. It was on these trips with her mother that Celina first met Henry and Manci Rosner, who became lifelong friends of her parents. Henry was a violinist and headed a well-known orchestra called Rosner's Players, which played at top clubs across Germany and Poland. He and his fellow musicians were preparing for that evening's performance when Felicja and Celina came into the cabaret. The Rosners would later be on "Schindler's List" as well.[27]

Unfortunately for Felicja, her position at the winery came to an end in 1937, when the family-owned business was liquidated because the owner's son showed no interest in continuing the company. She returned home and occasionally did freelance accounting work, but the job loss evidently did not have a negative impact on the family's comfortable, middle-class status.

Like other successful professionals of the era, the Karps regularly vacationed. However, in an unusual twist, Ignacy and Felicja usually did so separately, and Celina occasionally accompanied one or the other on these excursions. She once went with her mother to a spa resort, where Felicja would often go to relax and luxuriate in therapeutic water treatments, and she went on a vacation with her father to the Baltic Sea.[28]

They also visited relatives in Radomsko, although these trips were relatively infrequent. By the mid-1930s, several members of Ignacy's family had left Poland. His brother Felix had been a successful businessman with a lavatory manufacturing plant, but he was forced into bankruptcy after it was discovered an employee had been stealing from the company. Much like his and Ignacy's father Leon, Felix was a fervent Zionist. After closing his Polish factory, he moved to Jewish Palestine in 1931, where he again found success in business, this time making metal tubes. He also became one of the founders of Holon, a suburb of Tel Aviv. Two years later, Felix convinced his father and stepmother Paula to join him in Jewish Palestine.[29]

Ignacy had been a Zionist as well, but by the early 1930s, he, Felicja, and Celina had established roots in Kraków, and he had no interest in uprooting his young family and moving to Jewish Palestine. He had every reason to believe their good life in Poland would continue unabated, but there were ominous clouds forming over Germany, portending an uncertain future for the Karps and millions of others.[30]

Shortly after Adolf Hitler was appointed chancellor of Germany in January 1933, he and his Nazi Party rapidly consolidated their control over the state. Hitler soon took on dictatorial power and began rebuilding the German military, strictly forbidden under the terms of the Treaty of Versailles, which ended World War I. At the same time, he and Nazis were actively eliminating political rivals, and they soon took steps against Jews, starting in 1935 with the Nuremberg Laws. These consisted of two measures—denying Jews German citizenship and forbidding marriage or sexual relations between Jews and Germans. These laid the foundation for additional antisemitic policies and were followed by other laws and decrees further depriving Jews of their rights, property, and livelihood.[31]

Initially, Felicja and Ignacy knew little of Hitler or what was happening in Germany. Certainly, the Nuremberg Laws and the treatment of German Jews must have given them pause, but they and their Jewish friends could not imagine the state-sponsored antisemitism spilling across the border. Yet these events in Germany became fodder for the frequent ongoing discussions Ignacy and several other men from the apartment building had in the complex's courtyard.[32]

In March 1938, German troops entered Austria, where they received widespread support, and the Anschluss, Germany's annexation of Austria was quickly announced. It represented another German violation of the Treaty of Versailles, but the European powers who had guaranteed the peace did nothing. The move worried the Karps, especially after hearing of the widespread violence against Austrian Jews that followed. They grew more worried in mid-October, when German troops pushed closer to Poland, seizing the Sudetenland, a portion of land then in western Czechoslovakia and now in the Czech Republic. Two weeks later, the Nazis arrested and then expelled seventeen thousand Polish Jews living in Germany and put them on trains back to Poland, but the Polish government, which was becoming increasingly antisemitic, refused to accept them. Eventually, they were allowed into Poland and by November, made their way into the country's interior, where they were assisted by Polish Jews. Many went to Kraków, and Felicja and Ignacy were among those who helped them get situated in the city.[33]

Stories from these deportees of many atrocities against Jews in Germany, coupled with recent events, heightened Felicja and Ignacy's concerns even more, and they discussed the possibility of leaving Poland. The United States topped their list of potential destinations, as they could stay with Ignacy's brother David in Des Moines until the dire situation in central Europe blew over. But neither wished to leave their good life and beautiful apartment. More importantly, Felicja was not comfortable with leaving her family—her parents and a brother and sister in Radomsko and Gucia in Kraków—so she and Ignacy decided to stay. If something happened, Felicja reasoned, they could deal with it together as an extended family.[34]

Ultimately, the Karps "couldn't believe that the things happening in Germany could happen in Poland." So much so in fact, they went about their normal lives and spent generously on a new dining room set in 1939. This would have been an important purchase for Felicja who took great pride in her furniture and the apartment's decor. Celina recalled that the elegant "dining room table extended to seat eighteen, and there was service for twenty-four: china, crystal, and sterling."[35]

Yet the Karps' life was soon upended. Six months after German troops took the rest of Czechoslovakia, they invaded Poland. Early on Friday morning, September 1, Ignacy and Felicja awoke to loud booms. Since the previous night had been warm, the couple had left the apartment windows opened, and when they looked out, they expected to see rain that must be accompanying the thunder they thought they heard. But there was not a cloud in the sky, and the ground was dry. Ignacy also noticed several airplanes flying unusually low and thought maybe they were part of some sort of Polish military maneuvers. Then the emergency air-raid siren began to whine, and to the couple's horror, the two realized the city was under attack. More bombs went off.[36]

They turned on their radio and learned that Germany had declared war on Poland that morning, and their soldiers had crossed the border into the country. Confusion, panic, and dread set in. A few days later, Ignacy and Felicja heard that Radomsko had been bombed on Saturday, September

2, but they were unable to get any information about the status of Felicja's family. Two months would pass before she received a letter from a former maid from Radomsko giving her tragic news; the Wittenberg home had been leveled by a bomb, and her parents, a brother, a sister, as well as other relatives and friends who had gathered in the home's extra-large cellar, had all been killed.[37]

"People didn't know what to do," Ignacy later reported. But as he and Felicja were trying to figure out their first steps, they knew their daughter would need to give up her puppy Leda. Not surprisingly, Celina struggled with the decision: "That was very painful for me, and I could not quite understand why my parents were making me do this. But they felt we couldn't take care of a dog." When the family walked the dog to the animal shelter a couple of days later, they saw German planes bombing Kraków's radio station.[38]

Although Celina did not know it at the time, surrendering her dog marked the end of her childhood. More broadly, the regular rhythms of life seemed suspended as uncertainty now blanketed the city. News reports soon answered one question on the minds of all Poles. The country's defenses were not holding, and German troops were making rapid headway into the nation's interior; they would reach Kraków in a matter of days. But other troubling questions remained. How long would the invasion last? Would Germany occupy the country? And if so, what would that mean?

Two

OCCUPATION AND THE GHETTO

CELINA QUICKLY REALIZED THAT relinquishing her puppy was but a minor matter given the much more troubling events taking place around her. The eight-year-old obviously did not grasp the significance of these developments, but she sensed her parents' growing uneasiness. They exuded "a great fear," she remembered, and the ambiguity of the time was clear. "We didn't know what was going to happen." That uncertainty was a constant over the next few years. Anxiety ran high and terror became an everyday experience for the Karp family as Celina and her parents, along with three million other Polish Jews, tried to navigate the growing horror of Nazi occupation.[1]

A couple of days after the first bombs fell on Kraków, Ignacy and Felicja made a major heart-wrenching decision. German troops were bearing down on the city, and the couple agreed that Ignacy should join the large groups of Jews—mostly men—and other young Poles who were leaving Kraków and heading east. Two factors set off the exodus. First, there was the belief that the *Einsatzgruppen* (special forces—sometimes referred to as mobile killing squads—that included units of the Security Police, the *Sicherheitsdienst* or SD, the intelligence service of the *Schutzstaffel* or SS, the elite paramilitary corps of the Nazis) that followed Germany's regular military forces would massacre Jewish males they encountered but leave the women and children alone. Second, the Polish government had sent out an emergency call for all healthy men of draft age to travel east and join the nation's army, which planned to set up a defensive line in Poland's interior.[2]

Ignacy seemed motivated by both reasons. He hastily packed up food and clothing, kissed and hugged his wife and daughter and starting walking east, becoming part of the mass exodus of five thousand Jews and other young people hiking toward Russia. The experience was agonizing for Felicja, Celina, and Ignacy, for the three had no idea whether they would see each other again.[3]

Although Great Britain and France made good on their pledge to protect Poland if it were attacked and declared war on Germany, assistance from the two powers proved too little too late. German troops entered Kraków on Wednesday morning, September 6, and the city surrendered without a fight. Survivor Rena Ferber Finder, whose father had also abandoned Kraków and headed east with the many other Jews, described the Germans' arrival: "They marched through the city in parade fashion, their boots pounding on the pavement, while tanks rolled down the streets and shook the ground like an earthquake."[4]

Life in Kraków changed rapidly. Shortly after German occupation of the city began, Celina noticed that several family friends who used to discuss current events and politics with her father in the apartment's courtyard, began wearing swastika armbands. "It was frightening," she noted, "that people we considered friends and confided in were Nazis." Afraid and alone, she, her mother, and her aunt, Gucia Wittenberg, who still lived with the Karps, began wondering who they could trust.[5]

Food rationing was immediately instituted throughout the city, but Jews "were prevented from receiving rations in the breadlines." This was only the beginning of Jews being singled out. During the first week of occupation, Jewish businesses were ordered to display the Star of David. Education was disrupted as well. Jewish schools were closed, and Jews were not allowed to attend or teach in public schools, so Celina never started third grade. For a while, her mother and a few other Jewish families created a makeshift school and paid tutors to teach their children, but this only lasted a few weeks. From then on, Celina spent her days at home.[6]

She missed her friends, her teacher, and her lessons, but Celina was adaptable and soon got used to staying in the apartment. Because Felicja only did a little freelance accounting from home and could care for her daughter while working, she let the governess go. However, Felicja had no idea if or when Ignacy would return and worried about keeping the family afloat. She therefore went in search of a job and landed a bookkeeping position at the Hogo clothing company, the same firm where Ignacy had worked. This left Celina in the care of the family's maid. That did not last long either because new German restrictions forbade non-Jews from working for Jews, and the Karps' gentile maid was forced to leave. Fortunately, neighbors in the building picked up the slack and watched Celina while Felicja was at work.[7]

The war raged on throughout much of the country, made much more complicated for the Poles when Soviet troops joined the fight and invaded Poland from the east on September 17. Germany and the Soviet Union had signed a nonaggression pact that August with a secret protocol of the agreement calling for Russia to attack Poland after the German invasion, and the two would divide the country between them.

If Celina and her mother did not have enough to worry about at home, they were also afraid for Saul Karp, Ignacy's younger brother and Celina's favorite uncle, who was serving in the Polish army. Although they did not know it at the time, he and his unit were in the eastern portion of the country and were soon captured by Soviet troops. He spent the duration of World War II as a prisoner of war in Russia, but the Karps did not learn of his status until the end of the global conflict.[8]

By this time, Celina's father Ignacy was now in eastern Poland as well. His walk from Kraków had been horrible. Food was hard to come by and German planes were frequently overhead, killing anyone moving along the road. At some point, he apparently decided to forgo the government's plea to join the Polish army and continued east toward Russia. He reached the small town of Belz in southeastern Poland (now in Ukraine) on Friday, September 22. This was the beginning of Yom Kippur, and on Saturday he went to the synagogue to see the well-known Hasidic rabbi Aharon Rokeach. The following day, he saw Soviet planes flying west and learned that Russia had joined the war against Poland. This changed his plans. Eastern Poland and Russia no longer provided the haven he had expected, so he decided rather than staying where he was and ending up under Russian rule, he would return to Kraków to be with his family, despite the German presence there. Roughly two weeks later, he was back in Kraków, reunited with Celina and Felicja after being gone a month and a half.[9]

The fighting ended just thirty-five days after it began, with Poland easily defeated by Germany and Russia. As the victors had agreed, the two carved up Poland. This meant little to the Karp family, however, as the German occupation of Kraków had already altered their circumstances. Over the next year and a half, daily life grew more and more challenging with new edicts targeting the city's large Jewish population. Then it got worse, with the creation of the Kraków ghetto in March 1941.

Shortly after the invasion, Hitler and his lieutenants developed a plan to oversee the conquered territory. Western and northern portions of Poland would be directly annexed by Germany. The central and southern parts of the German-held territory were divided into four districts—Kraków to the south, Warsaw to the north with Lublin and Radom in between—of the civilian-run General Government of German-occupied Poland. A fifth district, Galicia, was later added. The city of Kraków, which came through the German attack largely unscathed, was named the capital of the General Government in late October, and Hitler handpicked Hans Frank, an early member of the Nazi Party who served as his personal legal advisor and the attorney for the party, as its top administrator.[10]

Frank established his official residence and headquarters in Kraków's Wawel Castle, the traditional seat of Polish kings, located in the city's Old Town district and close to the Karps' apartment complex. Soon he and other Nazi officials began issuing additional orders further removing rights and tightening their control over Jews in the General Government. On October 31, Joseph Goebbels, the Nazi minister of propaganda, called for the breakup of Polish media, which ended the country's free press. Many continued to get the news from BBC radio programming, but soon listening to foreign broadcasts was illegal, and in December 1939, radios were confiscated. Although some were able to hide their radios and continue using them, Nazi jamming devices made foreign broadcasts largely unintelligible in cities like Kraków. Ignacy later recounted the significance of the family's radio being seized: "Without regular radio broadcasts, we didn't know what was going on." This lack of reliable news meant, according to scholar Evgeny Finkel, "The majority had to rely on rumors, which were incomplete, contradictory, and generally unreliable."[11]

In November, Governor General Frank froze all Jewish bank accounts, permitting them to keep only $625 in cash. This issue was somewhat mitigated for the Karps, however, because when Ignacy returned to Kraków the previous month, he was able to return to his job as a manager at the Jewish-owned Hogo factory. Both he and Felicja now worked there, and they had money to buy necessities, but many Polish proprietors refused to sell anything to them or other Jews. Luckily, the Karps had several "good gentile friends," as Ignacy put it, who purchased any supplies the family needed.[12]

The following month, German leaders created the Kraków *Judenrat* or Jewish Council. Such groups of Jewish municipal leaders were used by the Nazis across their occupied territory in Europe to ensure that their demands and orders were implemented in Jewish communities. At the same time, Jews over twelve years old were ordered to wear a white band with a blue star of David on the right arm of their clothing. Those who did not comply were initially fined, but later Jews caught without armbands could be jailed or even hanged. Then came a series of edicts and regulations depriving Jews of their property and businesses. Many Jews had already lost possessions since the invasion began through looting and a variety of other arbitrary military and police actions. In early December, the Germans surrounded Kazimierz, the historic Jewish section of the city, and went through each house, seizing all property worth more than $625. Shortly after that, Jews were ordered to turn over their automobiles and motorcycles. These latter moves did not affect the Karps personally but undoubtedly heightened the family's concerns about what might happen next.[13]

That became clearer on January 24, 1940, when Jews were given five weeks to register all their remaining property with German administrators. As part of this order, Germany's Main Trust Office East announced policies for confiscating property. The agency had been created in November by a Nazi official and Hitler's designated successor, Hermann Göring. It was based in Berlin but would establish branch offices in each district of the General Government. The trust office could take over any property it deemed necessary for the public good. For Jews, the only property not subject to seizure were personal items of insignificant value.[14]

Once properties were expropriated, local trust offices were tasked with managing them before turning them over to carefully selected German trustees. The Jewish-owned Hogo manufacturing company was soon seized, and Ignacy and Felicja had their first experience with a German trustee running the factory. The new owner, Lukas, had been a leader in the *Sturmabteilung* or SA, a paramilitary unit of the Nazi party. He asked Felicja if she spoke German, and when she replied yes, he kept her on as a bookkeeper. Keeping her position at Hogo was important because without a job, Felicja would have been assigned manual labor work tasks such as scrubbing the sidewalk. However, she had to practice her German at night because she had not spoken it since her years at school.[15]

The Karps initially thought they were lucky to stay in their positions at Hogo, but these feelings soon faded as the trustee "initiated a reign of terror over his workers." Ignacy and Felicja kept their heads down and did their jobs. Early on, Ignacy recalled, the company fulfilled a German government order for mattresses and then one for caps.[16]

The couple hoped for better days, but matters only got worse. By the end of January 1940, Jews were no longer allowed to use public transportation; this included Kraków's streetcar system, which the Karps sometimes rode. That spring, Jews were forbidden from using Planty Park, where Celina had often played. At the same time, violence against Jews increased, and as Ignacy observed, "In the evening, we came home from work and stayed in. Being out on the street was dangerous. We were afraid all the time."[17]

It was also that spring when Hans Frank decided to push as many Jews as possible out of the city and into the countryside. He explained, "It is absolutely intolerable that thousands and thousands of Jews should slink about and have their dwellings in a town which the Führer had done the greatest honor of making the seat of the high Reich authority." His intent was to turn Kraków into "the town freest of Jews in the General Government."[18]

Frank wanted to decrease the number of Jews in Kraków from roughly sixty thousand down to those with essential business skills, which he thought would be between five to ten thousand but eventually increased that number to fifteen thousand. German officials called the policy a voluntary resettlement. It was to be managed by Kraków's Jewish Council, and Jews had three months to leave the city on their own or be forced out.[19]

Thousands of Jews complied and fled, but there were still too many there, so that August, German administrators formed a German-Jewish eviction committee that issued residency permits to Jews eligible to stay in Kraków. Ignacy and Felicja evidently received their residency permits or *Ausweis,* undoubtedly because of their business and accounting skills, and remained in their apartment in the city. Felicja's sister Gucia was a graphic designer and artist, and it is doubtful that she would have been viewed as an essential worker. But somehow, she remained as well, possibly obtaining a residency permit on the black market.[20]

As many Jews left the city, they were replaced by opportunistic business-people hoping to profit from the war. Among them were Oskar Schindler and Julius Madritsch, two men who would both become critically import-ant to the Karp family.

Schindler arrived first. He was an ethnic German born in 1908 in Svitavy, Moravia (in the Sudetenland region of the Austro-Hungarian Empire: it became part of Czechoslovakia and is now in the Czech

Republic). After gymnasium and then trade school, Schindler worked a variety of jobs, never lasting very long in any of them. He initially sold farm equipment with his father, worked for an electric company, and ran a driving school. He then enlisted and served in the Czech military, and after being discharged, returned to the electric company for a while before it went bankrupt. After being unemployed for a year, he operated a chicken farm, worked for a bank, and tried selling government property.[21]

Although married, Schindler was a womanizer, a heavy drinker, and a gambler. But the bon vivant was also known for his charm and eloquence. His ability to ingratiate himself to others may have helped when he began working for the Abwehr, the counterintelligence and counterespionage unit of the German military in 1936. Three years later, shortly after Hitler annexed the Sudetenland, Schindler joined the Nazi Party.[22]

Schindler evidently came to Kraków in mid-to-late September, shortly after World War II began. Here he hoped to profit from the conflict and resume his business career. Schindler quickly became involved in Kraków's budding black market, but he had other prospects in mind as well. His work for the Abwehr undoubtedly gave him connections, and they proved helpful in his acquisition of a confiscated Jewish company. His eagerness to obtain such a business may also have been influenced by his apparent orders from the spy agency to set up firms that could operate as Abwehr fronts.[23]

Schindler soon found what he wanted in Rekord, Ltd., a Jewish-owned enamel and tinware factory, which made products for the Polish military. It had filed for bankruptcy that summer and in November, Schindler leased it from the Polish Trade Court, which remained in operation after German occupation. The factory was in Podgórze, an industrial and working-class suburb of Kraków on the southern side of the Vistula River. He renamed the operation German Enamelware Factory Oskar Schindler, but soon referred to it as Emalia, and as Schindler had hoped, he began getting contracts from the German government.[24]

Yet it was Madritsch who would have a more immediate impact on the Karp family. When the war began in 1939, he was a successful, thirty-three-year-old Viennese businessman in the textile industry. A devout Catholic, Madritsch loathed the Nazis and had been upset when they annexed Austria the previous year, so when he was drafted by the German army in spring 1940, he looked for ways to avoid serving the Nazis on the battlefield. Madritsch soon discovered that he could delay being called up by obtaining a contract and producing shirts for the German military. He did so, making them at his Vienna factory, and postponed his service. Then, through several connections, Madritsch got himself appointed as a textile specialist for Kraków's Textile Trade Association and traveled to the city late that fall. There he was immediately disturbed by the Nazi persecution of the Jews.[25]

In December, Madritsch was appointed the trustee administrator of a Kraków confectionary business, and more importantly, two apparel manufacturers, including the Hogo firm. It is unclear what happened to Lukas, the first Hogo trustee. But Jews at the company were relieved that his iron-fisted management came to an end, and they soon realized their good fortune when Madritsch took over. He quickly gained a reputation "as a good man who treated his Jewish workers well." Celina recalled him as an "exceptionally decent human being," and her parents were surely pleased with this turn of events as well.[26]

But their life outside the factory continued getting worse. The same month Madritsch took over Hogo, Otto von Wächter, governor of the Kraków District, began rounding up Jews on the streets, whether or not they had an *Ausweis*. They were either imprisoned or sent to the ghettos in such cities as Warsaw or Lublin. The following two months, all Kraków Jews over sixteen years old were forced to spend a set number of days shoveling snow from the city streets. Wächter then issued new residency identification cards—*Kennkarten*—but to get one, Jews had to turn in their *Ausweis* and verify that they were employed.[27]

Bigger changes looked likely. There was growing speculation in early 1941 that more ghettos would go up throughout the General Government, and many Kraków Jews expected one to be created in the Kazimierz neighborhood, where Jews had lived for centuries. As the possibility seemed more and more certain, Felicja began looking into selling many of her prized household possessions, doubting she would be able to keep them if they were forced to a ghetto.[28]

Rumors became reality on March 3, 1941, when Wächter issued a decree creating a ghetto in Kraków's Podgórze neighborhood and requiring all the city's Jews to move there. The announcement was posted on walls and buildings, blared through loudspeakers on German vans, which drove up and down city streets, and published in the *Krakauer Zeitung*, a city newspaper. Wächter justified the move by saying: "Sanitary, economic, and law-enforcement considerations make it imperative to house the Jewish population of Kraków in a special, enclosed section of the city, the Jewish residential district."[29]

Wächter had selected a dilapidated, twelve-block area of Podgórze—bounded by the Vistula River to the north; a rail line connecting central Kraków with the Płaszów suburb to the east; Krzemionki Hill to the south; and the end of Podgórze's market square to the west—for the Jewish residential district; "the word ghetto," survivor Mietek Pemper wrote, "was never used."[30]

To make way for the Jews, the order required the 3,500 Poles to leave their three hundred or so apartments and homes in this section of Podgórze and relocate in Kazimierz by March 20. The city's Jews were given that same period to move into the ghetto. Individual Jews were only allowed to bring thirty kilograms (sixty-six pounds) of personal possessions with them. Therefore, like thousands of other Kraków Jews, Felicja went ahead and sold most of the family's furniture, silver, and china to gentile neighbors for anything they were willing to pay. Celina recalled this disposal of their household furnishings as "extremely hard on my mother," because "she was so proud of these things, and she and my father had worked long and hard to accumulate them." For Celina, the sale of these items and the subsequent move to the ghetto was "when I began to lose the sense of security I had as a child, which was replaced by the beginnings of fear."[31]

Felicja and Ignacy then gave Jan, a janitor at the Hogo company who Ignacy had taken under his wing, keepsakes, mementos, and family photographs that they hoped to retrieve sometime in the future. Jan also agreed to help the Karps move and borrowed a hefty Hogo pushcart to haul their larger items to the ghetto. The family packed up their remaining belongings—some smaller pieces of furniture, probably a few mattresses and blankets, household goods, pots and pans, clothes, and the like—and prepared to leave their apartment. Celina brought her favorite books and dolls as she, her parents, and her aunt joined the procession of Jews heading to the ghetto. The road was crowded with people walking with suitcases or bundles, pushing carts filled with a variety of possessions, or riding on horse-drawn wagons loaded with all their worldly goods. Like many others making the trip to the ghetto, the Karps almost certainly crossed the Pilsudski Bridge into Podgórze. It was only about a twenty-minute walk from the Karps' apartment to the ghetto, but this particular trek was especially grim and somber, taking place under the watchful eyes of German troops.[32]

The Jewish Council's *Wohnungsamt* or housing office was charged with making ghetto apartment assignments and had to house more than four times the number of people than had lived in the neighborhood previously. It therefore allotted space by window, employing the formula of four people per window. Many apartment rooms had two windows, often resulting in crowding eight people into such rooms. Celina, her parents, and her aunt were assigned a room in the two-room apartment. Another family lived in the kitchen, and a third family occupied the other room; all shared a small bathroom.[33]

This mandated move to the ghetto took place shortly before Passover—April 12-19 that year—and as historian David Crowe suggested, that was no accident. "The Germans often chose a period around a special Jewish holiday such as Passover or Rosh Hashana, to implement a major transfer or roundup. The idea was to use the period of strict Jewish religious observance to catch their victims when they were most off guard."[34]

Shortly after Passover, most of the barbed wire fencing originally surrounding the ghetto was replaced by a ten-foot brick wall, erected by forced Jewish labor. The wall was capped with a series of arches, which resembled Jewish tombstones. Building access doors along the ghetto border were also bricked over as were apartment windows above the wall that afforded a view of the city.[35]

Four guarded gates granted access to and from the ghetto. The main gate faced west and was on Podgórze Square. A blue Star of David was placed atop of this entrance above the words "Jewish Housing Estate" in Yiddish. All signs in the ghetto were changed from Polish to Hebrew except for the sign over the only Christian business in the ghetto, Tadeusz Pankiewicz's Under the Eagle Pharmacy.[36]

The ghetto's three other gates sat on its eastern side: one was at the end of Limanowskiego Street; one was at the intersection of Lwowska Street and Józefińska Street, which provided an entrance for larger vehicles and army units into the ghetto; and one at the northeastern corner of Kącik Street and *Plac Zgody.* Two trolley lines ran in and out of the ghetto through these gates, but streetcars made no stops within its confines.[37]

Quarters inside the ghetto were cramped, making everyday life difficult. Food preparation, for instance, was nearly impossible because the apartments' kitchens served as living space for families. Many addressed this problem by using a commercial bakery in the ghetto that rented out the use of its stoves and ovens. The Karps frequented this business, initially sending Celina with food dishes to bake or cook. But her trips alone to the bakery soon ceased altogether because of indiscriminate acts of violence against ghetto Jews. Survivor Malvina Graf recounted daily beatings: "SS men passing in the ghetto streets attacked and kicked Jews at random."[38]

Celina and her family therefore spent as much time as possible inside their apartment room, certainly making it seem even smaller than it was. And the tightness of their quarters was soon compounded when Gucia married dental technician Adolf Oberfeld, and he joined them in their assigned room. His presence also led to a steady stream of visitors, for he had brought his foot-powered drill to the ghetto and, using it and other instruments, he offered rudimentary dental care and tooth extractions to neighbors.[39]

The ghetto's crowded conditions and poor sanitation meant that disease spread quickly through the community. Although the Karps avoided any serious illnesses, Celina came down with the whooping cough shortly after she arrived in the ghetto. She probably contracted it through the children she spent some of her time with during her first few months there. While her parents and Gucia and her husband were at work, Celina was largely on her own during the first few months in the ghetto. Many of the other ghetto children were unsupervised as well, and with no school, they predictably met up in their new surroundings. Stella Müller-Madej, an eleven-year-old child when the ghetto opened, described the experience, saying she "kick[ed] around the ghetto as if [she] were in a bewitched world."[40]

In fact, normalcy seemed to be developing within its borders. Shortly after the ghetto was created, small businesses including cafes, salons, and bakeries opened. Plumbers, tailors, and others service providers soon hung out their shingles, and stores even offered appliances for sale. Three synagogues provided for the religious needs of its residents, while three hospitals, an old person's home, an orphanage, a post office, and a soup kitchen provided services as well. A grassy knoll on the ghetto's southside became a gathering spot for residents on Sundays, and there was even a restaurant and night club. Here violinist Henry Rosner and his brother Leopold, an accordionist, frequently played. Ignacy and Felicja certainly would have enjoyed seeing their friends perform, but such entertainment was expensive, and few Jews could have afforded it. Most of the club's patrons were therefore Nazi officials. The owner, Alexander Förster, a German Jew and SD agent, often entertained Gestapo officers there, and it is unlikely the Karps ever attended.[41]

Appearances notwithstanding, ordinary life did not exist in the ghetto. Although hindsight suggests that "the Jews of Kraków enjoyed relative safety until the summer of 1942," survivor Malvina Graf remembered that by the previous fall "the atmosphere in the ghetto became increasingly tense; the fearfulness of the people was everywhere apparent, reflected especially on their faces." Celina concurred: "The ghetto was a progressively frightening place."[42]

The Jewish Council oversaw the ghetto and served as the intermediary between the Jewish population and German authorities. The group was responsible for distributing food rations, maintaining public health, and assisting with ghetto security. To maintain order, the Jewish Council had its own police force—*Jüdischer Ordnungsdienst* or OD—but Ignacy and many others in the ghetto generally viewed them as Nazi collaborators and did not trust them. The OD were under the direct authority of the Polish police, and German police were also stationed at the ghetto. Both their office and that of the Jewish Council were near the main entrance at Podgórze Square.[43]

The largely unsupervised, unregimented daily life of Celina and most other ghetto children soon gave way to work when special cooperatives were established to employ child labor. Celina began toiling that spring in an envelope workshop, where she and other children folded paper into envelopes. Later, she was sent to a brush making operation. Here, she inserted bristles into predrilled holes in pieces of wood and then tied off each tuft with wire.[44]

Work, in fact, was the key to survival in the ghetto. Celina's parents were fortunate to remain at Hogo, now under Madritsch's control but still located in the Old Town district near their former apartment. Gucia and her husband were apparently able to get jobs at the company as well, probably through Ignacy's efforts, although how and when that occurred is not at all clear. Regardless, every morning, therefore, Ignacy and Felicja, Gucia and Adolf joined many of their friends and neighbors who also had special permits allowing them to work outside the ghetto, and together they proceeded through the main gate at Podgórze Square, crossed the river and headed to the old commercial area of Kraków. They returned in the evening, as did all who worked outside the ghetto, through the gate at *Plac Zgody*.[45]

It appears that Ignacy and Felicja were paid for their work at Hogo. Policies throughout the General Government varied and changed over the course of the early 1940s, but initially, Jews were to receive 80 percent what Polish workers in the same positions were paid. These regulations were often ignored by businesspeople, however, who were not willing to pay Jews at those levels. Still, Madritsch was widely known to be especially good to his Jewish workers, so Ignacy and Felicja were probably compensated as well as could be expected. Later, the *Arbeitsamt* or German Labor Office, which operated a branch in the ghetto, set wages at four to five Polish zloty per day, roughly equal to the price of two pounds of bread.[46]

Madritsch, meanwhile, had been thinking about expanding his textile operations. When the Jewish Council learned of this, it tried to persuade him to hire as many Jews as possible. Madritsch was amenable, but German officials in the labor office and the Gestapo often blocked these efforts, preferring he hire Poles. When the ghetto opened, Madritsch considered opening a much larger clothing factory in a building on the southwest side of the ghetto. He began talking about the idea with his general manager, Raimund Titsch, another Austrian from Vienna who was also known for treating Jews well. But he also sought the input of other Hogo managers, including Ignacy. And by this time, Madritsch had obtained a special permit to make goods for the military. This gave him the right the hire Jewish workers as they were now seen as essential to the German war effort.[47]

But then a new German decree changed Madritsch's fate, at least in the short term. It mandated that the management of trust companies would be reassigned to war veterans, and current trustees of draft age who had not fulfilled their military obligation were required to do so. Companies would be returned to displaced trustees once their military service was completed. Plans for the new factory were therefore put on hold, and Madritsch reported for basic training in late April and was posted in Vienna doing office work. Titsch, as the general manager, continued running Hogo and kept Madritsch apprised of the business and events in Kraków.[48]

Before the new trustee Heinz Bayer took over, he visited Madritsch in Vienna, where the two agreed to go forward with Madritsch's earlier plans for the ghetto factory and use his license to produce military goods with Jewish workers. Ignacy remembered the building selected for the factory as a "huge" three-story building located in the southwest corner of the ghetto, just to the south of the Jewish Council's office. It opened sometime in mid-1942 and eventually employed roughly eight hundred people. The factory produced German military uniforms and operated around the clock with two twelve-hour shifts.[49]

The stress of running the business, especially worrying about the persecution of Jewish workers, was too much for Bayer, who was sidelined with an eye infection that spring and soon unable to work. He resigned in August 1942. Fortunately, Madritsch was able to get several extended leaves beginning that spring to oversee the operations in Kraków. By August, the Wehrmacht considered his military service fulfilled, and Madritsch returned to his factory fulltime.[50]

When the Madritsch factory opened in the ghetto, the Hogo facility in Old Town was shuttered and operations were combined at the new larger facility. All the Hogo workers, including Ignacy and Felicja, remained in their same positions, and moved to the new, larger facility. Just as the Madritsch operation was growing, so too was Schindler's Emalia plant, a few blocks east of the ghetto. Like Madritsch, he was getting sizable military contracts and had expanded his workforce; Poles largely made the enamelware goods, including mess kits, while his Jewish workers mostly operated on the armaments side of the business.[51]

Unbeknownst to those in the ghetto, Nazi officials had been considering long-term options for dealing with the Jews in German-controlled territory. Earlier in 1940, German leaders resurrected the Madagascar Plan, an idea of sending Jews to the far away island of Madagascar—a French colony in the Indian Ocean off the southeast coast of Africa. It called for the deportation of four million European Jews to a settlement there. The proposal dated back to the 1880s when German political theorist and anti-Semite Paul de Lagarde first raised it, and by the 1930s, it had been discussed by some in France, Great Britain, Poland, and the American Jewish Joint Distribution Committee. But the British victory at the Battle of Britain in September 1940 essentially quashed the idea. Instead, Jewish ghettos were established throughout the General Government as a stop-gap measure while Nazi leaders mulled over solutions to what they saw as the "Jewish problem."[52]

Although interpretations of the coming of the Final Solution—the mass murder of European Jews—vary, Christopher Browning, a leading authority on the Holocaust, explained, "Most historians agree that there is not a 'big bang' theory for the origins of the Final Solution, predicated on a single decision made at a single moment in time. It is generally accepted that the decision-making process was prolonged and incremental."[53]

When Germany invaded the Soviet Union in June 1941, it inched toward such a solution when the *Einsatzgruppen* or mobile killing squads followed regular troops into Soviet territory and killed all the Jews they encountered. Shortly thereafter, Hitler expanded the authority of Heinrich Himmler, the head of the SS, to include all security matters over its occupied Soviet territory, and Himmler responded by sending additional special forces to assist in the killing of Jews. By the end of 1941, 500,000 to 800,000 Soviet Jews had been murdered.[54]

Before this mass killing of Jews began, Reinhard Heydrich, chief of the SD—the security service of the SS—and Himmler's immediate subordinate, sent Göring a letter proposing "the Final Solution to the Jewish Question." Göring and Hitler had tasked Heydrich with developing ideas to deal with the Jewish issue over the past couple of years, and that July, Göring ordered him to go forward with his Final Solution plans. In September, Hitler sanctioned sending German, Austrian, and Czech Jews to German-occupied Poland or Russia, where most would eventually be killed. The following month, Himmler directed Odilo Globocnik, SS and police leader for the Lublin District of the General Government, to oversee the program to murder the 2.3 million Jews in the General Government. This entailed the construction of three extermination camps—Belzec, seventy-five miles northeast of Kraków; Sobibor, two hundred miles northeast of Kraków; and Treblinka, two hundred fifty miles northeast of Kraków—which began late that fall.[55]

Then in January 1942, Heydrich hosted the Wannsee Conference—named for the site of the SS manor where it was held—in a Berlin suburb, bringing together top Nazi officials to discuss plans for the Final Solution. Heydrich emphasized that Göring had authorized him and the SS to manage the operation and explained that he and Himmler had been charged with the "central handling of the Final Solution" across Europe. Most of the meeting was largely informational, intended to ensure that all understood the plans. Some asked questions about details or implementation issues, but none raised objections.[56]

With preparations for the Final Solution underway, the Nazis soon started culling the ghetto population in Kraków. The process began in March 1942, when fifty Jewish intellectuals were arrested and transported to Auschwitz to their death. Located roughly forty miles west of Kraków just outside the town of Oświęcim, Auschwitz had been established in the spring 1940 as a prison camp in abandoned Polish military barracks. It initially held German criminals and Polish political prisoners. In the late summer 1941, the Nazis tested Zylon B, a poisonous gas, as a method of mass murder on Soviet and Polish prisoners. Satisfied that it was effective, the Germans built a gas chamber and crematorium at Auschwitz. The first transport of Jews sent to Auschwitz to be exterminated as part of the Final Solution took place sometime in the late fall 1941 or early winter 1942. At the same time, construction had begun on Auschwitz II-Birkenau, a much larger concentration camp/death camp about two miles away from Auschwitz I. The gassing operations were moved there in spring 1942.[57]

Meanwhile, the situation in the ghetto became much more dire that spring in late May when Operation Reinhard commenced. This was the code name used for the program to rid the General Government of Jews and a reference to Reinhard Heydrich, who died that June from injuries suffered in a Czech assassination attempt. The program's goal was to murder all Jews in the General Government, initially sparing those working in factories producing goods essential to the war effort.[58]

The first mass roundup and deportation of Kraków Jews to death camps under Operation Reinhard began on May 28 when the ghetto was sealed off by German police and SS guards. Adults in the ghetto were ordered to line up with their *Kennkarten* (identification cards). Skilled workers in essential jobs (or those who were successful at bribing officials) received a special stamp on their cards allowing them to remain in the ghetto. Those who did not receive the stamp, largely people over fifty-five years of age, were ordered to *Plac Zgody* with all their personal belongings on the morning of June 2. Rumors in the ghetto suggested that those deported were being sent to open work farms in Ukraine, but they were transported to the Belzec death camp. It would be several months before word of the extermination made its way back to the Kraków ghetto from Belzec escapees. An SS crew photographed and filmed the gathering at the square from the Under the Eagle Pharmacy's balcony to document the peaceful nature of the "resettlement program." The group was then put on a train at the Kraków Płaszów station for the trip to Belzec.[59]

Nazi officials, however, wished to reduce the size of the ghetto population even further. A much larger roundup of Jews without proper documents was announced the following evening. Ignacy and Felicja had evidently gotten the required stamp on their identification cards a couple of days earlier, and on Thursday, June 4, they were at work. The same must have been the case for Gucia and her husband. Many were not so fortunate, and without the appropriate identification cards, they were ordered to *Plac Zgody*, where armed German troops and police as well as Polish police surrounded the deportees. But panic and confusion ensued on this hot June day with soldiers and police firing into the crowd and beating people with rifle butts. An eyewitness recounted the brutality: "The ghetto resounds with shots. Firing guns in the hands of soldiers, the officers have revolvers, pokers, sticks or canes…the Germans are shooting like crazy at anyone at reach, whoever they choose."[60]

The massacre left hundreds dead in and around *Plac Zgody*. Once order was restored, German troops began marching those remaining to the train station. More were murdered along the two-mile route before the Jews boarded trains for Belzec and death. Survivors remembered the day as "Bloody Thursday."[61]

Ignacy and Felicja had been at work throughout the day and were unaware of the violence. They likely still worked at the Hogo factory north of the Vistula River because, according to Felicja, she and Ignacy returned to the ghetto to see corpses on the street. Workers coming back to the ghetto in the evening came through the gate at *Plac Zgody* (Peace Square; today it is called *Plac Bohaterów Getta* or Plaza of Ghetto Heroes) which was where the bloodshed had taken place; otherwise, they would have been coming home from Madritsch's new factory on the other side of the ghetto and probably would not have seen the dead bodies. Regardless, they rushed home, terrified they might not see their daughter, who had been ill that morning and had remained in bed.[62]

To their great relief, Celina was safe, still in her bed when they reached their apartment. But it had been a close call. Although she had been unaware of events taking place in the square, Celina had heard a commotion in the apartment building with people speaking German. She buried herself in the bed and remained as quiet and still as possible, hoping to be inconspicuous if anyone entered their apartment. Sure enough, a guard came in, but somehow, he did not notice Celina. Before leaving, however, he helped himself to Felicja's prized silver candelabra, one of the last cherished possessions the family owned.[63]

Celina had been lucky, but the incident shook Felicja. Then and there she vowed never to leave her daughter alone again as long as they remained prisoners of the Nazis. Honoring this pledge, however, would be difficult because Felicja and Ignacy had to go to work Monday through Friday, and Celina was on her own while they were at the textile factory.[64]

The only way Felicja could keep an eye on her would be to take Celina to the Madritsch facility every morning. But Celina had just turned eleven a few days earlier and was still a year shy of meeting the minimum age for a *Kennkarte* with a work stamp. She would need such a document to work in the factory with her parents. Felicja bribed a former neighbor then employed in the ghetto's labor office to alter Celina's records and push her birth date back by two years to 1929, making it appear that the youngster had just turned thirteen years old. The woman then apparently issued Celina a *Kennkarte* with a precious work stamp.[65]

A job was indeed "the bridge to life for Kraków Jews," and Felicja was not alone in trying to save a loved one with counterfeit employment papers. Some, like Felicja, used connections in the labor office, others changed dates on birth certificates, lied about their age, or forged their own work permits. Appearance also mattered. Parents worked to make their children look older with cosmetics or dress to obtain such permits. At the other end of the spectrum, older adults hoping to avoid deportation sometimes turned to hair dyes or makeup to appear younger and capable of work.[66]

The details of Felicja's efforts to get Celina the appropriate work documents are not entirely clear. She was either able to obtain them immediately, or she had already started the process of getting them because two days after "Bloody Thursday" the German officials ordered all remaining Jews to turn in their *Kennkarten*, with the Gestapo replacing them with new identity/work cards—the *Blauschein*. At roughly the same time, Ignacy, as a manager of the textile factory, probably had to scramble to line up a job for Celina at the business and must have prevailed upon Titsch, Bayer, or Madritsch (if he were there at the time) to give her a spot at the company. Finally, not everyone who had an old identification card received the *Blauschein*; bribes and/or the intervention of factory owners or trustees proved pivotal to their workers receiving the valuable document. Ignacy,

Felicja, and Celina, as well as her aunt and uncle, all got them, most likely due to the efforts of Bayer or Madritsch.[67]

Those who did not get the *Blauschein* were detained at the Optima factory in the ghetto, and it was announced that anyone without the new card would be shot on sight. On June 8, all those held at the Optima building were sent to the Belzec death camp. Over the course of the week, seven thousand Kraków Jews had been killed, and the ghetto population had been reduced to roughly eleven thousand.[68]

Celina joined her parents in Madritsch's factory and was put on a sewing machine working on German military uniforms. Like many others employed there, she had never sewn before and learned to operate the machine on the fly. Madritsch's deep religious convictions compelled him to save as many Jews as possible by hiring them as essential workers. He estimated that "60 percent of my workers had no clue about tailoring— there were doctors, lawyers, engineers, merchants, etc., and their families [working at my factory.]" And he worked closely with German officials at the textile trade association, possibly bribing them, to ensure his production numbers corresponded with all his workers pulling their full weight. These officials also kept profitable contracts for goods that were relatively easy to produce heading in Madritsch's direction.[69]

Madritsch was "a very kind man," Celina recalled, and Titsch "was wonderful." Both clearly cared for their workers, and they took a personal interest in Celina, most likely because of their relationship with Ignacy. They began calling her "Zenzi," the diminutive of the German name Kreszenz, which means to grow up or thrive. The two also took big risks on behalf of their workers, supplementing their limited food rations by sneaking in bread and other foodstuffs as well as essential items such as medications or soap under large bolts of cloth. Lewis Fagen, another worker at the factory, remembered Madritsch illicitly bringing in needed goods: "When my spectacles broke, he got me another pair of glasses. When we needed extra underwear or whatever, he was always smuggling it in."[70]

Shortly after Celina had started working and the June deportation, the physical boundaries of the ghetto were reduced by roughly a third. Much of the land south of the Limanowskiego Street, the main east-west thoroughfare was removed from the ghetto, and the Jewish Council's housing office relocated those now outside the ghetto's new, reduced boundaries. This included Celina and her family, who were moved to another apartment, where she and her parents shared a room, Gucia and her husband occupied the kitchen, and another family lived in the other room. Decreasing the size of the Kraków ghetto became part of a larger German plan that Heinrich Himmler ordered in July 1942. It called for the elimination of all ghettos in the General Government by December 1942, sending those remaining to either a death camp or a forced labor camp.[71]

To that end, the Nazis again took action against the Kraków Jews on October 28. The night before, special police surrounded the ghetto, and early the next morning, all in the ghetto were ordered to assemble near the main gate. Some heard of the coming selection and hid, but to no avail; they were rooted out and either killed or assigned to be deported. The rest were put through a seemingly arbitrary selection process, which determined who stayed in the ghetto and who would be deported. Children and the elderly were particularly affected in this roundup, with six hundred Jews killed on the spot, half of them children.[72]

Celina and her entire family were fortunate. They were selected as part of the fit-to-work group and remained in the ghetto. But the ghetto's population had been roughly halved, with six thousand Jews sent to the Belzec death camp. Again, the ghetto was physically reduced in size, and again, Celina and her family were moved into another apartment.[73]

Immediately afterward, construction began on a forced labor camp just southeast of the Kraków ghetto. It was one of several such camps developed as part of Himmler's plan to eliminate the ghettos and house workers essential to the German war effort. Although located in the Podgórze and Wola Duchacka districts, the camp was named Płaszów, possibly because its first prisoners came from a Jewish work camp in the Płaszów district, just to the east. The site for the camp was selected because of its proximity to the ghetto and a limestone quarry as well as being near industrial facilities and the Płaszów train station. Specifically, it would sit atop two Jewish cemeteries. Inmates from the ghetto built the camp and began living in some unfinished barracks in December, continuing construction of the facility through the cold, snowy winter under the harsh direction of SS guards. But their most gruesome task involved the desecration of Jewish graves. They were ordered to remove headstones and use them for paving some of the camp's roads.[74]

Rumors about the camp quickly spread throughout the ghetto, and those who remained soon understood it was being built for them. Conditions inside the ghetto were now growing worse. Beatings and threats of deportation became commonplace. At the same time, German officials realized the process of emptying out the ghettos in favor of slave labor camps or death camps was taking longer than expected, and they would not meet Himmler's target date of December 31, 1942. To expedite the imminent clearing and closing of the Kraków ghetto, it was divided into two sections early that month. A wooden fence and/or barbed wire separated the two areas. Those who had jobs, including Celina, her parents, and her aunt and uncle, were all assigned to Ghetto A, while those who could not work—elderly, the sick, and children—were put in Ghetto B. When the ghetto's children's home or *Kinderheim* opened in January, it was placed in Ghetto B.[75]

In February, Amon Göth, a thirty-five-year-old SS officer who had been involved in planning the roundups and deportations in Operation Reinhardt, became Płaszów commandant. He was charged with closing Ghettos A and B as quickly as possible.[76]

The following month on Saturday, March 13 at 11 AM, David Gutter, the head of the Jewish Council, announced the Nazi order that the Jews in Ghetto A had four hours to prepare for their move to Płaszów. The order also mandated that those in Ghetto B prepare for deportation the following day. After gathering what they could carry, those from Ghetto A reported to Plac Zgody. Some tried to escape during the process and were simply shot, with their bodies left on the street. Many, meanwhile, feared that their children would not be allowed at the forced labor camp, but Göth, who was on hand in the ghetto that morning, assured parents that he would send the children from the *Kinderheim* to Płaszów the following day. Few believed him and tried to sneak their children out of the ghetto. Others hid their children in their apartments or vacant buildings, but few escaped the Nazi dragnet. Göth himself and armed Gestapo and SS personnel were aggressive in searching those leaving the ghetto as well as their bags and bundles for hidden children. Most youngsters were found and sent to the *Kinderheim*. Then, to eliminate those deemed useless, SS officers murdered patients and infants in their hospital beds. And as the ghetto was viciously cleared, those who put up any resistance were beaten or killed.[77]

Survivor Bernard Offen remembered being "in the square for a large part of the day, while the shooting and terror surrounded us, later marching to the Płaszów slave-labor camp, carrying some clothing, food, and cooking pots, as hundreds of others were being shot in the streets." Celina saw her share of harrowing violence that day as well, but one grisly incident shook her to her core. She watched in horror as "Nazi soldiers swung infants and small children by their feet, bashing their heads against stone walls, brutally killing them." Traumatized by the carnage, Celina struggled to know how "God could have allowed that to happen to children." It was at that moment, she recalled, that she forever lost her faith.[78]

But then, after witnessing the gruesome scene, Celina, her mother and father, and her aunt and uncle were allowed to join the several thousand Jews who trudged five abreast out of the ghetto. They walked southeast about a mile-and-a-quarter along Wielicka Street to Płaszów.[79]

Ghetto B was viciously liquidated the following day. The process was much bloodier than the closing of Ghetto A because the people there had already been designated superfluous. Nearly two thousand were murdered outright, while the rest were deported to Auschwitz, where most met their end.[80]

All the children in the *Kinderheim* were among those murdered as Ghetto B was being emptied. A few days later, Felicja spoke with Madritsch about the awful episode and recalled that her soft-hearted boss broke down in tears when talking about the tragedy. The slaughter was made that much worse, Felicja later darkly explained, because "Göth kept his word; he sent all the dead children to Płaszów, and the parents had to bury them."[81]

Celina and her family would soon come to expect such ruthlessness from the commandant at Płaszów. They had been under the Nazis' control since September 1939. Conditions had grown progressively worse over the two-and-a-half years before they were marched off to the slave labor camp in March of 1943. Unimaginable atrocities surrounded them after Operation Reinhard began, but the Karps found ways to cope, going about their daily lives as best they could. Ignacy and Felicja, her sister and brother-in-law, and eventually Celina were fortunate to have worked under the supremely humane Madritsch and made it out of the ghetto. None of them had any idea what awaited them at the forced labor camp, but insecurity and fear clearly dogged them as they made their way to Płaszów. Years later, survivor Mietek Pemper expressed such uncertainty qualified by the benefit of hindsight: "As we left the ghetto, we still didn't know that a much worse situation had befallen us, that new depths of lawlessness awaited us."[82]

THREE
PŁASZÓW AND THE LIST

As MENACING AS LIFE in the ghetto became, it did not prepare Celina for what was to come. Fellow *Schindlerjude*, Moshe Taubé said of Płaszów, "The first day, everybody was crying. After all, the ghetto was half-humane surroundings. There were still streets, houses, freedom of movement inside the walls. Here, it was a prison." Conditions at all such German camps were terrible, but Płaszów was especially horrid because it was overseen by a "pathological sadist," commandant Amon Göth. Historian George Kren noted that Göth took "special pleasure in personally killing prisoners on a daily basis and was considered a monster even by Nazi standards." Celina found herself "petrified all the time" at Płaszów. Her mother Felicja explained that camp inmates thought "only of surviving."[1]

Survive was what Celina and her family did. They endured Płaszów as a forced labor camp and as it transitioned into a concentration camp in 1944. They even outlasted the monstrous Göth, who was arrested for corruption and murder that September. Once again, Julius Madritsch, Raimond Titsch, and Oskar Schindler played outsized roles for many in the camp, the Karps included. Together, the three were important in facilitating the family's exodus from Płaszów, getting them designated for work at Schindler's new factory to be erected in Brünnlitz, Czechoslovakia, now Brněnec in the Czech Republic. Celina's aunt was not so fortunate.

Even as Celina trudged to Płaszów, the tide of the war had changed. A month earlier, in February 1943, the Nazis suffered a major defeat by the Red Army at Stalingrad, which marked their furthest penetration into Soviet territory. From that point on, Soviet forces pushed the Germans out of the country as they made their way toward Berlin. This advance would ultimately impact Płaszów, inducing Nazi officials to cover up the crimes committed there and evacuate the prisoners.

But the Karps were unaware of this Soviet victory, and the dismantling of the camp was over a year-and-a-half away. In March 1943, Celina and her family were among the roughly six thousand Kraków Jews trying to navigate their new hellish environment that was Płaszów. Originally set on twenty-five acres, Płaszów had been designed to house four to five thousand prisoners. Two thousand Jewish inmates were already held there when ghetto inhabitants arrived, and the facilities were immediately over-whelmed. Expansion of the camp began that spring and continued over the next year to accommodate its seemingly ever-growing population.[2]

By 1944, Płaszów stretched over 198 acres and included more than two hundred buildings. It was surrounded by a double, electrified, barbed wire fence with enough voltage, survivor Malvina Graf wrote, "to cause instant death to humans." When squirrels tried to cross the wires, they "would be thrown ten feet into the air from the force of the electrical shock." Guards kept an eye on the prisoners from thirteen watchtowers—each equipped with a machine gun, searchlight, and a telephone.[3]

Inside the camp were several distinct sections: housing for German personnel, including the commandant's villa, known as the "Red House"; administrative offices; an industrial area with factory barracks and ware-houses; and the prisoner compounds, with separate sections for males and females. Adjacent to the men's barracks and the camp latrines was the infamous *Appellplatz*, or roll-call square. It was here all the Jews assembled twice a day for roll call, but it was also here they often experienced degrad-ing or deadly punishments.[4]

Płaszów was originally intended solely for Jews, but it soon incarcer-ated non-Jewish Poles as well. In July 1943, the Nazis established a work reeducation camp for Poles within the larger camp, separated from the rest of the facility by barbed wire. Most held here had committed minor offenses or were suspected members of the Polish resistance movement.

They usually served sentences of three to six months before being released. This section of Płaszów also interned some Roma families.[5]

Nonetheless, most of the inmates were Jews, and the number of prisoners at the camp grew dramatically over its existence. In the fall of 1943, there were twelve thousand inmates in Płaszów, but by the following July that had risen to seventeen thousand. Two months later, in September 1944, its prisoner population peaked at twenty-five thousand. An SS staff of 640 oversaw the inmates, with many of the guards initially coming from the ranks of Ukrainian collaborators or prisoners of war who had served in the Red Army and volunteered for such duty.[6]

When Celina arrived at Płaszów, she instantly realized how different it was from the ghetto. Instead of living in an apartment, albeit an overcrowded one, with her entire family, she and her mother were immediately separated from her father. He was taken off to the men's barracks area, which was cordoned off with barbed wire from the women's compound where Celina and her mother were assigned to a barrack.[7]

Over eighty such housing units stood in Płaszów when the Karps first entered (an additional hundred would be built over the next year). The crude, drafty, single story, wooden structures were roughly nine hundred square feet and each housed 150 inmates with rows of triple, wooden bunk beds crammed into the tight space. There were no mattresses, but most prisoners, Celina and her family included, had blankets and pillows they brought with them into the camp. The comforts ended there, however, as the barracks provided no privacy, had no indoor plumbing, and were infested with mice. They were hot in the summer and cold in the winter, with the only heat provided by a single wood stove in each structure.[8]

Since Ignacy and Celina and Felicja were sequestered in their respective, single-sex compounds, they only saw each other at the Madritsch factory where the three Karps still worked in their same jobs. But now they had to march five abreast out of the camp each morning to the plant, which initially remained in the ghetto, and back to Płaszów in the evening. Walking in such a formation was actually a blessing for Celina because her mother always put her in the middle amongst the other women to make her as inconspicuous as possible. Children were not supposed to be in Płaszów, and the Nazis made a great effort to keep most from moving from the ghetto into the work camp. Regardless, some were smuggled into the camp, and because Celina looked older than she was, had forged work documents, and was tall for her age, she had gotten into Płaszów with her parents. But Felicja worked hard to maintain the ruse of Celina's age, for if discovered, she would be sent to a death camp. Therefore, to appear older than she was, Celina always wore her hair up and wore high heels.[9]

There were other differences as well. Camp inmates were to be issued striped, prison uniforms, but supplies had run short, and Felicja recalled that guards applied yellow stripes to their civilian clothes instead. The stripes were to help guards easily identify prisoners and dissuade inmates from trying to escape. But this was a minor indignity compared to the hunger inmates were forced to endure.[10]

Food was extremely limited. Survivor Rena Ferber Finder explained that being "hungry in a camp meant a twisting, painful sensation in your stomach that made you dizzy and weak, and never went away. Our hope was that there would be enough food to keep us alive until the next morning." Celina's father Ignacy simply said there was never enough food. Each prisoner received a daily ration of just under fourteen ounces of bread, and meals generally consisted of a piece of the bread, chicory coffee and thin, watery soup. This was frequently supplemented with sago, an oatmeal-type dish made with barley. Celina was constantly hungry, and it was no wonder; historian David Crowe estimated that food rations at Płaszów provided each inmate with only seven to eight hundred calories per day. Bernard Offen, another survivor, remembered that in Płaszów he was "always dreaming of food, never imagining there could be enough food in the world to satisfy my hunger."[11]

Some became so desperate for food they would dig through the trash piled outside the inmate kitchen for something to eat. But a Ukrainian guard with a reputation for being particularly cruel would occasionally patrol this area and shoot any prisoner he saw rooting through the garbage for anything edible. Celina and her parents certainly suffered from the pangs of hunger like the rest of the inmates, but they received some additional food from Madritsch, who continued to purchase it on the black market and smuggle it into his factory for his workers.[12]

Still, the Karps were slowly starving and like the rest of the prisoners, they grew more and more frail. By 1945, the 5-foot-3-inch Celina weighed only about seventy pounds. This lack of adequate food combined with the crowded, dirty environment, made the inmates highly susceptible to disease. A typhus epidemic, for example, raged through the camp in early summer 1943, killing hundreds of prisoners. Celina avoided that outbreak but later caught scarlet fever and landed in Płaszów's hospital.[13]

She was very sick with a high fever in the hospital, and she was alone. Her parents were not allowed to visit her, but she treasured the few times she saw her mother "who waved to me through the window on the other side of the barbed wire fence." Loneliness, however, was the least of her or other hospital patients worries, and inmates desperately tried to avoid being sent there. While some indeed received treatment at the facility and returned to the workforce, many did not. Camp administrators often went through the list of ill patients and frequently ordered the chief physician to designate the sickest for extermination. Worse, Commandant Amon Göth unexpectedly came into the hospital one day, and for no apparent reason shot and killed every patient there.[14]

Then there were those like Celina who were treated for one malady at the hospital but because of its unhygienic conditions, came down with another illness while there. Just as she was recuperating from scarlet fever, Celina contracted typhoid fever. A Jewish doctor named Rosenberg treated her, and according to Felicja, he saved Celina's life. He also likely kept the diagnosis a secret. Jewish doctors routinely hid such cases from the camp officials because they knew of instances where the Nazis immediately shot those with typhus or typhoid fever. Fortunately, no one questioned Celina's illness, and she recovered after more than three weeks in the hospital. But she lost additional weight and was left with a heart murmur, liver damage, and jaundice.[15]

If this were not enough, the everyday stress of Płaszów made Celina "extremely tense," and she began experiencing migraine headaches. Fortunately, Julius Madritsch came to the rescue. He had continued looking after his workers and was especially attentive to Celina. Madritsch gave her "some little red pills" for the throbbing headaches, and although she did not know what they were, she recalled that the tablets "really helped."[16]

The harsh reality of the camp and the daily killing of Jewish inmates clearly led to Celina's anxiety and the debilitating headaches. But her dread was made that much worse by the violent and capricious Amon Göth who "enjoyed humiliating, torturing and murdering people."[17]

Like Madritsch, he was Catholic and from Vienna, where, in fact, the two had known each other as students. But the similarities ended there. Göth was born into a prosperous publishing family in 1908. He attended public school, and according to Madritsch, he was indulged by his parents and given "whatever he wanted." Göth had been sent to college to get an education intended to prepare him to take over the family's publishing business. Although bright, he was an indifferent student and dropped out after only a few semesters. But while there, he became interested in both fascism and Nazism. In 1925, Göth joined the Austria Nazi party's youth chapter before returning home to work at the family's publishing business.[18]

Two years later, he signed on with the Styrian Home Protection Organization, the most antisemitic branch of the Home Guard, the leading fascist competitor to the Austrian Nazis. In 1930, the top Nazi in Austria said that those in the party could no longer belong to the Home Guard as well. By that time, Göth had already applied for full membership into the Nazi Party and dropped his affiliation with the Home Guard. He became a party member in the spring 1931, a year-and-a half before Adolph Hitler became the chancellor of Germany in January 1933. He joined the SA (*Sturmabteilung*), a paramilitary unit of the Nazis, that year and after a two-year candidacy was accepted into the SS (*Schutzstaffel*), an elite Nazi paramilitary corps, in 1932.[19]

When the Nazis stepped up their terror and violence against opponents in Austria, the country's government outlawed the party in June 1933, and its leadership fled to Munich, Germany, where they set up an operation in exile. From time to time, Göth was sent into Austria covertly over the next couple of years, "smuggling weapons, money and information" to strengthen the Nazi position there. He was arrested a couple of times but made his way back to Munich in 1934. Although his activity is a bit unclear for the next four years, it appeared he returned to the publishing business.[20]

But after the *Anschluss*, the German annexation of Austria in 1938, Göth was back in Vienna working for the SS full-time. He gradually moved up the ranks. In 1940, he was posted in Upper Silesia, a province in western Poland seized by Germany in 1939, as an SS operational staff administrator. He remained in the area for two years, becoming an *Einsatzführer* or action leader for the *Einsatzgruppen*, the Nazis' paramilitary death squad before serving as financial administrator for the regional office of the Reich Commission for the Strengthening of Germandom, or RKF-DV—*Reichskommissariat für die Festigung Deutsches Volstums*. The RKFDV was responsible for the expulsion and resettlement of Poles and Jews in the conquered territories. Here Göth earned a reputation, according to historian David Crowe, "as a seasoned administrator but also an expert on Jewish resettlement and transfers."[21]

He was promoted to *SS-Untersturmführer* (second lieutenant) in the summer of 1941 and was transferred to Lublin, where he joined the staff of Odilo Globocnik, the police leader of the Lublin district the following summer. Over the next six months, Göth was involved in Operation Reinhard, the program of roundups, deportation, and execution of thousands of Jews. Göth's work impressed his superiors, and in February 1943, he was appointed the commandant of Płaszów. Raimund Titsch, the general manager of Madritsch's textile operations noted that Göth's brutal reputation preceded him, and Płaszów's Jews knew him as the "Bloody Dog of Lublin."[22]

Leopold "Poldek" Pfefferberg, the *Schindlerjude* who inspired author Thomas Keneally to write the bestselling *Schindler's List,* said of the commandant: "When you saw Göth, you saw death." And Göth was impossible to miss. A large, obese, man—6 feet 4 inches tall and more than 330 pounds—he towered over most at the time. He was often seen patrolling Płaszów, sometimes walking, sometimes riding his horse, but almost always accompanied by his two large, vicious dogs—Rolf, a Great Dane, and Ralf, a mongrel that some believed was German Shepherd-Siberian wolf mix. Göth had trained both to attack people on command, and Felicja was among the many inmates who saw him "set the dogs" on prisoners. *Schindlerjude* Roman Ferber thought Göth sent the dogs after people "if he didn't like your looks." Several of these attacks proved lethal as Göth sometimes allowed the dogs to "rip people apart."[23]

Another *Schindlerjude,* Josef Bau explained that Göth "ran the camp through extremes of cruelty that are beyond the comprehension of a compassionate mind, employing tortures which dispatched his victims to hell," while survivor Malvina Graf noted that "the mere sight [of Göth] was enough to evoke fear." His secretary Mietek Pemper wrote, "As much as possible, the inmates hid, changed the direction they were walking, or otherwise inconspicuously avoided Göth." But sometimes, avoiding Göth was not enough. His villa overlooked part of the camp's stone quarry, and he occasionally shot workers laboring there with a rifle from the home's balcony. Fortunately, Celina was never assigned to the quarry, yet Felicja constantly worried that her daughter might inadvertently draw Göth's attention when she encountered him. "A day didn't go by," she remembered, "that he didn't kill someone. I was afraid Celina might be shot and told her not to make faces or cry [in his presence]."[24]

But Celina did not require such warnings; she was terrified of Göth: "He was an incredibly evil human being; we knew never to look at him in the face because he might kill you. I looked down whenever he walked by."

Seeing Göth, she added, elicited "an unbearable fear." His random acts of violence, frequently without the least provocation, kept all the inmates on edge. Ignacy, for instance, saw Göth come inside his barracks, pull out his pistol, kill several inmates, and leave. On another occasion, Göth stopped to inspect the work of an inmate who was painting a barracks. Apparently displeased, Göth shot and killed him. Sometimes, his indiscriminate acts of violence were larger in scope. On Yom Kippur—the holiest day of the year in Judaism—1943, Göth and his SS lieutenants pulled fifty Jewish men out of their barracks and shot them.[25]

The commandant's penchant for killing led Celina to think the worst when one day, she glimpsed him talking with her father. The discussion continued as Ignacy and Göth and his dogs then walked down the road and out of her sight. She worried that she would never see her father again and was overcome with relief when she spotted him at the factory the next day. Celina never learned why Göth had stopped her father but decided the conversation must have been about work at Madritsch's factory.[26]

Public punishments and murders took place regularly on the *Appell-platz*, while all the inmates were gathered at roll call and were meant to intimidate the prisoners. Göth would sometimes walk through the lines of prisoners shooting those who did not measure up to whatever standards he had on that given day. He was known to have shot and killed inmates who were not standing straight enough, and in one instance, he shot an inmate because he said he was too tall. On another day at roll call, he shot an inmate because his coat was too long. As this man laid dying, Göth urinated on him. Celina saw these cold-blooded *Appellplatz* killings or heard the gunshots, and she also saw many brutal whippings at roll call. When Göth personally whipped prisoners (generally with twenty-five lashes), he required them to count out each strike, and if they made a mistake, the count would start over. She also witnessed several hangings.[27]

Maybe the most infamous took place on the *Appellplatz* in August 1943 and involved a teenage boy named Haubenstock and an engineer named Krautwirt. Göth had chosen to put the fifteen-year-old to death because he had been heard singing a Russian song. The rope was put around his neck, and the hangman pulled him up from the chair. He hung suspended for a moment before the rope broke, and he tumbled to the ground alive. His pleas for mercy went unheeded, and Göth ordered him hanged again. This time he died, but just to be sure, Göth shot the teen. This ghastly scene was followed by another, when Krautwirt, standing on a chair waiting for the noose to be placed around his neck, slit his wrists with a razor. He was hanged anyway, even as the blood poured out of his veins.[28]

Surrounded by such regular violence, Celina lived in constant dread that she or her parents would be the next to be tortured or killed. Luckily, that never happened, but the possibility hung heavily over her. Celina did find two respites from this terrible fear, however. First, there were books smuggled into the camp by inmates, which circulated among the prisoners. She had always loved to read and delighted in books provided through this informal, underground library. Celina especially enjoyed adventures and novels set in the wild, which "took me to a different place," she noted, if only in her mind and only momentarily. Such books included James Fenimore Cooper's *The Last of the Mohicans* and Jack London's *The Call of the Wild.*[29]

The other reprieve from the terrors of Płaszów was her time at Madritsch's factory, still located in the ghetto. Here a couple of miles away from the camp and under the watchful eyes of Madritsch and Titsch, Celina and her parents enjoyed a modicum of protection from Göth's terror. But this was about to change. Madritsch had been in the midst of expanding his operations over the past couple of years because, he explained, he had been encouraged to do so by the Jewish Council in Kraków. In early 1942, he opened a second textile factory in the Bochnia ghetto, twenty-seven miles east of Kraków, and later that year, he opened a third sewing facility in the Tarnów ghetto, another twenty-five miles east of Bochnia. When the Kraków ghetto was closed in March 1943, many of Madritsch's workers asked him to transfer them to the Tarnów operation, rightfully believing life in another ghetto would be much better than living in the Płaszów labor camp. Madritsch cajoled (and most likely bribed) Göth and others in the SS for permission to send 232 men, women, and children from his Kraków shop to the one in Tarnów.[30]

For whatever reason, Celina and her parents remained in Płaszów, and although conditions were much less harsh in Tarnów, the workers transferred there did not benefit long because Göth liquidated that ghetto (and removed all Jews from Bochnia as well) that September 1943. Those Jews were either sent to Płaszów to work or Auschwitz to their death.[31]

This left Madritsch with the one remaining factory, the one in the Kraków ghetto. Six months earlier, he had asked Nazi officials for permission to move this business to Płaszów. The move became critical for Madritsch as of September 1, when Göth announced that Jewish prisoners would no longer be allowed to leave the camp at all. He finally received approval in mid-September, and Madritsch transferred all his equipment and material from both the Kraków and Tarnów facilities (it is unclear what happened to his business in Bochnia) into six industrial barracks in Płaszów. He became the only private entrepreneur to operate there, and with two thousand workers, Madritsch's enterprise was the largest business enterprise in the camp.[32]

When the operation was moved to the camp, Celina and her parents remained in their same jobs they held in the other facility—Celina stayed on a sewing machine doing piece work, Felicja did accounting in the office, and Ignacy continued as one of the factory's managers. Even though it was now situated within the confines of Płaszów, the business was a relative "oasis of peace" amid the arbitrary violence in the camp. Here Celina felt protected and shielded as much as one could be from the capriciousness of Göth. And Madritsch continued looking out for his workers, still providing them with extra food under the ruse of a "performance bonus" and, when possible, smuggling in various and sundry items to better the lives of his workers.[33]

The other preferred place for inmates to work remained Oskar Schindler's Emalia factory, near the former Kraków ghetto. But even before

Madritsch began considering moving his facility, Schindler was interested in changing his factory arrangement as well. Once it was clear that the ghetto would be cleared and the inmates moved to Płaszów, Schindler worked to persuade Göth and other Nazi bureaucrats that his plant and the surrounding land should be converted into a sub-camp of Płaszów, and to that end, he had purchased lots adjacent to the factory. Here, he explained, he would add barracks for his workers so they could stay there as opposed to marching back and forth over the roughly two-mile trek between Płaszów and the factory. Schindler eventually succeeded, getting Göth and others to agree to his sub-camp plan, and it appears that construction of the facility began late in the spring 1943, several months before Madritsch got approval to move his operations into Płaszów.[34]

Both Madritsch and Schindler had relied on generous bribes and their relationships to Göth to make these changes happen, and although they continued to watch over their employees, general conditions for the thousands of inmates at Płaszów remained about the same. Little changed in fact when the labor camp was designated a concentration camp in January 1944. Construction of gas chambers and a crematorium began but soon ceased as the structures were ultimately considered unnecessary because of the proximity of Auschwitz, which was only fifty miles away.[35]

There was one significant change at the camp, however. Intially, despite Göth's best efforts to keep children from entering the camp, many parents smuggled them in when the ghetto closed. The children were kept hidden, and if they were discovered, they were generally shipped off to a death camp.

Life for these children was so dangerous that parents soon tried to sneak their youngsters out of the camp, and Celina heard of several successful such efforts. She and her mother personally helped get one child out of Płaszów. They launched their plan one morning, when Celina, her mother, and three women walked five abreast as they always did on their way to Madritsch's factory, still located outside the camp. The small child to be taken out of the camp had been put in a burlap bag, which was secured to the leg of one of the women and covered with her skirt. With her secret package so attached, she walked in the middle of the group of five women toward the factory. It was a risky move; if they were caught, the women and the child would have been killed. Luckily, they evaded detection and arrived at the building safely. They handed the child over to a Polish Catholic family, who came to the factory for the exchange and had agreed to care for the toddler for the duration of the war.[37]

Eventually, Wilhelm Chilowicz, the camp's top Jewish administrator, arranged a deal with Göth that all children in the camp would be tolerated and a special barracks, the *Kinderheim*, was arranged for them in March 1944. There was even a playground installed in front of it. Unfortunately, the accord did not mean they were safe for very long.[38]

In early spring 1944, Göth received a telegram asking if he could temporarily house prisoners from Hungary before they were sent to sub-camps of Auschwitz. Göth replied that he could take ten thousand prisoners if he were allowed to make space by ridding the camp of those who were ill, elderly, weak, or too young to work. When he got the okay, Göth ordered the camp's head physician, Dr. Max Blancke, to hold a health roll call to identify those to be sent from Płaszów to extermination.[39]

On Sunday morning, May 7, 1944, all inmates were called to the *Appellplatz* for regular roll call. When it was over, they were told to remain in place, while the children's barracks was surrounded and Auschwitz II-Birkenau's chief medical officer, *SS-Hauptsturmführer* (captain), Dr. Josef Mengele was there writing down the names of all the children. Inmates and survivors referred to Mengele as the "Angel of Death" for the casual manner he affected during prisoner selections, pointing to the left or right and thus deciding whether individuals went to the gas chamber or remained alive. With a doctorate in physical anthropology, a medical degree, and an interest in genetics and pseudo-scientific racial theories, he joined the Nazi party and the SS in the late 1930s, before serving in the war on the Russian front. After being wounded, he was transferred to Auschwitz in 1943, where he began conducting diabolical experiments on prisoners, especially twins. Unfortunately, this would not be the last time Celina would see the "Angel of Death."[40]

This day, however, Mengele did not send anyone to death. When he was finished drafting the list of children, all the women were ordered back to their barracks, and Göth told the men that going forward they would be assigned work based on physical abilities. Those with limited capacity would be given easier jobs. The inmates were then ordered to strip naked and file past tables where the medical staff and Blancke gave each inmate a physical grade.[41]

The male inmates were then dismissed, and Blancke moved to the grounds of the women's barracks and repeated the medical inspection process for the female prisoners. Fortunately, Celina had no remaining visible blemishes from her bouts with scarlet fever or Typhoid fever—for anything that could be considered an imperfection, even a mole or birthmark, could have had her singled out for extermination—and she along with her entire family passed this inspection.[42]

After the regular roll call the following Sunday, all inmates were again told to remain on the *Appellplatz*. Heavily armed guards stood by each barracks and along the camp's main road, which ran by the roll call area. When Göth and his assistants arrived, the names of those who had been singled out during the previous week's medical inspection were read, and they were escorted away by SS guards. At the same time, the 294 children from the *Kinderheim* were marched in rows five abreast and pushed into waiting trucks. Guards whipped any who tried to move out of the line. Terrified children began to scream, and parents began to yell, but there was nothing they could do as guards and a barbed wire fence separated them from the trucks and their sons or daughters.[43]

As the trucks pulled away with the children, Celina noted that the SS played the German lullaby *"Gute Nacht, Mutter"* ("Good Night, Mother") over the camp loudspeakers. It was all "so sadistic," she recalled, "You can't imagine." Others agreed there was music but recounted the details differently. *Schindlerjude* Stella Müller-Madej, for instance, thought the song was "*Mama, komm zurück*" ("Mama, come back"), while Dr. Aleksander Bieberstein, another *Schindlerjude* believed it was "*Mutti, kauf mir ein Pferdchen*" ("Mummy, buy me a pony"). Survivor Bernard Offen remembered that a variety of German lullabies were played, "to keep the children calm," he thought, "but perhaps also as part of the guards' sense of humor knowing that the children's parents would know what was really going on."[44]

Some children, those of Jewish Council officials, for example, were spared, while a few others received enough advanced warning and hid in the camp latrines. One was *Schindlerjude* Roman Ferber. He explained: "The pit was twelve feet deep. You couldn't have jumped in it or you would have drowned. People would sit on boards with holes, and the stuff would fall inside. There were crossbars [under the boards], and this was where we used to hide." He felt it was the safest place in camp because the stench "was so repulsive that the guards wouldn't go near it."[45]

Women inmates discovered the hidden children later that day. They left them there for a while, caring for them and feeding them until it was safe to bring them out, and then they successfully hid the children in the camp's *Krankenstube* or sick room. These few children were among the lucky ones, for 1,400 prisoners were deported to Auschwitz and their death after the health selection.[46]

By that summer, the Soviet military's push into eastern Poland led to a flurry of activity in Płaszów. Plans were made to evacuate, shut down, and dismantle the camp ahead of the Red Army's arrival. On August 6, there was another large selection, resulting in 7,500 to 8,000 inmates being sent to Auschwitz. It was another close call for Celina. Initially, she, her mother, and her aunt Gucia (her uncle was evidently not selected and remained in the camp) were chosen for deportation, when just in the nick of time, Celina's father Ignacy intervened. He ran up waving papers that likely indicated they worked at Madritsch's factory, which had been deemed vital to the war effort. With that, the guards allowed him to pull his daughter and wife out of the line heading to the boxcars earmarked for Auschwitz. Gucia, however, was in a different line, and Ignacy was unable to save her.[47]

Celina and her parents did not learn of her fate until after the war. Gucia evidently spent five weeks in Auschwitz before she and several thousand other inmates were put on a train and sent to the Nazi concentration camp at Stutthof, just outside the Polish town of Sztutowo near the Baltic Sea and twenty-five miles east of Gdańsk. When Russian troops began bearing down on this area of northern Poland in early 1945, the Nazis began evacuating prisoners from the camp. That January, Gucia was among the five thousand inmates who were marched in the brutally cold winter to the Baltic Sea. There is some dispute about what happened next. Some suggested the prisoners were put on a ship, which was then scuttled, killing most onboard. More likely, however, and the story Celina recalled, was that Gucia and the others were ordered to walk into the icy water, where the guards shot and killed them with machine guns.[48]

By late summer 1944, Nazi officials were preparing to destroy evidence of the mass murders that took place at Płaszów, which maintained three execution and burial sites adjacent to the camp. The main one, Hujowa Górka, had been dubbed "Prick Hill" by the prisoners because it was visible from most parts of the camp. Mass graves here and at the other two locations held the two thousand Jews killed when the Kraków ghetto was liquidated, and all the inmates murdered in Płaszów. Others buried there included many sent to the camp for execution from Kraków's Montelupich prison. From the fall of 1943, inmates from this penitentiary arrived at Płaszów several days a week. Once at the camp, they were taken to Hujowa Górka, ordered to strip and lie down in a ditch, where they were shot and killed. Then a dentist or dental technician, often a Jew, would remove gold crowns and teeth from the dead. This grisly job might well have fallen to Gucia's husband, Adolf Oberfeld, whose dental training would have made him an ideal candidate, but there is no way to be certain.[49]

To rid the camp of any sign of these crimes, Wilhelm Koppe, the SS and Police Leader for the General Government ordered the exhumation and burning of the thousands of bodies of largely Jewish prisoners. Nazi efforts to cover up their mass murder of Jews began in 1942 when word of the horrendous activity spread to other European nations and the United States. That June, *SS-Standartenführer* (colonel) Paul Blobel was put in charge of *Aktion 1005* (Operation 1005), a code name for destroying evidence of their extermination of the Jews. Overseen by the SS, *Sonderkommandos* or special command units made up of Jewish and Soviet prisoners were forced to dig up and burn the corpses, crush any remaining bones, and scatter the ashes.[50]

Such work began at Płaszów in the fall of 1944, and 170 camp inmates were detailed for the grizzly job. Witnesses to the horror said seventeen truckloads were filled with human ashes, which were spread over the site and throughout the camp.[51]

Göth had been responsible for the deaths of many of those who had been buried on Hujowa Górka, but he also had other crimes to cover up. He had enjoyed a luxurious lifestyle supported by theft. Much of his wealth came from the items taken from Jews when the Kraków ghetto was closed. In Płaszów, Göth continued stealing. Instead of turning over valuables confiscated from inmates and the gold extracted from the mouths of murder victims to the SS, Göth kept this for himself. He also operated on the black market, selling large allotments of food, intended for the prisoners, for his personal gain.[52]

Jewish administrator Wilhelm Chilowicz had helped the commandant in many of these illicit activities (becoming quite wealthy himself), and Göth, now aware of an SS investigation into camp corruption, thought it best to kill Chilowicz to silence him. But such arbitrary action, once a Göth staple, became much more difficult since Płaszów became a concentration camp earlier that year in January. The SS put stricter controls in place, and Göth no longer had absolute power over the camp. If he wanted to execute someone, he needed to get it approved from his superiors. He therefore asked for permission to put down a fictitious revolt and kill the instigators. His request was granted.[53]

To play out the subterfuge, Göth either gave Chilowicz a gun or had it planted in his barracks. He then searched the barracks and found the gun on August 12, 1944. The next day, Celina saw Chilowicz and his wife Maria in the Madritsch warehouse. When she heard that Göth was on his way there, she quickly hid among some large bolts of fabric. It was a smart move. Once Göth arrived, he shot and killed Chilowicz. Then, when Maria came running into the room to see what had happened, the thirteen-year-old Celina saw Göth shoot her as well. The teen was horrified and struggled to keep quiet. Fortunately, Göth did not see her and left, going on to kill several others that day who could have testified about his illegal activities. But the horrors were not over for Celina. Shortly after the shootings, she remembered that Göth made the inmates line up and file past the dead bodies situated between the men's and women's barracks. There by the bodies, according to Stella Müller-Madej, was Göth on horseback and two inmates who held a sign that read, "Everybody who puts up resistance will die this way." The prisoners were then all marched to the *Appellplatz* to watch the hanging of two young men.[54]

A month later in September, Göth was arrested for abuse, corruption, and murder and taken to prison in Breslau (now Wrocław) in western Poland. Leadership of the camp passed to SS officer Arnold Büscher. Celina must have been aware and happy that Göth was gone, but she does not recall it. Instead, she remembers that the camp seemed to be in chaos as preparations were being made to close it down, and although she could not know it at the time, she would have one last encounter with Göth several months later.[55]

Ever since July, rumors had spread throughout the camp about its impending closure. Schindler had been ordered to prepare to move the armament portion of the Emalia factory to Germany. A few months earlier, Madritsch had been told he would have to close his textile enterprise in favor of an arms factory, but he successfully worked with friends in Berlin and lobbied to get an agreement, keeping his business in operation through August.[56]

Schindler also went to Berlin to grease the wheels so he could continue to operate his armament business. He soon found the complex he wanted—an old textile mill in Brünnlitz, ten miles from his hometown of Svitavy. The facility had been owned and operated by the Löw-Beers, a Jewish family, but once Germany occupied the area, it was confiscated and turned over to the Hoffman brothers, two businessmen from Vienna, who eventually bought the mill. As he had often done, Schindler schmoozed, flattered, and bribed Nazi officials until he finally got the okay that fall to move his enterprise to an unused portion of the Hoffmans' complex.[57]

While he was awaiting final approval, Schindler had asked Madritsch to join him and transfer his textile business, along with his Jewish laborers, to Brünnlitz as well. Madritsch had originally tried to move his sewing operation to Drosendorf, a small Austrian village near the present-day Czech Republic's border. When this did not materialize, he accepted Schindler's offer and sought approval for the move. But Madritsch failed to get the necessary permission. Nazi officials told him that uniforms, which his workers produced, "are not a decisive factor in the war, one can fight in civilian clothes, [and] Jewish workers can only be made available to produce ammunition!" He was also likely turned down because there was already an SS uniform factory located in the large Brünnlitz industrial complex.[58]

At that point in early August, Madritsch gave up trying to move his factory. And as the work wound down at his Płaszów operation, most of his two thousand workers were slowly shipped out to Auschwitz or Mauthausen, a Nazi concentration camp in Austria, twelve miles east of the city of Linz. Their evacuation was part of the much larger effort to empty out the camp before its closure. Göth had been aggressive in sending prisoners to other camps since July, and by September, Płaszów's inmate population had dropped to roughly seven thousand, down from twenty-five thousand in July.[59]

But Madritsch was permitted to keep a skeletal crew of roughly three hundred men and two hundred women employed into October to clear out and clean up his factory barracks. Ignacy was among those who were retained, surely because as one of the facility's managers, he could oversee its decommissioning. And since he remained, Madritsch or Titsch kept Felicja and Celina on the job and in the camp as well.[60]

A couple of months passed before Schindler won final approval in late September or early October to relocate his armament enterprise to Brünnlitz. He had also been working closely with Nazi officials, and no doubt providing them with persuasive inducements of expensive gifts, to obtain the right to select the workers for his new operation. He succeeded here as well.[61]

Once Schindler had these authorizations in hand, the now famous lists of workers destined for his new operation were drawn up. But unlike the story told in Thomas Keneally's book, *Schindler's List* or Steven Spielberg's film of the same name, Schindler was not "the principal author of the list," and had little to do with its details. Rather, Schindler provided general instructions about the list to Franz Müller, the SS officer in charge of inmate work assignments. Those he wanted for the Brünnlitz enterprise included the Jewish laborers who were still at his Emalia plant and Jews skilled in metal work. Göth's inmate secretary Mietek Pemper noted that Schindler also wished for families to be kept together, and he wanted the spouses and children of those bound for Brünnlitz added to the list as well.[62]

Müller, however, was preoccupied with the ongoing efforts to shut down the camp and did not care which workers left Płaszów for Schindler's new operation. The task of compiling the list, therefore, fell to Marcel Goldberg, Müller's Jewish inmate clerk. He drew up two lists, one for men and one for women, and Pemper typed the documents.[63]

Goldberg had a free hand in filling a number of the slots and accepted bribes to put people on the list, but many spots were already determined by Schindler's guidelines and the workers that the Brünnlitz camp's incoming commandant, Josef Leipold, wanted to bring with him from his previous posting at an aviation plant. Included among those that Schindler expected to be sent to his new business were some workers from Madritsch's sewing factory. That list of sixty some odd workers grew out of conversations Schindler had with Madritsch and Titsch during a party at Arnold Büscher's—the new Płaszów commandant—villa in October.[64]

Schindler first spoke with Madritsch at the party about saving some of his workers by providing names of those he would send to work in the Brünnlitz armament factory. According to Schindler, Madritsch was not interested and apparently believed little else could be done to help. When Schindler pushed the issue, Madritsch told him: "Dear Oskar, spare yourself your words; it is a lost cause. I am not investing another dime in it."[65]

But Schindler and Titsch conferred later that night, and Madritsch's general manager hurriedly drafted a handwritten note of sixty-two of their sewing factory employees to include among the thousand workers bound for the Sudetenland. Schindler referred to those on this list as his "factory tailors." Madritsch, meanwhile, claimed that he had given Schindler a list of one hundred names.[66]

Regardless, when the Madritsch-Titsch list was soon typed, it contained only sixty names, forty men and twenty women. The document appeared on letterhead from Madritsch's former confectionary company and included a handwritten notation signed by Titsch that read, "Inventory about people of our company who were taken over by the Schindler Company at our request." It was dated October 1944 and included Marcel Goldberg's signature at the bottom. Historian David Crowe attributed the discrepancy in the number of names that landed on the list to the "whims of Marcel Goldberg" and reported that only fifty-three of those on the Madritsch-Titsch list made it to Brünnlitz. In general, Goldberg kept most of the prominent people Schindler, Madritsch, or Titsch suggested but then made his own adjustments, removing some and adding others to the transport lists.[67]

Celina, her mother and father, and her uncle Adolf Oberfeld were on the hastily drawn Madritsch-Titsch list, certainly because it included those Madritsch and Titsch knew best—largely their managers and supervisors—and their family members. Ignacy and Felicja were likely aware that they and their daughter had been placed on the list, but Celina cannot remember when she learned the news.[68]

Her parents probably told her before those plans were announced to the entire camp on October 15, 1944. Early that morning, all prisoners were ordered to the *Appellplatz* for roll call. With the inmates standing at attention, a Nazi official read the names of the thousand Jews—seven hundred men and three hundred women—being sent to Schindler's new factory. The women were then dismissed, and roughly four thousand Jewish men were lined up to board rail cars and leave the camp. The seven hundred bound for Brünnlitz were put into the train's first seven cars; the rest filled in the remaining cattle cars and were heading to Gross-Rosen, a concentration camp in a German village of the same name; today it is the town of Rogoźnica in southwestern Poland, roughly forty miles northeast of Brünnlitz. About two thousand women, included Celina, Felicja, and the three hundred other *Schindlerjuden*, would depart Płaszów the following week.[69]

Celina was thrilled to be leaving Płaszów. She and her parents had endured the nightmarish camp for nineteen months. Although she was not sure what to expect, she understood that the spots she and her parents had on the transport lists to Schindler's factory in Brünnlitz were lifelines from almost certain death.

Four
Auschwitz, Brünnlitz, and Liberation

CELINA ONCE REMINISCED ABOUT having been on "Schindler's List": "I don't know whether it was chance, luck or fate," she said, "but it saved me." In October 1944, however, the initial notion that she had been lucky soon evaporated. A week after her father and the other men were shipped out of Płaszów, Celina, her mother Felicja, and the rest of the Schindler women were ordered onto railcars along with hundreds of other female inmates. The boxcars were cold and crowded. Felicja said they were "packed in like sardines," without food, water, or bathrooms. But to be out of Płaszów and bound for Schindler's operation, Celina and the rest were more than willing to put up with these aggravations.[1]

Later that night, the train came to a stop. But when the doors opened, Celina did not see the factory or Schindler. Instead, bright spotlights shined in the inmates' eyes as SS guards and *Kapos*—inmates, frequently German political prisoners, who were appointed as prison guards in exchange for special privileges—with rifles and whips were yelling, "*Raus, raus, macht schnell* (Get off, quickly)." The guards' large German Shepherds were barking and leaping at the women as they were forced off the railcars. They were told they were in Auschwitz, and Celina remembered a foul smell in the air. She had heard about the death camp, and when she saw the five tall chimneys rising from nearby buildings, she asked her mother, "Are those the [crematoria] chimneys we've been talking about?" "Yes," was the reply, but as Felicja recalled, they were not in use that night although they were the next day when she saw smoke billowing from them.[2]

Like Celina, Rena Ferber Finder, another young *Schindlerjude*, recalled a "terrible stench like rotting meat," as she was led away from the boxcar. She also remembered what she thought was falling snow until she realized it was human ash coming from the chimneys. Whether or not the crematoria were in operation when they arrived mattered little; the women were shocked not to be in Brünnlitz. Bewildered and scared, Celina thought "we're someplace we're not supposed to be—Auschwitz."[3]

Terrified, she asked her mother another poignant question, "If they take me to the gas chamber, will you go with me?" Of course, was the answer, and that was just what the thirteen-year-old needed to hear. Celina had grown particularly close to her mother, especially because Felicja had essentially become her sole parent ever since she had been separated from her father at Płaszów a year-a-and-a-half earlier. Knowing she could count on her mother helped Celina tamp down her fears and get her through their three-and-a-half-week stay at Auschwitz.[4]

Like most of the Schindler women, Celina and her mother believed their arrival at Auschwitz had been a terrible mistake, but the temporary stop had been planned. It was part of the SS policy to first quarantine prisoners before moving them between camps. Thus, inmates were sent to secure locations where they were searched, shaved, and disinfected before being transported to their final destination. The women would have been sent to the Gross-Rosen concentration camp because, administratively, Schindler's operation in Brünnlitz was one of its sub-camps, but it no longer had a women's camp, so they were sent instead to Auschwitz, which was the next closest concentration camp.[5]

Apparently only one woman, Helen Sternlicht Rosenzweig, knew of the planned Auschwitz detour. She had been one of Göth's maids, and Oskar Schindler told her of his planned factory in Czechoslovakia and said that she would be on the list of Jews to work there. He took down the names of her two sisters and had them added to the list and then told her that there would be a quarantine stop at Auschwitz before the women would be taken to Brünnlitz.[6]

At least one other *Schindlerjude*, Stella Müller-Madej, recalled that a woman on the train had told her mother that they were heading to Auschwitz. Actually, the women were being sent to Auschwitz II-Birkenau—the largest of the camps in the Auschwitz system, which combined the complex's killing center with a concentration camp and included a camp for women—but the Nazis had no reason to tell the women anything about the journey, and nearly all expected a direct trip to Schindler's new factory.[7]

Once forced from the train, the women trudged through the mud and cold to the sauna building—so dubbed because this was where inmates received disinfection baths—for registration and quarantine as the female SS guards shouted and taunted them: "Płaszów scum! We shouldn't be wasting our time with you." There, after stripping off all their clothes, the humiliating experience began: the women were subjected to invasive, full body cavity searches and then had all their bodily hair removed with old and dull "rusty scissors and razor blades," which left them with bloody cuts and sores. Many cried out in pain.[8]

The episode was too much for Celina, who began whimpering when her hair was being shorn and sobbed, "They're cutting all my beautiful hair." Her mother whispered back, "Don't cry about your hair, pray for your head, and you'll have your hair [back eventually]." For some unknown reason, Celina's thick, chestnut brown hair was clipped short but not shaved like most of the other women. After the haircutting, she and the rest of the Schindler women were deloused, which sometimes involved being bathed in hot steam, but Müller-Madej remembered that it merely consisted of guards hitting the women's newly shaved heads with rags soaked in some kind of disinfectant.[9]

Still naked, the women were then pushed into a large shower room and an iron door was closed behind them. They had heard about the gas chambers and anxiously stood and waited. "We were petrified," Celina remembered, "We didn't know if it would be water or gas." Nothing happened; their worry rose, and then water fell from the showerheads. Hysteria broke out when the women realized they would survive their first few hours at Auschwitz. Celina was overjoyed but kept what she saw as good fortune in perspective, understanding that the shower only meant "we had another day."[10]

When the iron door opened, the women were hurried out of the shower into a room where they were ordered to pick up a pair of wooden clogs and take an outfit from a pile of civilian clothes (all with a red stripe painted on the back) and get dressed. Few women were lucky enough to pick clothes that fit, with most getting clothes too big or too tight. One woman happened to select a "ballet dress," and once she had it on, she began dancing around the room. Felicja could only conclude that stress had gotten to the woman, and she "had lost her mind."[11]

Once situated, the Schindler women did some work while at Auschwitz including cleaning the latrines and barracks or sweeping snow, but much of their time was spent inside their barracks except for the hours outside in the cold lined up at roll call three times a day. Still, there was a "temporary sense" to their stay, and before long rumors spread to other inmates that these women were heading to a labor camp. The Schindler group's intended destination, however, did not keep the horrors of the camp at bay.[12]

The next day, Celina faced Josef Mengele, the camp's chief physician. He held a two-hour selection of the 2,000 women who had arrived from Płaszów the previous evening. Most, including all the Schindler women, were ordered back to the barracks, but the "Angel of Death" sent 235 women he deemed unfit for work to the gas chambers. Regrettably, Celina soon had a much more terrifying encounter with Mengele.[13]

One morning, guards came into Celina and her mother's barracks and said they needed twenty or so women to peel potatoes. Although Felicja had earlier pledged never to leave Celina alone as long as they were held by the Nazis, she and her daughter were famished, and she saw an opportunity to pilfer some food scraps for them. Celina begged her not to go, but Felicja assured her it would be fine, and she and the other volunteers left with the guards. But camp officials had not sought out the women for kitchen work. Instead, they were taken to the infirmary where nurses drew blood, which, ironically was used to provide plasma for wounded German soldiers.[14]

After Felicja left, guards returned to the barracks and marched Celina and the rest of the women to a different building where another selection took place. The women were ordered to strip and walk past Mengele, who was waiting in a heavy fur coat with a yellow pencil in hand, which he pointed in one direction or the other as each woman passed by. He directed those he wanted to live to the right. With great sighs of relief, they quickly picked up their clothing and rushed out of the building. But Celina was notably skinny, and Mengele steered her to the left, where those intended for the gas chamber stood. Frightened beyond belief, Celina knew she was in the wrong group.[15]

But then for whatever reason, Mengele reconsidered his decision and ordered those designated for death to file past him a second time. When it was Celina's turn to pass by Mengele again, she stopped, looked up at him with tears in her eyes and said in German, *"Lassen Sie mich"* ("Let me go"). Remarkably, Mengele pointed her to the right, and she gathered up her clothes and ran from the building sobbing uncontrollably. "I'm thirteen years old and I've just been given life by Dr. Mengele," Celina observed years later. "I don't know what made me do it; I wouldn't be this brave now."[16]

As Celina and the Schindler women struggled through such terrors, they hoped they would eventually be taken to the Brünnlitz factory. They also wondered how the Schindler men were faring, wrongly believing the men had been sent directly to the plant. But the Schindler men had likewise gone through a quarantine experience as well. They left Płaszów a week before the women, and as Celina's father Ignacy remembered, conditions on the railcars were awful. "There was no food or water, and we couldn't sit because we were jammed in so tightly." At least one man, Emanuel Taubé, had a nervous breakdown.[17]

After twenty hours, they were ordered off the train, shocked to learn they were at Gross-Rosen, a Nazi concentration camp roughly two hundred miles northwest of Płaszów. *Schindlerjude* Leon Leyson, then just fifteen, recalled, "None of us had any idea what our being in Gross-Rosen meant. Why were we there? How had this happened? Was this part of Schindler's plan that he kept to himself? Was it merely temporary, or was it our last stop?"[18]

Much like the women, the men went through a registration process where they were forced to strip naked, undergo full body searches, and had all their bodily hair shaved off. Ignacy thought the hair would be used to make soap or stuff mattresses. They were deloused and sent to the showers where, like the women, they were unsure they would come out alive. Then, naked, they had to run through the cold to a storehouse where they were issued used shirts and pants, a cap, and either wooden clogs or leather shoes. The clothes were mismatched and ill-fitting; Ignacy received two left shoes.[19]

Gross-Rosen proved a hellish experience. Besides facing daily uncertainty, the seven hundred men spent time in two cramped rooms when they were not forced to do calisthenics outside for most of the day. At mealtime, each room of prisoners was given fifty bowls of food to pass around among their fellow inmates. German criminal inmates guarded the Schindler men, and beatings were common. Unlike their female counterparts, however, the men's concentration camp stay was mercifully brief, and on October 21, after only five days, the men were put on a train for a twenty-one-hour trip to Brünnlitz.[20]

They reached Schindler's sub-camp in the large industrial complex at noon the following day. Some of the men remembered that Oskar Schindler was there to greet them when they arrived. Others recalled seeing his wife Emilie Schindler and the camp commandant, Josef Leipold. The men then saw the unfinished factory facility. Schindler had had 250 railcars of material sent from Emalia, and the men's first job would be to erect the munitions plant by putting the equipment and machinery in place. Because the men's barracks had not been built yet, nor had their bunks arrived, the men slept on straw spread out on the second floor of the factory building for the next few weeks.[21]

As the men were setting up the machinery, they worried about what had happened to the Schindler women, who, in many cases, were their wives, daughters, or mothers. Schindler, of course, knew the women had been sent to quarantine, but when they failed to arrive shortly after the men, he became concerned as well and soon worked to secure their release from Auschwitz.[22]

Schindler's effort to free the women and bring them to Brünnlitz most likely took place behind the scenes. This included many phone calls to his contacts in Berlin, the Army Procurement Office, and Gerhard Maurer, head of the office in charge of prisoner labor. Schindler may also have had his girlfriend and secretary Hilde Albrecht travel to Auschwitz with gifts and bribes for camp officials to get the women out of the concentration camp and sent on to Brünnlitz, although leading Schindler biographer David Crowe is skeptical of this because of the danger involved. Whether or not Albrecht made the trip, Crowe and Robin O'Neil, a historian who has written extensively on Schindler, agree that there is no evidence that Schindler himself ever drove to Auschwitz to bribe officials to free the women. Hence the scene depicting Schindler doing so in Thomas Keneally's book and Steven Spielberg's film, *Schindler's List*, they argue, is pure fiction.[23]

Regardless, as Schindler labored to get the women out of Auschwitz and to his factory, they were languishing. After several weeks at the camp, Celina and her mother found themselves standing in line, waiting to get their left forearms tattooed with their prisoner serial number. Contrary to popular belief, the Auschwitz complex—encompassing the Auschwitz I, the main camp; Auschwitz II-Birkenau; and Auschwitz III-Monowitz, a labor camp—was the only Nazi concentration camp facility that tattooed serial numbers on its prisoners. Officials there opted for this permanent identification method rather than sewing numbered patches on inmates' clothing (the method used at all the other camps) because mortality rates were high at Auschwitz, and the tattoos made identifying corpses much easier.[24]

Yet even some at Auschwitz were not tattooed. This included those like the Schindler women who were quarantined there before being sent on to another camp. Initially, in fact, the Schindler women were housed in the Auschwitz II-Birkenau's transit camp, but when that portion of the facility was liquidated in early November, they were transferred to the women's camp. Maybe it was this move that required them to get tattoos. As the Karps moved up the line closer to the tattooist, Celina asked her mother if it would hurt. "No," Felicja replied, "it's just like a pinprick."[25]

But before they were to get their tattoos, the guards suspended the process, and Celina, her mother, and the other Schindler women were directed to join the rest on the transit list. The three hundred women were then lined up and marched by the crematorium before being directed onto boxcars of a waiting train bound for Brünnlitz.[26]

The trip was not without drama. Felicja had not been feeling well the last couple of days and became very ill with a fever, chills, and a cough in the crowded boxcar. It turned out to be pneumonia. While Celina was doing her best to comfort her mother during the journey, the train stopped and then restarted several times, heightening fears among the women. One stop occurred because the German army needed their locomotive, and the train had to await another. When another locomotive was hooked up, they were underway again only to screech to a halt shortly thereafter. Many "went crazy," Müller-Madej recalled, terrified they were back at Auschwitz. Soon, however, the train started moving, and the next time it stopped, Müller-Madej was certain they were going to be killed. But once again, it began moving.[27]

Nearly two days later, the train came to yet another stop. Anxiety ran high throughout the boxcars, but when the doors opened, there was no shouting and no barking dogs. Instead, guards were giving directions for the women to line up and exit the train. Then a car pulled up and out stepped Oskar Schindler and an SS officer, probably camp commandant, Josef Leipold.[28]

Celina and the rest of the women soon realized they were in Brünnlitz, and a wave of relief swept over them as they walked in their standard rows of five a short distance to Schindler's factory building. When they were inside, they saw a large group of men beyond a screen on the plant's main floor. Initially, neither the women nor the men recognized each other because of their further emaciated condition and shaved heads. But once they did, shouting and yelling broke out. The women and the men were pointing at each other, crying out each other's names, and whooping with joy. Celina, her mother, and her father all choked back tears as they had nearly given up hope of ever seeing each other again. As the celebratory reunion continued, the women were served soup. They then were led upstairs where the men slept, and where separate living quarters had been arranged for them as well. The bunks had still not arrived, and as the men had been doing, the women slept on straw, which had been laid on the floor. That did not matter to Celina, though, for she remembered how the heat from the factory below kept the quarters warm and comfortable.[29]

Schindler then spoke to the women: "I know you have been through hell on your way here. Your appearance says it all. Here also, for the time being, you will be forced to suffer many discomforts, but you are brave women." These "discomforts" centered on the limited amount of food he had available for the workers and the spread of disease. He concluded his remarks by providing some details of the camp and saying that those who were ill or had injuries should see the camp doctors. Felicja most likely followed this directive and went down to the infirmary, located in the factory's first floor, to seek treatment for pneumonia. Fortunately, she made a full recovery, but it was without the benefit of medication, such as the relatively new antibiotic penicillin, because the camp's medical supplies were woefully short.[30]

Soon after her mother recuperated, however, Celina fell ill because of the liver damage she had suffered from scarlet fever. Intense stomach pain, nausea, and vomiting made her extremely weak and landed her in the infirmary. There she was looked after by inmate doctors and Emilie Schindler, who had started helping with the sick. Schindler often made farina, a nutrient-rich, Cream of Wheat-like porridge for patients, and she did so for Celina while the teenager was in the hospital. After a couple of weeks of care and convalescence, Celina was back working on the factory floor, but in her mind, it was Emilie Schindler's cooking and compassion that saved her life.[31]

Once Celina was well and working, she rejoined Niusia Horowitz, another teenage inmate, cleaning the plant's large machines. Later, Celina learned to operate a lathe and then worked calibrating some of the equipment. She and the other workers were manufacturing antitank shells, but as both Celina and Felicja recalled, they understood Schindler's intent was that nothing leaving the factory would work. This, however, was probably not possible. Given his contracts with the Armament Inspectorate and the Wehrmacht, Schindler had to manufacture functioning munitions or his operation would surely have been shut down. But Leon Leyson remembered that "we produced almost no usable ammunition," and in fact, over the course of the facility's operation, the factory only delivered one wagonload of antitank shells.[32]

Still, this production level was exceedingly low, but Schindler and his staff were adept at explaining the numbers by maintaining that they had had startup problems. They then kept officials at bay by delivering phony production reports. And when inspectors came to see the facility, Schindler turned on his charm. He schmoozed, gave generous gifts, and boasted about (false) production levels while leading them on tours of the factory floor as workers were scurrying about humming machines. The ploy succeeded, and the factory remained opened, which kept workers away from Nazi death camps.[33]

Of course, the factory was operated as part of the Gross-Rosen concentration camp and watched over by a garrison of one hundred SS staff and guards. The women clearly had to be careful, but conditions at Brünnlitz were unquestionably better than those they had endured at Płaszów or Auschwitz. And while Schindler had leased a lovely villa nearby, he and his wife Emilie chose to live in an apartment he had constructed inside the factory, which made it easier for him to protect his workers from SS personnel. He regularly plied the guards with gifts of alcohol and cigarettes to keep them friendly and later explained that he "had the guards and supervisors under control, which primarily guaranteed humane treatment of my inmates, often against the will of the camp commandant."[34]

Indeed, Celina and the other inmates were relatively safe at Brünnlitz as long as they took precautions around the SS guards and the commandant, who the camp doctor Chaim Hilfstein said, "was dangerous and had to be watched." They also had to tread carefully around certain *Kapos* who could be brutal. Here, *Kapo* Willi stood out as particularly cruel. He had come to Brünnlitz in March 1945 with several Jewish prisoners from another labor camp, and after violently beating an inmate with his whip on his first day there, he became Commandant Leipold's "favorite *Kapo*."[35]

The beating happened on a day Schindler was away from the camp, but when he heard about it, he pulled Willi aside, telling him that the inmates' health was important because they were doing work critical for German soldiers. He therefore could not do anything that might negatively affect their ability to work. Schindler then threatened to have him arrested if he hit a prisoner again. Whether the warning restrained Willi at all is unclear, but he remained "the most feared *Kapo*" in the camp.[36]

Besides trying to protect his workers from the guards, Schindler did his best to keep them well fed. Initially, he was able to provide inmates three meals a day totaling roughly two thousand calories each, an ample amount by concentration camp standards. But that caloric amount fell after the first of the year when food supplies began to dwindle. Breakfast usually consisted of watery coffee and bread; lunch was thin soup with few vegetables and sometimes bits of horsemeat; and for dinner, inmates were given more soup, bread, and occasionally small pieces of cheese. [37]

By winter 1945, the lack of food became a problem for the entire camp, and that spring, the inmates' meals dropped down to two a day. Schindler spent a growing amount of time trading for food and other necessary items. Meanwhile, inmates grew hungry and sought ways to supplement their food rations. Leon Leyson "scrounged for food every day." He became friendly with the kitchen staff, who let him collect leftover bits of food from kettles used to cook the daily soup.[38]

As food grew scarce, Celina scrounged for anything edible as well. But like other female inmates, she spent some of her free time knitting desirable woolen items, which could be traded for food. On one occasion, for instance, Celina knitted underwear and a camisole for a Czech woman who worked in the camp kitchen and received two loaves of bread for the clothing. Celina and her mother shared the one loaf, and she sneaked the other to her father. He had made Celina's knitting needles, and the yarn she and the others used had been stolen from the adjacent Hoffmann mill. When Hoffmann discovered the theft, he was ready to report it to the SS, only to be dissuaded from doing so by Schindler, who bribed him to stay quiet.[39]

While working in the armament plant, Celina regularly saw Schindler on the factory floor, where he chain-smoked and was frequently joined by dignitaries and other officials. Two visitors stood out in Celina's mind. First was Raimund Titsch, the general manager of Madritsch's former textile mill. When Titsch saw Celina, he came over to talk with her. During the conversation, he asked if she needed anything. Celina said she would like other shoes; she only had the pair of wooden clogs from Auschwitz, and her feet were always cold. Much to her delight, a week later a shipment of wooden-soled shoes with leather uppers arrived for all the women inmates. Celina was never sure if Titsch or Schindler was responsible for the shoes, but they were a godsend and provided much better protection against the cold.[40]

The other caller Celina remembered was former commandant Amon Göth. The last time she had seen the sadistic and unpredictable Göth was in Płaszów before his arrest, and as she had always done, she averted her eyes and cowered as he walked by. But this time it was completely different.

Göth had been released from prison on his own recognizance in October, while the investigation of his crimes continued. The following spring, 1945, he came to see Schindler about boxes of personal items that the businessman had agreed to store for him. Many inmates panicked when they heard of Göth's visit. Mietek Pemper, who had been Göth's inmate secretary, was shocked to see him. Schindler, however, reassured Pemper and a few others, "He's no longer the same Göth. He can't hurt you anymore." Rena Ferber Finder had that sense and thought he looked much less intimidating because he had grown thin and was wearing civilian clothing. Celina had the same impression and because she felt safe under Schindler's auspices, she was emboldened enough to glare directly at Göth. She felt triumphant: "It was a very good feeling to look the monster right in the face."[41]

Shortly after Göth's departure, the Russian advance drew closer to the camp. Local Czechs kept the inmates informed of their progress. Schindler knew of the situation and was concerned that Leipold would liquidate the camp and kill the inmates before the Red Army arrived. Indeed, both Celina and her mother remembered that graves had already been prepared to dispose of the inmates' remains; Stella Müller-Madej said that Leipold frequently took Schindler into the nearby forest to show him the progress being made on the ditches for that purpose. Schindler thus decided to get rid of Leipold to protect his workers.[42]

Celina did not have a clear memory of these efforts, but both her parents did, recalling in separate 1981 interviews that Schindler sent Leipold a falsified telegram ordering him to the front. Müller-Madej similarly believed that Schindler created fake documents calling for Leipold and the guards to head to the front lines.[43]

Another version of Schindler's work to push Leipold out involved getting him drunk and convincing him to volunteer for duty at the front. But the commandant had a change of heart when he was actually ordered to the front. He explained to Schindler that one of the reasons he did not want to go was that he did not know how to use grenades. Schindler replied that he had some hand grenades stashed away, and he could show Leipold how to use them.[44]

The noise of Leipold practicing with the grenades was very loud and caught the attention of Field Marshall Ferdinand Schörner, in charge of the German Army Group Central, who was stationed nearby. He came to investigate, and Schindler told him Leipold was playing with grenades instead of heading to the front. Schörner ordered Leipold to the front at once. But Leipold refused to go. A few days later, Schindler hosted a raucous party for SS officials. Everyone got drunk, except Schindler, and when the party wound down, he drove Leipold to the front. A truck with his SS guards followed.[45]

Although the details of Leipold's exit from the camp are a bit ambigious, Schindler clearly played a major role in ousting him. The commandant and the guards were replaced by older and milder SS men for the last days of the war. Yet Schindler did more to safeguard his workers. He had been covertly amassing weapons such as rifles, pistols, and even a few machines guns and hand grenades (some of which he had let Leipold use) to arm a secret Jewish self-protection force made up of inmates to guard the camp as the war wound down. He then created a committee to organize and oversee the group, which had established contacts with the Czech underground operating outside the camp.[46]

But Schindler knew that while his workers would probably be safe when the Soviets arrived, he would solely be viewed as a Nazi and either be killed or arrested. Consequently, he and his wife Emilie prepared to flee prior to their arrival. On the evening of May 8, the day the war officially ended, Schindler gathered all the workers, staff, and guards in the factory to say goodbye. He spoke about the Nazi's defeat and the freedom the inmates would now enjoy. He also emphasized that not all Germans were bad and asked that the gathered Jews not seek retribution, which he suggested would be meted out by the authorities. Then he thanked his German staff and the current SS guards, who he said had behaved with "extraordinary humanness and correctness." He continued, explaining that it might be safer for the guards to abandon their posts and leave camp immediately, before facing the Russia army. They did, and the camp was then protected by the inmate defense group Schindler had established.[47]

Schindler added that he and his wife would be leaving the village in a few hours. The inmates presented him with a token of their appreciation, thanking him for protecting them over the past few years. It was a gold ring, crafted by prisoners who had been goldsmiths, by melting down gold fillings donated for the cause by inmate Simon Jereth. Inside the ring was an inscription in Hebrew: "Whoever saves a life saves the whole world." Schindler left shortly after midnight.[48]

Before he left, Schindler had done one last thing for his workers. Over the past several months, he had used bribes to buy supplies and had accrued eighteen truckloads of goods for his workers. The stockpile included bolts of wool and khaki cloth, leather, sewing equipment, including thread and scissors, men's shoes, and vodka. After Schindler left, the warehouses were opened, and each *Schindlerjude* was given some material, sewing equipment, a pair of shoes, and vodka. Schindler's thinking was that the former inmates could make some clothing and use the other items to barter or sell for necessities during their first weeks of freedom. Celina recalled getting two bolts of fabric and five pairs of scissors, which, she said "proved invaluable."[49]

Late in the morning on Wednesday, May 9, ten or so hours after Schindler left, Celina, her parents, and many other inmates were gathered together in the camp when they saw a lone Russian soldier ride up to the gates on a white horse. He asked who they were, and many responded that they were Jews from Poland. He replied: "Brothers and sisters you are free. Take off your [prison] numbers [sewn on your clothes]. *Schindlerjude* Moshe Taubé remembered that the soldier was a Jew and spoke Yiddish, which led him "to be mobbed" by the inmates and "kissed from head to toe."[50]

More Russian soldiers arrived and amid the excitement, confusion, and commotion of liberation, some of the Jews that had come into the camp with the *Kapo* Willi sought revenge. They had experienced his brutality well before Brünnlitz, which included his killing of a number of their fellow inmates. Willi was seized, and with a Russian soldier overseeing the process, charges against the *Kapo* were drafted. Some wanted Willi to be tried for his crimes, while others just wanted him hanged. Later that afternoon, Willi was strung up with wire thrown over a factory beam and hanged. Celina witnessed the particularly horrific scene and broke down in tears. A Russian soldier standing nearby did not understand her crying over the execution of the cruel German *Kapo*. He was angered by what he thought was sympathy of Willi and pulled out his pistol, threatening to shoot Celina.[51]

Fortunately, Celina's father Ignacy was right there and immediately intervened. He spoke to the soldier in Russian and soon calmed him down. Ignacy said that his daughter was just a terrified child who had experienced years of terror, and the gruesome hanging was more than she could bear. The soldier seemed to buy the explanation and holstered his gun. Felicja breathed a sigh of relief; she was certain her husband had saved their daughter's life.[52]

Then it was Felicja who protected the family. With the camp open, local Czechs came in with food and some supplies for the newly freed inmates. "They were wonderful, warm people," Celina remembered. But some of the starving Jews, who had been so hungry for so long, gorged themselves and became very sick with diarrhea. A few even died because their diminished digestive tracts could not handle the volume or richness of the food. When the Karps were given a loaf of bread and some butter, Felicja carefully doled it out, one unbuttered piece at a time, for the butter, she feared, might make them ill. The three savored the bread, and because they were eating small amounts at a time, none of them got sick.[53]

Maybe one of the most difficult initial adjustments for Celina, though, was getting used to walking by herself or with someone else "because we always had to be in fives." Whenever she was out walking, she would be thinking, "Where is my five." And when Celina and her parents strolled down to the village that first weekend after liberation, she recalled, "It was so strange to be able to walk out of the camp to begin with."[54]

Yet that same weekend, some sense of normalcy was restored. The first Friday after liberation, many of the Schindler women took back a Jewish religious ritual that had been absent from their lives in the camps over the past few years. They picked up candles from the camp warehouse and late that afternoon went down to the bank of the nearby Zwittawa River (now the Svitava River). There, just before sunset, they followed the tradition of lighting candles to usher in the Sabbath. It was "a sight to behold," Felicja remembered.[55]

But attaining any lasting normality would be a lengthy and challenging process. Having survived and now finally free from the horrors of the Holocaust, Celina and the rest of the former inmates were plainly "disoriented and uncertain." After a few days of getting their footing in camp and spending time in the village of Brünnlitz, most were ready to leave. The Karps joined the exodus, hoping to return to their homes, locate lost family members and friends, and rebuild their prewar lives cruelly stolen by the Nazis.[56]

Celina and her mother,
Felicja (later known
as Phyllis) Karp, 1931.
Courtesy of Celina Biniaz.

Celina and father, Ignacy
(later known as Irvin)
Karp in Krakow, 1933.
Courtesy of Celina Biniaz.

Karp family shortly before Celina's grandfather moved to Jewish Palestine, later Israel. Celina is seated next to her grandfather on the far right. Her parents are standing behind her, circa 1934. Courtesy of Celina Biniaz.

LEFT: Celina and her family at the building of Piłsudski Mound in Kraków, circa 1935. The monument was erected to honor Polish leader Józef Piłsudski. Left to right: Gucia Wittenberg, Felicja's sister and Celina's aunt, Felicja, Ignacy, and Celina. Courtesy of Celina Biniaz. RIGHT: Celina before her first day of school, 1937. Courtesy of Celina Biniaz.

View of the arched entrance to the Kraków ghetto, circa 1941. United States Holocaust Memorial Museum, courtesy of Instytut Pamieci Narodowej.

Jewish women at forced labor camp at Płaszów. Behind them is a barrack owned by Julius Madritsch's clothing firm, where Celina and her family worked, 1943-1944. United States Holocaust Memorial Museum, courtesy of Leopold Page Photographic Collection.

Ignacy Karp, a manager of the Madritsch factory, overseeing the unloading of cloth by Jewish prisoners in Płaszów, 1943-1944. United States Holocaust Memorial Museum, courtesy of Leopold Page Photographic Collection.

Oskar Schindler visiting with an SS officer at a dinner party in Kraków, April 8, 1942. United States Holocaust Memorial Museum, courtesy of Leopold Page Photographic Collection.

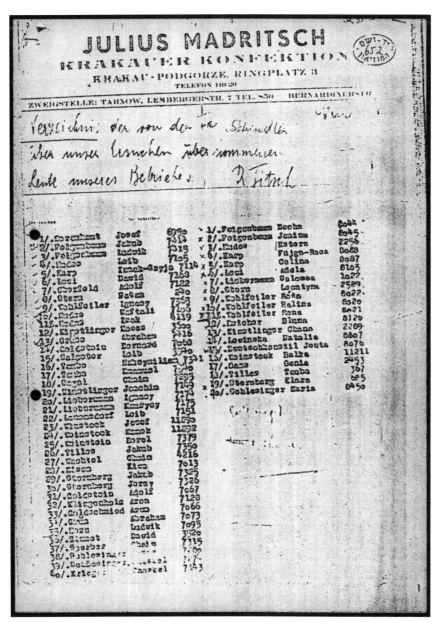

The Madritsch-Titsch list of workers to be sent to Oskar Schindler's factory in Brünnlitz. Celina, her parents, and uncle, Adolf Oberfeld are included on the list. ITS Digital file, 1.1.19.1/0004/0002, accessed at the United States Holocaust Memorial Museum Digital Collection, March 4, 2020.

KL Groß-Rosen – AL Brünnlitz – Namensliste d. weibl. Häftlinge / 2. Blatt

Lfd. Nr.	Art	H.Nr.	Name und Vorname	Geb.-Datum	Beruf	Einsatz d.H.
61.	Jü.Po.	76261	Garde Mira	7. 8.1899	Metallarbeiterin	Fa.
62.	"	2	Garde Irena	2. 4.1918	"	Fa.
63.	"	3	Geller Anna	8. 9.1912	"	Fa.
64.	"	4	Geminder Pela	18. 7.1914	"	Fa.
65.	"	5	Geminder Helene	16. 5.1910	Schreibkraft	Fa.
66.	"	6	Geminder Lora	5. 1.1923	Metallarbeiterin	Fa.
67.	"	7	Gerner Eidl	22.11.1896	"	Fa.
68.	"	8	Gerner Pela	17. 1.1921	"	Fa.
69.	"	9	Getzler Syda	13. 5.1913	"	Fa.
70.	"	76270	Ginter Ernestine	16. 1.1910	"	Fa.
71.	"	1	Glockenberg Rosa	4. 1.1920	Schreibkraft	Fa.
72.	"	2	Goldberg Salomea	18.12.1918	Metallarbeiterin	Fa.
73.	"	3	Goldberg Syda	8. 3.1922	"	Fa.
74.	"	4	Goldmann Hinde Debora	6. 7.1892	"	Ha.
75.	"	5	Goldstein Cypora	15. 1.1899	"	Ha.
76.	"	6	Grajower Sara	30. 7.1923	"	Fa.
77.	"	7	Grünberg Leonie	23.10.1919	"	Fa.
78.	"	8	Grüner Hanka	3.11.1905	"	Fa.
79.	"	9	Grüner Helena	20.12.1927	"	Fa.
80.	"	76280	Grünspan Sabina	24. 1.1918	"	Fa.
81.	"	1	Handelbaum Mala	24. 7.1917	"	Fa.
82.	"	2	Grünwald Sabina	26.11.1911	"	Fa.
83.	"	3	Grosner Gustawa	22.10.1908	"	Fa.
84.	"	4	Groß Zipora	26. 3.1916	"	Fa.
85.	"	5	Groß Zelma	26. 6.1912	"	Fa.
86.	"	6	Großbard Paulina	3. 8.1925	"	Fa.
87.	"	7	Güns-Sperling Bronia	21. 8.1915	"	Fa.
88.	"	8	Guthers Augusta	18. 5.1897	"	Fa.
89.	"	9	Haubenstock Zofia	14. 5.1921	"	Fa.
90.	"	76290	Haubenstock Maria	12. 4.1917	"	Fa.
91.	"	1	Finder Eugenia	13. 7.1915	"	Fa.
92.	"	2	Heilman Sara	20.11.1910	"	Fa.
93.	"	3	Hendler Lea	10. 5.1908	"	Ha.
94.	"	4	Henig Chana	6. 6.1902	"	Fa.
95.	"	5	Herzog Lea	12.12.1922	"	Fa.
96.	"	6	Herzog Estera	15. 6.1899	"	Fa.
97.	"	7	Heublum Mina	11. 1.1897	"	Fa.
98.	"	8	Hilfstein Miriam	25. 1.1897	Schneiderin	Fa.
99.	"	9	Hirsch Helene	3. 9.1911	Metallarbeiterin	Fa.
100.	"	76300	Hirsch Anna	29. 3.1915	Schneiderin	Fa.
101.	"	1	Hirsch Helga	1. 7.1923	Metallarbeiterin	Ha.
102.	"	2	Hirschberg Sali	18. 5.1903	"	Fa.
103.	"	3	Hirschfeld Folda	21. 4.1921	Schneiderin	Fa.
104.	"	4	Holländer Rachela	23. 3.1917	Metallarbeiterin	Fa.
105.	"	5	Holzmann Perl	14. 3.1910	Schreibkraft	Fa.
106.	"	6	Horn Estera	24.11.1918	Metallarbeiterin	Ha.
107.	"	7	Horowitz Bronislawa	22. 4.1930	"	Fa.
108.	"	8	Horowitz Malina	13. 3.1929	"	Fa.
109.	"	9	Horowitz Rosa	15. 5.1912	"	Fa.
110.	"	76310	Horowitz Ruchel	14.12.1906	"	Fa.
111.	"	1	Horowitz Bela	10. 3.1920	"	Fa.
112.	"	2	Horowitz Sara	24. 6.1888	"	Fa.
113.	"	3	Hudes Estera	10. 3.1910	"	Fa.
114.	"	4	Ickovics Pela	21. 2.1918	"	Fa.
115.	"	5	Israeli Stella	4. 3.1910	"	Fa.
116.	"	6	Jereth Chaja	12. 7.1892	"	Fa.
117.	"	7	Karmel-Poß Adela	5. 4.1921	"	Ha.
118.	"	8	Karp Celina	28. 5.1923	"	Fa.
119.	"	9	Karp Feiga Raca	15. 9.1905	"	Fa.
120.	"	76320	Katolik Cyla	14. 5.1914	"	Fa.

Female prisoners, Schindler's List. KL Gross-Rosen/detachment Brünnlitz status, October 21, 1944. Celina and her mother are listed near the bottom of the page. (#'s 118 & 119). ITS Digital file, 1.1.11.1/0048/0044, accessed at the United States Holocaust Memorial Museum Digital Collection, March 26, 2021.

Celina and her friend Jadzia Bauman shortly after the war in Kraków, 1945. Courtesy of Celina Biniaz.

The *Englisches Institut Mindelheim* convent where Celina was tutored by Mater Leontine, Mindelheim, Germany. Building is pictured here in 2019. Courtesy of Fabian Vetter.

Celina and Mater Leontine, 1947.
Courtesy of Celina Biniaz.

Celina, middle, with her friends
Angelika Bloch on the left and
her sister Hanelore on the right,
Mindelheim, Germany, circa 1946.
Courtesy of Celina Biniaz.

LEFT: Celina skiing in Mindelheim, Germany, circa 1946. RIGHT: Celina on a slide in the Bremen refugee compound where she, her parents, and many other displaced persons were housed before traveling to their new homes. Courtesy of Celina Biniaz.

On the SS *Marine Marlin* shortly before departing for the United States, 1947. Felicja and Celina are standing on the left next to two other passengers. Courtesy of Celina Biniaz.

Celina, Dottie Isaacson, an old friend of Felicja's, and Felicja in New York City, shortly after the Karps arrived in the United States, 1947. Courtesy of Celina Biniaz.

In New York City, Celina and her parents after they arrived from Europe, 1947. Left to right: Celina's aunt, Augusta Karp (partially cut off in original photo), Felicja Karp, David Karp, Celina's uncle, Celina, and Ignacy Karp. Courtesy of Celina Biniaz.

FIVE
FROM DP TO U.S.

A FEW DAYS AFTER THE Karps returned to Kraków in late May 1945, Celina turned fourteen. Liberation had given her the chance to celebrate her birthday for the first time in years. She remembered how special going to a movie theater used to be and decided that was all she wanted for her birthday. Her mother helped arrange it. Celina borrowed a blouse and skirt from their landlord, but she was so gaunt she had to wrap the skirt around herself twice and hook it together with a safety pin to make it fit. She then headed down to the theater and saw *Mad About Music*. The 1938 American film starred Deanna Durbin as a fourteen-year-old at a girls' boarding school in Switzerland. Durbin's character enjoyed a life Celina could hardly imagine, and she found the light-hearted musical "absolutely charming."[1]

But her escape from reality was brief. After the movie, Celina walked by a full-length mirror in the theater lobby and saw her reflection, something she had not seen for several years. She was shocked: "I couldn't believe what I saw. My hair had started to grow out, and I was as skinny as anything and looked awful, like a skeleton really." Indeed, historian David Nasaw observed, "Jewish survivors were distinguishable by their pallor, emaciated physiques, shaved heads, lice-infested bodies, and vacant look in their eyes." Celina recalled, "We were known as *katzetniks*, because the German word for concentration camp was *katzet*....I weighed only 35 kilos, which is a little over 70 pounds so...nobody could mistake me for anything else other than a concentration camp survivor."[2]

Like thousands of other survivors, Celina, her parents, and probably her uncle, Adolf Oberfeld, had decided to head back to their prewar home in

Kraków. They had heard a rumor that Gucia (Felicja's sister and Oberfeld's wife) had survived the war and was in the city waiting for them. There they also assumed they could piece their lives back together, get Celina back in school, reconnect with other family and friends, and restart their careers. But making the two-hundred-mile-trip to Kraków would be difficult because bridges were destroyed, and trains were not running in or out of Brünnlitz. Ignacy asked the town mayor for help and likely offered him some of the products Schindler had given the family. The mayor provided the Karps with two horses, a guide, and travel passes to Prague. That city was out of their way, but they understood that railroads were operating there, and the family anticipated they could ride a train from Prague to Kraków.[3]

They left Brünnlitz on May 13 or 14. It is unclear how far the guide escorted them, but Celina remembered that they walked a lot and hitched rides whenever possible. Although destruction was widespread, Czech people along the route were extremely generous and helpful, giving the family food and providing them with shelter at night. As they had hoped, once in Prague they were able to stow away on a train bound for Kraków.[4]

After traveling for eight to ten days, they finally arrived in Kraków. Ignacy looked up Jan, his friend and onetime Hogo janitor who had held some of Karps' photographs and mementos during the war. Jan was thrilled to see Ignacy and the family and must have been amazed they survived. He welcomed them into his home, fed them, and then gave them a place to stay for the night. He also returned their keepsakes.[5]

Over the next day or two, Ignacy and Felicja went to see their old apartment and were not at all surprised to see it occupied. Ignacy noted that it had been rented by a communist party official. Felicja, however, had a much more specific recollection of an encounter at the apartment. When the Karps knocked on the door, a woman answered, and Felicja told her she used to live there. The woman was uninterested, but Felicja persisted saying that she had stored some valuable items inside and wanted them back. The woman said there was nothing there, but Felicja talked her way into the building, went down to the coalbin, and retrieved the cloth-wrapped package with two silver candlesticks she had hidden before being forced into the ghetto. The woman grabbed them and said they were hers. Felicja gave in, saying, "You can keep them." Maybe worse was the woman's chilling response. As she shut the door on Felicja, she hissed, "Hitler should have finished you off."[6]

Unfortunately, such antisemitism was rife in Poland. When *Schindlerjude* Rena Ferber Finder and her family were preparing to return to their Polish home, Russian soldiers warned them, "When you get back to Kraków, don't go out at night. Some Polish people don't want you there, and there could be trouble." But the Karps were eager to reestablish themselves in the city and hoped to put down roots again.[7]

To that end, Ignacy and Felicja rented a room in an apartment near their old building from a woman they knew before the war. They paid for the room with some of the items Schindler had given them. Another Jewish couple the Karps knew from the Madritsch factory and then Schindler's Brünnlitz plant rented another bedroom in the same apartment. The Karps very well may have helped them secure the room. Sadly, this couple was soon dealing with tragic news. They had entrusted the care of their two daughters to a Polish Catholic family when they were sent to Płaszów in 1943. But when they reconnected with the family to get their children, they learned that one had been killed in a car accident during the war.[8]

Ignacy, Felicja, and likely Oberfeld had also gone down to the recently established Jewish community center located in a former school. Its prima-ry purpose was to register returning Jews and connect them with missing family and friends. The Karps and Gucia's husband were not among the fortunate few who discovered that their loved ones were alive or saw notes posted along the office walls with contact information for them. They may not have learned anything on that first visit, but they eventually heard of Gucia's death, probably through someone at the center.[9]

One of the family's other major concerns was to get Celina back in school. She had just completed second grade a few months before Germany invaded Poland in 1939, which interrupted her education for the duration of the war. "I could read but I couldn't do anything else," Celina recalled, "so the priority…was to fill in the gaps in my education. I had not held a pencil in my hand in all those years, five and a half years." Her parents therefore hired a local woman to tutor their daughter, hoping she could make up several years of schooling in a few months and get admitted into the girl's gymnasium (secondary school).[10]

Celina was "ashamed" that she "knew nothing" and welcomed the return to learning, happily going to her tutor's house daily. She eagerly soaked up everything and passed the gymnasium entrance exams that summer. In September, Celina became one of two Jewish students admitted to the Queen Jadwiga Private Gymnasium for Girls, where she began the equivalent of eighth grade.[11]

But she did more than just study that summer. Celina also "focused on retrieving a normal life" and worked hard to recover all she had missed over the past six years. She wanted to be a regular teenager, and on weekends she got together with some newly made friends, went to an occasional movie, learned the steps to swing dancing, and reconnected with a Jewish friend from her prewar childhood named Jadzia Bauman.[12]

Jadzia's parents had been good friends of Ignacy and Felicja as well, but sometime after the Germans invaded Poland, Jadzia, her sister, and mother fled Kraków. All blonds, they obtained forged Aryan papers claiming they were Polish gentiles and went east to Warsaw, thinking no one there would guess they were Jews. Jadzia survived the war, but her mother and sister did not. Her father had been sent to a concentration camp, but he survived. He would eventually reunite with Jadzia, who had returned to Krakow after the war and was living with her aunt. There she became reacquainted with Celina.[13]

That summer, while Celina studied and adjusted to the regular rhythms of teenage life, her parents took a trip to Vienna on behalf of businessmen Julius Madritsch and Raimond Titsch. The provisional government in Austria had begun a denazification process, and Ignacy and Felicja appeared before the Vienna Court of Appeal in the city's Soviet zone, testifying to Madritsch's and Titsch's efforts to save Jews during the war. When her parents came back to Kraków, Celina thought they seemed flush with cash, and she always wondered if either Madritsch or Titsch had held valuables for them during the Holocaust and returned them in Vienna.[14]

After Celina started school that fall, the Polish government offered Ignacy a job. He was asked to run a factory in Breslau, a German city that became the Polish city of Wrocław after the war, and went to inspect the facility, roughly one hundred fifty miles northwest of Kraków. But while he was considering the position, widespread pogroms broke out across the country. Such "violence against the Jews," historian David Nasaw wrote, "was homegrown, endemic, and encouraged by popular support. It was not carried out in the middle of the night, but often in broad daylight, in public view. Local officials could not halt the violence even had they tried to, and they rarely did."[15]

Ignacy and Felicja already knew that reestablishing themselves in Kraków would be difficult, but they now feared for their safety. Ignacy turned down the job offer, and he, Felicja, and Celina prepared to leave Poland in favor of Germany and the American zone of occupation (encompassing the states of Bavaria, Bremen, Hesse, and Württemberg-Baden) where they thought they would receive assistance and be protected. From there they eventually hoped to make their way to Israel (then Palestine) or the United States.[16]

They were not alone. Thousands of Jews who returned to Poland after the war had similar experiences and flooded displaced persons (DPs) camps in Germany. Rabbi Abraham Klausner, a Jewish U.S. Army chaplain who arrived at Dachau days after liberation and became an outspoken advocate of Holocaust survivors in these camps over the next few years, reported in December 1945 that about 40 percent of the twenty-five thousand Jewish DPs in Bavaria "fled from Poland and have come to whatever sanctuary this area has to offer. At the present time, the Polish Jews are arriving in large numbers and as difficult as it is, we manage to share our misery with them."[17]

The DP camps had been ill prepared for the large numbers of refugees and were soon overwhelmed. Klausner lobbied tirelessly to improve conditions at the camps, noting at one point, "It is better to be a conquered German than a liberated Jew." Earlier that June, President Harry Truman had sent attorney Earl Harrison, the U.S. representative to the Intergovernmental Committee on Refugees to Europe, to investigate the situation in postwar Europe. Klausner met Harrison in Munich and persuaded him to visit some DP camps, including a nearby one in Landsberg. Harrison's trip resulted in a blistering report that August, highly critical of the U.S. Army's management of the camps. He wrote, "As matters now stand, we appear to be treating the Jews as the Nazis treated them, except that we do not exterminate them."[18]

General Dwight Eisenhower, commander of U.S. forces in Europe, responded by making some changes in the camps. The United Nations Relief and Rehabilitation Administration (UNRRA) took over their administration, but conditions only gradually improved and significant problems remained at the end of the year. The Landsberg camp, for example, had originally been built as a German army camp intended to accommodate 2,500 soldiers, but as of December 1945, it housed 6,300 displaced Jews. In addition, an American journalist wrote that month, "[Building] windows are broken, although there is bitter cold. Blankets and clothing are insufficient. The food is unpalatable and inadequate. Only cold water can be had for washing. The floors of the washrooms are sheeted with ice. The pipes are rusty or broken so that only one toilet is available for every hundred persons."[19]

There is no way to know if Celina or her family were aware of these issues at the DP camps, but by the fall, they were ready to abandon Poland for one of these centers in Germany. Celina hated being forced to leave school again, and in her words "went back to being stupid." And she was unhappy to have to say goodbye to her friends, especially Jadzia, who gave

Celina a photograph of the two of them and a note pledging never to forget her. The friends stayed in contact for the next few years. Jadzia ended up emigrating to Israel with her father, and she and Celina ultimately fell out of touch.[20]

But getting out of Poland and eventually into Germany would be a lengthy, challenging, and costly process. National borders were either closed or carefully guarded, and many roads, railroad tracks, and bridges had been damaged during the war and remained unusable. The first leg of their journey was to Czechoslovakia. Oberfeld, however, did not make this trip with the Karps, and they soon lost track of him. Records suggest, however, that he made his way down to Italy by the end of 1945 and eventually relocated in Israel, where he died in 1950.[21]

Ignacy and Felicja struggled to find a way into Czechoslovakia. They finally made a deal with a Russian soldier, paying him to smuggle them and Celina across the border. He was trucking newspapers to the Czech city of Bratislava (now the capital of Slovakia) 280 miles southwest of Kraków, and the family hid under a tarp below the newspapers, in what must have been a long and uncomfortable journey. Celina remembered how nervous they were at the border crossing. They had to remain perfectly quiet and still while guards checked the driver's travel documents and the back of the truck. Evidently, nothing looked amiss, and Celina and her parents breathed a sigh of relief when the truck started moving again.[22]

As before, the Czech people were welcoming and helpful, providing them with a meal here and lodging there. The Karps probably spent a few days in Bratislava before making their way two hundred miles northwest to Prague by walking and hitching rides. They arrived sometime in late October or early November and found lodging at several places over the course of their week or two stay. Maybe their most interesting overnight accommodation was in a large municipal laundry, which Celina remembered as "especially nice and warm."[23]

While in Prague, Ignacy and Felicja ran into a woman they knew from their past. She put the family up for a few nights and, most importantly, paid the postage on urgent letters Ignacy wanted to mail. One went to his younger brother Felix in Jewish Palestine, and the other went to his older brother David in the United States. He told them that he, Felicja, and Celina had survived the war, gave them the woman's contact information, and asked for their help in getting the family out of Europe.[24]

They also became reacquainted with a man they had known in Kraków who, for a fee, agreed to smuggle them into the American zone in Germany. It was late November when he drove them through Czechoslovakia, and after it was dark, took them across the border through the Bavarian Forest into Germany. He then dropped them off in Hof, a town 175 miles north of Munich. From there, the Karps walked and hitchhiked the 200 miles south to Landsberg, where one of the largest centers for Jewish DPs in the American zone was located.[25]

Conditions at the Landsberg DP camp were poor when the Karps arrived at the end of November, and Felicja was adamant that they find somewhere else to stay. She had had enough of camps and wanted Celina to have a more normal experience in some type of private lodging. As they worked to find other accommodations, however, they spent a couple of weeks at the camp, which Celina observed "was not pleasant, but provided food and a place to stay." While there, Ignacy and Felicja met three or four other Jewish couples who were also concentration camp survivors and were seeking alternative housing as well.[26]

They may have checked with the representatives of the Joint Distribution Committee about boarding possibilities, but somehow the Karps and the other couples were directed to Mindelheim, a small town twenty miles west of Landsberg. There they visited the mayor, who first suggested they seek refuge in a nearby army camp. When none were interested in the idea, the mayor made some inquiries around town and soon found them all rooms to rent from local German families. Interestingly, the idea of housing Jewish DPs in the private homes of Germans had been floated the previous month by U.S. Army chaplain Abraham Klausner.[27]

By mid-December, the Karps took up residence in Mindelheim. They were given a room to rent and kitchen privileges in a fourth-floor apartment above a bank. Their landlord, a widow named Frau Gattemeier, was the bank's caretaker. During an early conversation, Gattemeier explained to Ignacy and Felicja that she knew nothing of the Jewish experience during the war. Before long, however, Felicja learned that was a lie after becoming acquainted with the bank president and his wife, who also lived in the building. The woman laughed when Felicja told her of Gattemeier's assertion, saying that she certainly knew all about German treatment of the Jews because her husband had been a guard in a concentration camp before being killed. Still, Gattemeier and the Karps got along well, and she soon rented them a second room, so Celina did not have to sleep in the kitchen.[28]

The space was tight, but Felicja recalled they were happy to take it, and she dearly hoped the much more ordinary housing arrangement and the small-town setting would restore a sense of normalcy for Celina. Serendipitously, Gattemeier's teenage nephew soon moved into the apartment as well and helped Celina with her German language skills. Happily, the move to Mindelheim proved even better for the family and Celina than Felicja ever could ever have envisioned.[29]

Local city officials provided the Karps with food ration cards, but townspeople, who Felicja believed felt guilty about the war, gave the family "more and better food than the ration cards merited." Even when foodstuffs were in short supply, the Karps seemed to be able to get most of what they wanted, including eggs, milk, white bread, and even some meat. And Felicja had noticed a change in Celina's eating habits. Before the war she had been a picky eater; now, Celina ate anything and everything.[30]

The Karps also began getting aid from a variety of nonprofit organizations. Felicja remembered that they received some clothes from the Hebrew Immigrant Aid Society (HIAS), an international immigrant and refugee service founded in New York City in 1881. They also started receiving relief packages from UNRRA and other charitable organizations containing staples like canned meat, cheese, sardines, and shortening as well as highly sought-after things such as coffee, cigarettes, chocolate, and soap. These provided the family some comfort and gave them valuable items to trade for other services they needed.[31]

Another pillar of restoring normality was restarting Celina's education again, and Felicja and Ignacy immediately began looking for tutors for their daughter. They soon found one to teach her Latin and another for mathematics. Celina also took violin lessons, an embroidery class, and gymnastics. But it was her math tutor and her gymnastics class that left lasting impressions on her.[32]

The mathematics teacher was a former Nazi, and Celina felt especially compelled to do well "to show him a Jew could excel in math." It was also somewhat empowering as Celina felt good "that he was dependent on whatever money I was giving him." As for gymnastics, the years in the concentration camps had taken their toll, and Celina was still very weak. "I had no strength in my arms," she remembered. "I couldn't do the parallel bars, and one of the German girls started making fun [of me]. She made a remark, something like, 'Why are you proud of being Jewish.'" Antisemitism, Celina knew, remained a fact of life.[33]

Her parents also needed a language teacher for Celina. Early in their search, they happened upon the *Englisches Institut Mindelheim,* a Catholic convent in town run by an order founded in Britain known as the English Sisters, which included a school for girls. There they met Mater Leontine Thoma, a seventy-nine-year-old, semi-cloistered nun who was a retired English teacher. She agreed to take on Celina and teach her German and English.[34]

"I gave up my chocolate for learning," Celina told the *Des Moines Register* in 1947, describing how she gave candy and other items from relief packages to the convent in exchange for Mater Leontine's tutoring service. But the two got off to a rocky start. They initially found it impossible to communicate because Celina only knew a few words in German, and Mater Leontine did not speak the teenager's native Polish. Mater Leontine quickly found a solution, arranging for a Czech woman to translate for them for a week or so. After that, Mater Leontine developed a system to start Celina down the road to fluency in both English and German by pointing to objects and identifying them in both languages. Soon the two were having simple conversations, and they then began working on grammar and punctuation. Celina learned rapidly because, she said, she was "starved" for knowledge.[35]

Mater Leontine also introduced her new charge to a local teenage girl named Angelika Bloch. Angelika and her younger sister Hanelore were from a prominent local family and were taking English classes with Mater Leontine. Celina and Angelika became fast friends, and they could practice their new language skills with each other. The two also spent a lot of time together. In winter, they frolicked in the snow and cross-country skied, and they went to the movies all year long. Some of Celina's favorites were *I Married a Witch*, starring Fredric March and Veronica Lake; *Kitty Foyle* (*Fraulein Kitty* in Germany) with Ginger Rodgers; *Keys to the Kingdom*, featuring Gregory Peck; and *Young Tom Edison*, starring Mickey Rooney. As they did for so many, American films such as these introduced Celina to American culture.[36]

Angelika's family (she and her sister lived with their mother and grand-father; their father, a Jewish attorney had been killed during the war) also became friendly with Celina's parents. They hosted them for several teas and dinners at their lovely home while the Karps were in Mindelheim.[37]

But Mater Leontine did much more for Celina than teach her two lan-guages or introduce her to Angelika. The elderly nun took an immediate interest in Celina, Linka as she called her, and the two quickly developed a remarkably close connection. Like many survivors, Celina had grown angry and bitter after her World War II experience. She was filled with hatred and did not easily trust people.[38]

Mater Leontine, however, was patient, gentle, and kind. She had en-tered the convent years earlier as a young woman after a love affair ended. She knew little of the outside world or of the war that had just ended.

She offered Celina unconditional acceptance. "My being Jewish meant nothing to her," Celina observed. Mater Leontine did not judge the fragile adolescent and provided her a safe place to discuss the trauma she had suffered over the past few years. "I know I must have told her things about what happened. I remember sitting in a garden with her and talking…. She was instrumental in making me feel good."[39]

Celina's time with Mater Leontine helped restore some of her self-esteem, left in tatters by the Nazis. "She was the first person who treated me like a human being. She gave me value." Equally important, Mater Leontine helped Celina get past her hatred. "She taught me how to get through hate, figuring out that hate is very corrosive and only hurts you, not the person you're hating, and the only way you can move forward in your life is by confronting all the hate and anger and working through it."[40]

Such guidance from the nun and Celina's experience with many warm, thoughtful townspeople in Mindelheim proved healing, and she came to realize that "not all Germans were ogres." But it was Mater Leontine who deserved the credit for renewing the teenager's faith in humanity: "She was an incredible influence," Celina observed. "I say she was my salvation because she showed me a way of moving on."[41]

As Celina was getting to know Mater Leontine, she and her parents were also enjoying the companionship of other Jews in town, most of whom had come with the Karps from Landsberg. They spent a lot of time together, often picnicking and sometimes dancing in the evening. Most of the group ended up emigrating to what became Israel. Celina soon lost track of these people, but her parents kept in touch with them over the years. On their sixtieth wedding anniversary in 1989, Ignacy and Felicja went to Israel with Celina and enjoyed a "wonderful" reunion with these friends from their time in Mindelheim.[42]

Meanwhile, Ignacy had continued working to get the family to either the United States or Jewish Palestine. Although the United States did not throw open its doors to the DPs of Europe, President Harry Truman addressed the issue when Congress did not, announcing a new directive in late December 1945. While the order did not increase the country's immigration quotas, it gave priority to displaced persons seeking immigration visas to come to the United States. A month or so after the directive, both of Ignacy's brothers, Felix and David, contacted him through the woman who had mailed his letters to them from Prague.[43]

Each was overjoyed that Ignacy and the family had survived and was prepared to sign the necessary affidavits for visas and bring them to Israel or the United States, respectively. More immediately, both brothers began sending the family relief packages. When combined with those from UNRRA and the food they obtained with their ration cards, the Karps were eating well for the first time in years. And they began gaining the weight they had lost because of little nutrition, overwork, and the extreme stress of life in the ghetto and then the labor/concentration camps. By the time they arrived in the United States in June 1947, Ignacy had gained back seventy-five pounds; Felicja, twenty-three pounds; and Celina, fifty pounds. She had also grown three inches since the war ended, and now stood at 5 feet 6 inches.[44]

By March 1946, Felix Karp had filed all the necessary documents—including required affidavits swearing that he could financially support the family and they would not become a public burden—to bring his brother and his family to what was soon to become Israel. Evidently, he had been working with three distant cousins—Bela, Fela, and Samuel Blumenstein—in Paris to facilitate the process. Sisters Bela and Fela both worked for the American Joint Distribution Committee (AJDC), and it seems that they arranged for the Karps to go to Paris and meet up with their brother Samuel, who would escort them to Jewish Palestine. Late that month, the AJDC in Paris had French travel visas ready for the Karps and notified Ignacy of the plan in early April.[45]

When Ignacy got the news, he had already received the affidavits from Felix. But by then, he, Felicja, and Celina had decided they preferred moving to the United States and were afraid going to France might hurt their chances to immigrate to America. They therefore turned down the French travel visas. The affidavits Felix sent did not go unused, however. They were apparently stolen, and another family surreptitiously used them, traveling under the Karps' names to Israel.[46]

Even as they chose not to go to Israel, Ignacy received word that the affidavits from his brother David had arrived, and the Karps were instructed to go to Munich, pick up the documents, and register for their visas. All three went to the city in late April. There the Karps joined a long line of DPs waiting to get into the U.S. Consulate to apply for visas. But when Ignacy showed officials the letter asking the family to come to register, they were ushered right in. They filled out the paperwork and went back to Mindelheim for another year before spots became available under the country's immigration quota system for them to come to the U.S.[47]

Late the following March 1947, the Karps were instructed to return to Munich. Here it appears they stayed for a little over a month at the city's Munich Emigrant Assembly Center, located in the Deutsches Museum. While they were waiting for their visas, they happened to see Oscar Schindler down a city street. Ignacy went over and spoke to him, telling the businessman they were in town to get their visas and would soon be leaving for the United States. Schindler was pleased to speak with Ignacy, but he was especially thrilled the family had made it through the challenging postwar years and would be starting anew in America.[48]

The three had to wait nearly three weeks before their visas were ready, and they picked them up at the consulate on April 21. After that, they went back to Mindelheim briefly to pack up a few remaining items and say their goodbyes. Celina found it especially difficult to leave Mater Leontine but promised to write. After she arrived in the United States, Celina and the elderly nun corresponded regularly over the next two-and-a-half-years until Mater Leontine passed away in December 1950. Mater Leontine's impact on the teenager had been profound, and even though seventy years have passed since she died, Celina still tears up when she thinks of her mentor and close friend.[49]

The Karps soon returned to Munich and the assembly center. On May 1, they were put on a train for the 360-mile trip to Bremen, in preparation for their upcoming journey to the U.S. The trip took all day, Celina remembered, and they rode in boxcars again, but unlike the war years, the cars were not overcrowded, and the doors were not locked from the outside.[50]

Once there, they were taken to Camp Grohn, a U.S. Army base, which housed a large DP facility. Here several thousand refugees stayed for brief periods before beginning their travel overseas to their new homes. Many, like the Karps, were bound for the United States, and in preparation for the move, numerous DPs took English classes at the camp, where students also learned aspects of American culture. The courses were taught by volunteers with the Church World Service Language Institute, a U.S.-based relief organization. Although Celina had a good grasp of English because of Mater Leontine's tutoring, neither Ignacy nor Felicja spoke the language, and they both probably got an introduction to it here in one of these classes.[51]

Celina and her parents spent nearly a month at the Bremen camp before taking a short, forty-mile train ride to the North Sea port of Bremerhaven, where they met the SS *Marine Marlin*, the ship that would take them to the United States. It was built in 1945 as a troop transport and designed to carry 3,500 soldiers, but the following year, it was leased by United States Lines, reconfigured to accommodate a little over 900 tourist class passengers, and began ferrying refugees and soldiers from Europe to the United States. The Karps boarded the ship on May 28, 1947, Celina's sixteenth birthday. "We were thrilled to be going," she remembered, "what a birthday present!" But her excitement was tempered with trepidation and "mixed feelings about going to something unknown."[52]

Like the trips of many other Jewish refugees on the ship, the Karps' trip was underwritten by the American Joint Distribution Committee. The journey was not without its difficulties, however. A pipe to one of the ship's boilers burst, and as Ignacy recalled, they were without warm food for a few days before repairs were made. They also encountered rough seas in the North Atlantic, and "everyone got sick but me," Celina remembered. But with some pleasure she added, "so I got to eat everyone's ice cream!" Then there was her first encounter with Coca-Cola, which had become synonymous with the American way of life. Celina had never tasted it and was eager to do so. But when she was given one on the ship, she hated it and wondered, "How could anyone drink that awful stuff?"[53]

The Karps arrived in New York on Saturday, June 7. Thirty-four years after making the trip, Felicja explained that she and Ignacy believed they had survived to give Celina a new beginning. When their ship entered New York Harbor and she and her husband caught their first glimpse of the Statue of Liberty, they must have felt the door to their daughter's new life was beginning to open. Just as the famous statue greeted the Karps, it had welcomed millions of other immigrants to the country for decades, serving as a beacon of freedom, hope, and opportunity. And so it was for Celina, who was mesmerized by the "amazing" statue and could only imagine how her new life in America would unfold.[54]

Shortly after their arrival, the Karps told a reporter, "We were just lucky" to have survived the war years. But it was clear Celina and her parents were ready to put that chapter behind them. They were overjoyed to be in the New World for a new start and embraced their new home with a vengeance. So much so, in fact, they agreed on the ship "that once in the USA, we would try not to speak Polish, only English" to facilitate their adoption of the American way of life.[55]

SIX
IOWA: A NEW BEGINNING

SEVERAL DAYS AFTER THEY arrived in New York City, Celina and her parents experienced a classic American road trip with her uncle and aunt as David Karp drove them in his brand-new, navy-blue Cadillac eleven hundred miles to their new home in Des Moines, Iowa. They most likely headed south on U.S. Highway 1 from New York through the heavily populated corridor in New Jersey and Pennsylvania to Philadelphia, where they picked up U.S. Highway 30 and probably took it all the way into Iowa. Along the route, Celina experienced local diners, restaurants, roadside motels, and a frequently changing landscape. Once out of greater Philadelphia, she passed through rolling hills, forests, and small towns, perhaps catching a glimpse of Amish families in their horse-drawn buggies around Lancaster, Pennsylvania. Just to the west she went by the Civil War battlefield of Gettysburg followed by an industrial belt of cities including Pittsburgh and Canton, Ohio. Endless farms in Indiana and Illinois ensued until the Karps crossed the Mississippi River into Iowa. There fields of corn and soybeans dominated the terrain before they finally reached Des Moines. No wonder the wide-eyed sixteen-year-old was "amazed at the vastness of America."[1]

But beyond the nation's scale and scope, Celina was soon struck by the liberty and rights Americans enjoyed: "Everything is so free here," she observed. "You can say what you want, believe what you want, and do what you please." Although adjusting to the new home and culture would take a while, it seemed like the perfect place for Celina to reconstruct her life.[2]

Before Celina and her parents reached Iowa, however, they were introduced to big city life in New York. There they stayed at the then popular Hotel Chesterfield at 130 West Forty-Ninth Street in Midtown Manhattan. Celina was mesmerized by the neon lights on Broadway and Times Square: "I had never seen a city like New York. It was so colorful and beautiful after dark Europe. We walked around New York City, and I enjoyed it immensely." She was also fascinated by all the people milling about who seemed to be "living such a normal life," something she longed to do.[3]

Maybe her first taste of normality in America came at a breakfast in Manhattan. Celina was clearly startled by the wide variety of foods available on the restaurant menu. When she saw that tomatoes were listed, she immediately craved them. She had loved them as a child but had not had one since the war broke out in 1939. She asked for sliced tomatoes for breakfast. The server looked askance, but her uncle immediately said, "If she wants tomatoes for breakfast, then she can have them."[4]

As Celina was relishing the New York experience, her mother was having difficulty and unable to sleep. It was not the city so much as her struggle to accept her new life. "I couldn't sleep because I couldn't believe I was free. I would go to the hotel window [late at night] and stare out. I went for walks at 2 AM and saw a lot of people on the streets." Her anxiety was evidently eased somewhat by Dottie Isaacson, her closest childhood friend from Radomsko, who had moved to New York years earlier and visited with Phyllis and her family a couple of times while they were in the city.[5]

Isaacson lived in the Bronx. She and her mother came to the United States about 1920, but she and Phyllis corresponded over the years, and the two even saw each other once before World War II, when Isaacson returned to Poland to see friends and family. Somehow, Phyllis got back in touch with her after the war, and when the Karps arrived in New York, Isaacson, her six-year-old son Richard, and her husband Samuel met them at the Chesterfield. She also had the Karps out to her Bronx apartment, and Richard remembered how sophisticated Celina seemed "in a European sort of way," and that she brought him a toy gift.[6]

Besides reminiscing with Phyllis and telling the Karps all about America, Isaacson also invited the family to stay with her in the Bronx and offered to help them get established in the city. Phyllis appreciated the overture, but she thought the much smaller Des Moines would be easier for Celina to navigate and believed she would get a better education there.[7]

They therefore stuck to their original plan, and after the short stay in New York, David drove the clan to Des Moines. The trip took roughly three days, and they arrived in mid-June. Celina was not initially impressed; the heat and humidity were almost too much for her to bear. Although temperatures were not especially high for the Midwest, it was particularly muggy that month, and all Celina could think was that she "had landed in absolute hell. I was shocked by the humidity in Des Moines. I remember sitting by the open windows at night and not being able to sleep. The air did not move at all," and Celina broke out with a heat rash.[8]

Worse, Iowa was inundated with exceptionally high rainfall that month, causing flooding in Des Moines and much of the state. Celina could not believe this was her new home and must have explained her dismay to Mater Leontine, her mentor, teacher, and good friend in Germany, as the nun's first letter to Celina in the United States commented on the disaster: "Your new home in such a terrible flood could not give you a very favorable impression." But then Mater Leontine offered encouragement, "Meanwhile, I hope, you have a flood of sunshine too."[9]

There was soon plenty of sunshine, the floodwaters receded, and Celina found some relief from the oppressive heat. She and her parents stayed with David and Augusta for their first few weeks in Des Moines. By that time, David was the owner of a successful automobile parts business, and he and his wife lived in a large, three-story, clapboard house in the thirteen hundred block of Eleventh Street, a mile northwest of today's MercyOne Des Moines Medical Center. Much more important to Celina, however, the Karp home stood just around the corner from a Reed's Ice Cream stand, which she discovered a day or two after coming to Des Moines.[10]

She had developed a real sweet tooth for ice cream a few weeks earlier on the SS *Marine Marlin* while crossing the Atlantic, and the rest of that summer, Celina stopped by the ice cream stand almost every afternoon as a respite from steamy weather. There, she remembered, "they would cut off a huge chunk of ice cream" from a tube of the frozen dessert and "put it in a cone for ten cents. I wanted to try every flavor."[11]

Two of David and Augusta's three children were home when Celina and her parents arrived: Harold, who had just graduated from Drake University, and Basil, a graduate student in political science at the University of Chicago, who was back for the summer. Their recently married daughter, Sylvia Gaynor, and her husband Nathan soon drove from their home in Michigan to meet their European relatives as well. Celina loved spending time with her newfound cousins and could not get over "how good looking they all were."[12]

But it was Basil who really took Celina under his wing. A couple of days after she arrived, he took Celina to the city's North High School (which he and his two siblings had attended) where they visited with the principal and discussed her placement for the fall. Celina had brought all the notebooks showing what she had learned from the nun and her other tutors in Mindelheim. The principal was impressed and told Celina she could enter North High that fall as a senior if she took U.S. history and American literature in summer school. She readily agreed and enrolled in the classes, which were offered at Des Moines's East High School.[13]

Celina enjoyed being in a classroom again, even if it was only a summer session. Basil immediately recognized that his younger cousin was "very bright" and happily tutored her along the way. He taught Celina common U.S. idioms and phrases, gently moving her away from the King's English Mater Leontine had taught her to a more standard American English. And it was Basil who helped her learn the Palmer Method of penmanship, then the standard cursive handwriting system in the United States.[14]

He also introduced Celina to the national pastime, taking her to a couple of Des Moines Bruins baseball games. The Bruins were a Class A minor league affiliate of the Chicago Cubs and had just reestablished professional baseball in the city that spring. Their games were played at Des Moines's Pioneer Park, now called Principal Park. She thoroughly enjoyed the outings, but most of the sport was lost on her. Try as she might to understand it, "the intricacies of baseball…went over my head completely."[15]

If Celina and her parents were not the first Holocaust survivors to come to Des Moines after the war, they were some of the earliest arrivals. They were among the 23,000 European Jews who entered the United States from late 1945 through 1947 under President Harry Truman's immigration directive of December 1945. Even after Congress increased the number of refugees who could enter the country with the Displaced Persons Act in 1948, only about 100,000 Jewish survivors had come to the United States by the end of 1952.[16]

By midcentury, there were roughly 3,000 Jews living in Des Moines. It was the largest such community in Iowa but made up only about 1.5 percent of the city's population. Just shy of 50 percent of those were born in Des Moines, with 5 percent coming from elsewhere in Iowa, and 20 percent from other states. With nearly three-fourths of these residents born in the United States, a locally done report noted, it was the most "native" Jewish community in the country.[17]

These factors initially made the Karps somewhat of an oddity in Des Moines. Celina recalled that urban Iowans "were used to people coming from the farms. We were the first [immigrant] city people. They kept asking [me]: 'Do you know what electricity is? Running water? Did you have a toilet?' It was strange because we had all these things, and in some ways lived a more sophisticated life in Poland. My parents had gone to the theater, the opera, concerts, all the time."[18]

Meanwhile, a couple of days after Ignacy and Felicja arrived, David suggested the two Americanize their names to ease the transition to their new home, and from that point on, they were known as Irvin and Phyllis.

Shortly after that, David and Augusta hoped to introduce the two to Des Moines by having a few of their close Jewish friends over to meet them. The conversation must have taken place in Yiddish for David did not remember enough Polish to translate. Everyone evidently enjoyed the evening until someone asked Irvin and Phyllis about their wartime experience. The two tentatively began describing some of what they had gone through when awkward, nervous laughter broke out among the guests. Irvin and Phyllis quickly realized that those in the room could not comprehend what they had faced during the war or more broadly the mass genocide. And it was clear they were not interested in hearing about it. One woman dismissed their story by saying that such things could never happen in the United States; Phyllis replied, "I hope and pray it doesn't, but German Jews had said the same thing."[19]

Very shortly afterward, the *Des Moines Register* got wind of the Karps' story, and a reporter interviewed Irvin, Phyllis, and Celina for a human-interest piece, which ran with a large photograph of the three the following week. It recounted their experience during and after the war but was vague on specifics. Either the Karps, it seems, were becoming more reticent to talk about their treatment at the hands of the Nazis because of the way their conversation at David and Augusta's house went, or the reporter believed readers would be averse to such details.[20]

The Karps' experience was hardly unique. As historian Peter Novick explained, for the first fifteen or so years after the war, survivors were repeatedly told to focus on their new lives and the present and future, not the Holocaust and their pasts. One survivor, for instance, remembered his aunt telling him: "If you want to have friends here in America, don't keep telling them about your experiences. Nobody's interested and if you tell them, they're going to hear it once and then the next time, they'll be afraid to come see you. Don't ever speak about it."[21]

Indeed, American Jews were largely downplaying the wartime experience of European Jews. They were focused on assimilating into American society, and "as an increasing number of Americans came to think of Jews as not significantly different from other Americans, an increasing number of American Jews came to think of themselves in the same way." They were therefore not interested in Jews being singled out as the primary victims of Nazi atrocities, which would separate them as distinct from Americans, even as they were integrating into society.[22]

Moreover, the changing international framework pushed Americans to minimize the Holocaust. As the Cold War ensued and the bipolar worldview became dominant, the United States' loyalties shifted. The Soviet Union, our World War II ally, became our totalitarian enemy, while Germany, our wartime enemy, became an integral part of our defense against the spread of communism. This, Novick argued, made "the Holocaust the 'wrong atrocity' for purposes of mobilizing the new consciousness" for fighting our new communist menace.[23]

Irvin, Phyllis, and eventually Celina thus rarely talked about their Holocaust years and got on with their new life. While Celina was in summer school, her uncle David hired Irvin as a bookkeeper at his Karp Auto Parts, located in downtown Des Moines in the block where the Krause Gateway Center now stands. Phyllis went through an employment agency and found a bookkeeping job as well, but because she was soon exploited there, she would only tell a later interviewer that it was at "a Jewish-owned company." Instead of handling the firm's financial records, managers utilized her as a shipping clerk, where she spent her days receiving, stacking, loading, and "carrying forty-pound packages."[24]

There was a silver lining for Phyllis though. A fellow worker at the business, "a lovely gentile woman," told her she needed to speak English. She offered to help Phyllis with the language and correct her usage and grammar. Phyllis enthusiastically accepted the assistance and began working on her English by trying to read the newspaper at night and then talk with the woman about it the next day.[25]

Phyllis and the family remained with David and Augusta for six weeks before finding another place to live. The man who delivered Jewish baked goods to the Karp household told Irvin about a widower who was alone in a large home and might be looking for boarders who could help around the house. Such an arrangement appealed to Irvin and Phyllis because they still had very little money and could not afford to pay rent. They met the man and as expected, he offered to take the family in as tenants if they would regularly clean the house and cook dinner every evening. The couple readily agreed and moved into the home at 1015 Third Street (no longer standing, but it would have been near the present-day Wells Fargo Arena).[26]

Irvin continued at Karp Auto Parts, but Phyllis eventually left her job to take an actual bookkeeping position at the Roycraft Company, an appliance distributor on Walnut Street, a half-mile south of David's business. The Karps aggressively saved most of their two incomes, and after living with the widower for about two years, they bought a small, two-bedroom, clapboard bungalow on Thirty-Seventh Street in Beaverdale, a neighborhood northwest of downtown. This was the first time they had had a place of their own since 1941, when they had been forced out of their apartment and into the Kraków ghetto, and they were rightfully proud. "Only in America," Phyllis later recalled, "could we have made a comeback like we did."[27]

The two also started participating in the community. They began attending David and Augusta's synagogue, Tifereth Israel Synagogue, although they were not initially very active because they were working so much. Phyllis would eventually become more involved at the synagogue, especially in its Women's League. Irvin found time to join several service organizations. Probably encouraged to do so by David, he became involved in the Home Masonic Lodge and the Des Moines Scottish Rite Consistory, and he also joined his brother in the Zionist Organization of America and B'nai B'rith, an international Jewish advocacy and service group. Through these connections, their jobs, and neighbors, Irvin and Phyllis made many friends in Des Moines; a few were fellow survivors, most were not.[28]

Celina, meanwhile, started as a senior at North High that fall, remembering, "it was incredibly wonderful to be back in school again." Even though it was a relatively large, three-year high school, and her class was a little over three hundred students, Celina stood out. She still had a thick accent, and many knew something of her background as a displaced person. And for the moment, the teenager was still talking about her wartime experience. Shortly after the semester began, the *Des Moines Tribune* ran a front-page story about Celina. Here she provided the broad outlines of her years in the ghetto and the labor and concentration camps and even offered some detail of her terrifying encounter with Dr. Joesef Mengele at Auschwitz. She also must have mentioned the episode to some classmates or teachers at North High because the school's drama club soon adapted events in Celina's life into a radio drama, highlighting the Mengele incident. The program was broadcast on Des Moines's KRNT radio station (then owned by the Des Moines Register and Tribune Company, hence its last three call letters).[29]

But Celina was trying to fit in and get on with her life, and like her parents, she too became aware that most people were not interested in the Holocaust or could not understand it, so she soon stopped talking about her World War II years. North High classmate Lou Hurwitz recalled Celina as "trying to become integrated and doing a good job of it." He said she "never mentioned her past" but was "very gregarious and open," and made a lot of female friends. Boys evidently were another matter. Celina's aunt Augusta tried to help her assimilate in this regard by suggesting she wear lipstick and makeup; things Celina had never done before. Augusta also tried to arrange a date for her niece to meet some boys, but she "was too shy for that."[30]

Yet Celina did socialize and got involved in extracurricular activities. Like most of her classmates, she attended school football games, happily telling the *Tribune* reporter of her first game, "It was fun! North won 6-0. We made a touchdown!" In addition, she joined the school orchestra, playing the violin she had brought from Europe, which her parents had bought for her from a Roma family in Mindelheim. She also served on the school's social committee, the senior party committee, and she joined the Latin club, where she was elected vice president.[31]

Academics, however, were where Celina shined. Hurwitz thought Celina was "brighter and more studious than the rest of us.... Her mind was like a vacuum; she took everything in quickly." Jean Lory, another North High classmate, noted, "Celina was so eager for knowledge and such a good student." She and Celina were only casual friends, but it was her father, Ellsworth Lory, a social studies and English teacher at the school, who played the most formative role in Celina's life at high school.[32]

Lory had Celina in a U.S. government class, and the two soon developed a special relationship. Celina found him "a fantastic teacher" who was "unbelievably smart and caring," while Lory later described her as "a brilliant Jewish girl…an escapee of the Nazi gas ovens, who risked her life to read (a reference to Celina reading contraband books at Płaszów). What a contrast she was to the boys who boasted they never completely read a book."[33]

"The [high school] teacher that always stands out in my recollections was Mr. Lory," Celina observed. He introduced me to what it meant to be an American. His civic lessons were not just a historical review, but rather a thorough introduction to the rights and responsibilities of citizenship." But Celina had great respect for all her teachers at North and found them and the school staff nothing but warm and welcoming.[34]

When not involved with school, Celina remained busy by working at Gaylard's, a women's clothing store in downtown Des Moines, every Saturday. Paying $2 per day, the job gave her pocket money and some savings for college, a stepping-stone in her plan to become a physician.[35]

Her grades at North High were outstanding—she would graduate second in her class—and suggested she could be admitted into an elite college or university, but Celina knew little about individual schools or the process of applying for scholarships. Luckily, Essie Whirry, North High School's girls' advisor, took Celina under her wing. Whirry was a Grinnell College graduate, and she thought the small, selective, liberal arts college, located fifty-five miles east of Des Moines, would be perfect for Celina. Whirry encouraged her to consider the institution, and when Celina expressed interest, she drove the teen to visit the school and meet some faculty and staff.[36]

When she and Whirry arrived at the campus, Celina was impressed with everything she saw. Grinnell officials were equally impressed with Celina and her academic records. Whirry easily convinced college administrators to admit the stellar North High student that fall with a full academic scholarship and campus jobs to cover room and board. Celina was thrilled, but before she had much time to savor this good fortune, she was getting ready to take advantage of another opportunity: the Encampment for Citizenship, a residential summer program in New York City designed to bring together young people from diverse backgrounds and encourage critical thinking, civic activism, and participation in the democratic system, had invited her to attend.[37]

The organization had been founded two years earlier in 1946 by Algernon Black, a social critic and head of the New York Society for Ethical Culture, and Alice Pollitzer, one of New York City's leading civic activists. Originally lasting six weeks, the program was first held at the Fieldston School in the Riverdale neighborhood of New York City's borough of the Bronx. Celina learned of the Encampment from Isaac "Jay" Hurwitz—an older brother of her classmate, Lou Hurwitz—who had been selected by North High teachers to attend the Encampment the previous year. He found the program valuable and thought it would be a perfect way for Celina to learn more about the country.[38]

When Celina expressed interest, Jay used contacts there and secured Celina an invitation to the Encampment as well as a full scholarship. All Celina needed to do was pay for a roundtrip train ticket to New York City, which she happily did with money from clerking at Gaylard's.[39]

The Encampment proved a "fascinating experience" for Celina, expanding her understanding of what it meant to be an American. Participants included a diverse group of students from across the United States and several foreign countries as well. Encampers attended lectures and discussions on critical thinking, leadership, political activism, and democracy. They even had tickets to attend the fourth day of the 1948 Democratic National Convention held that summer in Philadelphia. Unfortunately, Celina and the rest did not get to go; the party gave Harry Truman the presidential nomination earlier than expected, and the convention ended the day before they were scheduled to attend.[40]

One of the Encampment's major focuses was on the country's struggle with race relations. Celina knew little of the issue and found discussions on the topic eye-opening. She and the other white students also had the opportunity to live in the dormitory and interact and work with African American students on a variety of simulations in the hope of breaking down stereotypes. But her most memorable experience that summer was meeting Eleanor Roosevelt.[41]

Near the end of the program, Encampment leaders drove their students to Hyde Park for a day of workshops and a picnic that political figure and former first lady Eleanor Roosevelt held at her estate. Roosevelt was one of the leading supporters of the organization and hosted the annual event for the Encampment for several years. Officials handpicked a few students to introduce to Roosevelt. Celina was selected because she was a Holocaust survivor and was elated to meet the larger-than-life political figure and former first lady[42]

Shortly after returning home, Celina headed to Grinnell to begin college late that summer. At the time, the school's enrollment had swelled to 1,140, a record high, largely due to the more than 300 World War II veterans who were attending the college on the GI Bill. This also helped reduce the proportion of Iowa students at the school to a "record-low proportion of just under 32 percent." As a result, atmosphere at Grinnell, according to then student and late author Curtis Harnack was "a very cosmopolitan place in the best sense: fellow students often hailed from far places, different backgrounds. ... There was a refreshing absence of discrimination regarding money, status, family prestige, and ethnic groupings."[43]

The small school seemed perfectly suited for Celina, and her initial impression was overwhelmingly positive. "I thought I'd ended up in paradise... I saw these students, in such an academic atmosphere, that I truly felt enriched." But she soon became disenchanted. Although there were a few other Jewish students on campus, Celina recalled, several of them "kept quiet" about their Judaism to be accepted. And while there were several African and African American students at Grinnell, the college was overwhelmingly white and Protestant; "There was not much diversity," noted Nick Piediscalzi, who also began at Grinnell in the fall of 1948, and Celina felt the pangs of discrimination almost immediately. She had a single room in the Cleveland Hall dormitory, and she never knew "if it was that I spoke with an accent or had a very meager wardrobe, but in the next room was a girl who objected to being next to me and was actually moved."[44]

Shy and quiet, Celina was "quite self-contained," according to friend and fellow student Carolyn "Kay" Swartz (Bucksbaum). When coupled with her Holocaust experience, which, Celina said, "made me old beyond my years," she had difficulty finding a niche at the college. Likewise, her mindset was quite different from that of typical American teenagers who seemed to her to take college for granted. She saw college as a privilege and was frustrated by many undergraduates at Grinnell who she thought "failed to appreciate" their education.[45]

One of the highlights of her first year at Grinnell did not actually involve the college at all and must have seemed like an extension of the Encampment—Celina got to see President Harry Truman. On September 6, the incumbent presidential candidate began his second whistle-stop campaign tour of the year. By the time the tour ended on October 31, Truman had traveled nearly 22,000 miles through the Midwest, West, and Northeast and given 275 speeches.[46]

The president's seventeen-car train, dubbed the Truman Special, made its way to Iowa early in the morning on September 18, and began a dawn to dusk, seven-stop run through the state. After Truman made brief, back platform remarks to people in Davenport, Iowa City, and Oxford, his train pulled into Grinnell at 8:55 AM. Celina and many Grinnell students were part of the throng of seven thousand that had gathered—more than the town's entire population—to catch a glimpse of the president. College president Samuel Stephens introduced Truman, who referred to himself as a "synthetic" alumnus of Grinnell, since he had received an honorary degree from the institution four years earlier.[47]

Truman then told the crowd how much he enjoyed Iowa, reminding them that he was from nearby Jackson County, Missouri, which was "just like this Iowa country." His comments were brief and lasted only a few minutes, but before the train pulled away, the crowd enjoyed seeing five-year-old Kathleen Meldrem present the president with an ear of corn, symbolic of the state's agricultural abundance. Photographers captured the moment, and the image of the smiling president holding the child and the ear of corn graced newspapers across the country the following day. But Celina had witnessed the scene firsthand and was delighted "to be part of the political scene that day."[48]

In addition to some of the social challenges Celina faced adjusting to college life, she had started Grinnell with every intention of becoming a doctor, and her premed courses were particularly difficult. The situation was made that much tougher for Celina because her "English was not great at all," and she had to work especially hard in her classes. "That first year was intense," she recalled, but her hours of study paid off, and she did well in the classroom.[49]

When not in class or studying at the library, Celina worked in a variety of on campus jobs. During her four years at Grinnell, she served food in the dining hall, worked at the switchboard, the student union, and the library, and acted as a dormitory monitor, letting women into the building after the doors were locked at ten PM. And like many other college students, when she went home each summer, Celina worked in Des Moines. The first year back she got a job at Roycraft, the company where her mother was a bookkeeper. Between her sophomore and junior year, Celina sold dresses at the Younkers department store downtown, and the following summer, she did clerical work at an insurance company.[50]

Fortunately, Celina's time at Grinnell began improving after she returned to campus for her sophomore year. She made good friends, became more involved in campus organizations, began dating, and changed her major. She changed dormitories that fall, moving into Haines Hall where she shared a suite with two bright, ambitious young women, Kathy Jantzen (Wood) and Jane Miller. The two were both from Quincy, Illinois, and already knew each other. Celina, Jantzen, and Miller hit it off almost immediately and became fast friends, remaining so the rest of their lives. Both the young women were Methodist, and Celina even joined them at Sunday church services sometimes when she was not working.[51]

Her roommate that spring semester was Lillian Robinson (Bellamy), an African American exchange student from the Hampton Institute (now Hampton University), a historically African American university in Virginia. The two schools introduced the pioneering exchange program in 1947, with up to three Hampton students studying at Grinnell every spring semester through 1954 and vice versa. Grinnell housing officials asked Celina to room with Robinson, and she promptly accepted. College administrators approached her because, Celina believed, they thought she and her parents would be much less likely to object to having an African American roommate than most others at the college. It was a fortuitous pairing; the two became lifelong friends and their families got to know each other as well.[52]

Celina also befriended Andrew Billingsley, another African American, Hampton exchange student. He was also a World War II veteran who ended up staying at Grinnell to graduate. Billingsley would go on to become a sociologist, author, college professor, and serve as the eighth president of Morgan State University in Baltimore, Maryland. Celina recalled that he was in "need of companionship," and she appreciated his older, more mature perspective. The two did many things together on campus and sometimes ventured into town to see a movie at the local theater. While college administrators were happy Billingsley had friends like Celina, they evidently worried about how locals would react to seeing these two students—a white woman and Black man—together in town. Celina was therefore called into the dean of students' office. The dean not only reprimanded her for going off campus with Billingsley but threatened to take her scholarship away if Celina went into town with him again. From then on, the two confined themselves to campus.[53]

She had begun dating as well. No serious relationships ensued, but Celina did develop several close friendships with other young men at Grinnell besides Billingsley. One was upperclassman John Stoessinger. Jewish and originally from Vienna, Stoessinger, his mother, and step-father had escaped the Holocaust by getting visas to Shanghai, China, shortly after the Germans marched into their home of Czechoslovakia in 1939. They spent the war years there, and after the conflict was over, a U.S. serviceman told Stoessinger that he had gone to Grinnell College and suggested the teenager apply. He did, received a full scholarship, came to the United States, and started at Grinnell in 1947.[54]

Celina met him in 1948, during her first year at the school, and the two soon became good friends. Their shared European past was certainly part of the connection, and they regularly conversed in German rather than English. They also both enjoyed dancing. After graduating from Grinnell in 1950, Stoessinger went on to get a doctorate in international relations from Harvard and became a distinguished scholar and teacher, political analyst, and award-winning author before passing away in 2017.[55]

Meanwhile, Celina grew more active in campus organizations as well. She joined the Latin club, the League of Women Voters, and the dance company, even using her sewing skills to help make skirts for the group. But the biggest change in her life at Grinnell came after she had to dissect a pig in a biology class. That was it. Celina realized then and there that the medical field was not for her, and she changed majors. She had thought her introductory philosophy class with Neal Klausner was interesting and decided to major in the subject.[56]

As she became increasingly integrated into the Grinnell community, Celina really began enjoying her college experience. "I loved the atmosphere," she would exclaim. And with a new major she found fascinating, she hoped "to find what it was in reasoning and in the world that created the kind of circumstances that I experienced."[57]

The philosophy department put her in contact with a small number of smart young men also majoring in the subject. Celina was the only woman among the handful of philosophy majors in her class. Harold Harrison, a fellow Grinnell student at the time remembered the group of philosophy majors "as a competitive bunch," but Celina held her own and excelled. One major, Nick Piediscalzi, now a retired minister and professor of religion at Wright State University was impressed with Celina, saying she was a "serious and articulate student" who was "quite verbal and participated actively, especially in upper-level courses." While Ken Sayre, another major and now an American philosopher and professor emeritus at the University of Notre Dame, found Celina "very cosmopolitan and very bright."[58]

The study of philosophy helped Celina work through some of the horrific episodes of her life, but she did not find a reasonable explanation of the Holocaust. As she told an audience of Grinnell undergraduates in 2017, "I'm still looking for it." But she remained absorbed by the study of philosophy, and her interest and intelligence captured the attention of Klausner, one of Grinnell's two professors of religion and philosophy at the time. A favorite of many students, the charismatic Klausner was in Sayre's words, "gregarious, stimulating, and inquisitive. He was a distinct presence on campus." Klausner saw great potential in Celina, and she found him engaging, thought-provoking, and "a delightful human being." The two developed a close relationship—Celina would regularly correspond with him until he died in 2010—and he encouraged her to go to graduate school and eagerly wrote her letters of recommendation.[59]

One was to Smith College, where Celina had applied to its master's program in social work. Ever since dropping the idea of going into medicine, she was not sure what she wanted to do after college, but she found this field interesting, and it was one of the few options open to women in the 1950s. Smith not only accepted her but offered her a full scholarship. So, shortly after graduating Phi Beta Kappa in June 1952, Celina headed east to Northampton, Massachusetts, and began the college's accelerated social work program that summer.[60]

Her plans changed in August, when Celina received word that she had won a Necchi graduate fellowship for displaced persons to Teachers College, Columbia University in New York City. She had not initially planned to apply for the award because it was highly competitive, and hundreds would be seeking the two available scholarships. Klausner, however, ensured she did, telling her, "If you don't [apply for it], I won't write you any other letters of recommendation."[61]

She complied, and Klausner wrote what was certainly a glowing letter of support. Surely Celina's stellar academic record and strong candidacy carried the day, but it may have been her poignant application essay that finally swayed the judges. In it she noted that education "is the strongest tool in man's struggle for betterment." She then went on to explain that she had learned the value of education during the war. Almost everything had been taken away from her, she wrote, except her education, and "it was this that made me realize how important education is for the survival of our society."[62]

At first, Celina was unsure whether to accept the award. She was enjoying the program at Smith and had just been assigned to what sounded like an interesting internship in Baltimore that fall. But when she asked the head of the social work program for advice, Celina was told it was a great opportunity, and she should accept the prize. Celina ultimately agreed and made plans to head to New York that fall.[63]

Maybe the award and attending Columbia were fated for Celina, as the scholarship had been created by Leon Jolson, a man whose path had paralleled hers in many ways. Jolson was a Polish Jew who survived the Holocaust and spent a couple of years as a displaced person in Europe before immigrating to New York City in 1947. Then their stories diverged. Jolson was nearly twenty years older than Celina and relying on prewar experience and connections, he soon established a very successful business—Necchi Sewing Machines Sales Corporation, the sole distributor of the Italian-made device in the United States. He rapidly grew wealthy, and to celebrate becoming an American citizen in April 1952, he gave $10,000 to Columbia's Teachers College to establish the fellowship for other refugees.[64]

Then, as if scripted in Hollywood, the same day the winners of the award were announced, Celina's parents became American citizens themselves, in a ceremony at the federal courthouse in downtown Des Moines. Coworkers at Roycraft had decorated Phyllis's desk with a cake and U.S. flags to mark the event, but Celina getting the Necchi Fellowship must have seemed like the real gift. When told his daughter was a recipient of the scholarship, her father Irvin, who still struggled with English said, "Is that so? Very fine; we're glad she got it!" Clearly, Irvin did not have the words to convey the immense pride and excitement he was feeling that day.[65]

The Necchi Fellowship closed this period of Celina's life. What a chapter it had been. She had arrived in Iowa just two years after suffering through the Holocaust. In the Hawkeye state, she adjusted to a new reality—freedom, a new home and culture—and learned what it meant to be an American. She had long understood the importance of education and took advantage of such opportunities. Her agile mind and thirst for knowledge led to academic success, first at North High School and then Grinnell College. This opened doors for Celina, and although she had enjoyed all that Iowa had to offer, she did not imagine her future in the state. Such ambition took her to the East Coast where her life would continue to unfold.

SEVEN

NEW YORK AND THE AMERICAN DREAM

WHEN CELINA RETURNED TO New York in 1952, she was hardly recognizable from the anxious, teenaged, displaced person who first stepped foot in the city five years earlier. Now a poised, acculturated, young woman with a degree from a fine liberal arts college, Celina had embraced her new country and come back to the big city when the Neechi Fellowship and Teachers College, Columbia University beckoned. Although she did not know where these would lead, Celina was looking forward, eager to join the millions of other Americans ready to enjoy the postwar prosperity as they sought out their piece of the American dream.

New York was a unique, exciting place to be at midcentury. As Celina had noted in 1947, it was so different than the war-ravaged cities she had known in Europe. The gateway for immigrants coming to the United States, New York City was teeming with energy, activity, and optimism. But it was much more than that. World War II had ushered in the so-called American Century, publisher Henry Luce's term to describe the nation's new global dominance, politically, economically, and culturally. And for many, New York City was its very epicenter. British writer J. B. Priestley, explained at the time, "The New York City of forty years ago [was] an American city, but today's cosmopolis belongs to the world, if the world does not belong to it."[1]

By the late 1940s, the city was the nation's largest metropolis, the world's largest port and financial center, and home to many of the world's largest companies. It was a leader in media and publishing and had become the international center for art and culture. Symbolic of its prominent position, the city was chosen by the United Nations as the site for its permanent headquarters, completed in 1952. Author E. B. White wrote that New York was on its way to "becoming the capital of the world."[2]

It was in this vibrant, global center of a city that Celina took up residence late in the summer of 1952. When she first arrived, she stayed with her mother's old friend, Dottie Isaacson, in the Bronx, before arranging a room at the International House. International House (I-House) was perfectly suited for Celina and seemed like something of an extension of the Encampment she had attended several years earlier. A private, non-profit residence, it had been established in 1924 to bring together graduate students and scholars from all over the world. While there, residents attended or worked at one of several of the city's nearby schools and universities— Columbia University, Teachers College, New York University, Julliard School, or the Union Theological Seminary, for example—and took part in I-House programming designed to promote diversity of thought and build mutual understanding, friendship, and respect from people of all cultures and countries. Only about a third of its residents were from the United States.[3]

Celina studied philosophy of education while at Teachers College, where she found her professors first rate. She had the good fortune of studying with some of the leading minds of the day, including Lawrence Cremin, who was widely regarded as an outstanding teacher who "exuded knowledge and enthusiasm for issues in America's educational past." Outside the classroom, Cremin was a prolific author who won the Bancroft Prize in American History in 1962 and a Pulitzer Prize for history in 1984, and he served as the president of Teachers College from 1974 to 1981. Celina also took courses with John L. Childs, a noted progressive and proponent of John Dewey's idea of a pragmatic education, emphasizing a curriculum relevant to the students and involving their active participation.[4]

Fellow students enhanced her time there as well. The program included many extremely bright people, and Celina thought Teachers College a "heady" experience. The courses and interaction with classmates would indeed be helpful to Celina's teaching career fifteen years down the road, but it was her stay at International House that ultimately proved more important, for it was here she met Amir "Bini" Biniaz, her soon-to-be husband.[5]

Bini had been born in Tehran, Persia (renamed Iran in 1935), in July 1925, the firstborn child of a prominent, secular Muslim couple. His father was a colonel in the army, his mother a homemaker. After being educated in top private schools—an Armenian primary school and a Zoroastrian secondary school, which included the equivalent of a couple of years of college—Bini went to study law at the University of Tehran. But he longed to escape his autocratic, imperious, physically abusive father and leave the country.[6]

He got the chance in early 1946, when a U.S. Embassy official issued him a visa. Bini had tutored this State Department staffer in Farsi, and to return the favor, the diplomat paved the way for the twenty-year-old Iranian to come to the United States with the necessary travel permit. That April, Bini landed in New York, a little more than a year before Celina and her parents arrived. He found a room at the I-House but was only there a few weeks before he was drafted into the U.S. Army. He volunteered for the airborne division and spent his year of service at Fort Benning, Georgia. There he ultimately became a jumpmaster or expert paratrooper who trained others to parachute from airplanes.[7]

After being discharged, Bini returned to New York in the spring of 1947. He took a couple of night courses to earn his requisite New York high school diploma and enrolled in the City College of New York—a public, tuition-free institution at the time—in the fall. Instead of continuing his study of law, which would require him to learn a different legal system, he decided to pursue his interest in the sciences and majored in biology. Bini graduated in three years because of credits he had earned from the University of Tehran. That fall, he took advantage of the GI Bill, which covered his tuition and living expenses and enrolled in dental school at New York University.[8]

Although Bini did not live at International House, he had maintained a nonresident membership because he enjoyed the various social and cultural activities it offered. It was here at a dance in December 1952 that he and Celina met. Bini remembered the encounter and the evening, "She was a great dancer, great conversationalist, and the most intelligent person I had ever met." Celina recalled him as "tall, dark, and handsome" with a quick mind and a great sense of humor. It was, she said, "love at first sight."[9]

A whirlwind romance ensued. The two were engaged at the end of April and planned a September wedding. Celina, meanwhile, completed her master's degree at Teachers College. Her Necchi scholarship was renewed for another year, but she declined the honor, planning to work to support the couple while Bini finished dental school.[10]

That summer, Bini returned to his job at the Ramapo Summer Camp in Rhinebeck, a small town one hundred miles north of New York City. He had worked at the residential camp designed to serve children and teens with behavioral, emotional, or learning difficulties every summer since 1948, when he found a camp counselor position there at CCNY's employment office. By 1952, Bini was its head counselor, and Celina joined him at Ramapo that summer, working as dance counselor. Besides providing Bini and then Celina employment, the camp also introduced them to Robert "Bob" and Jean Thomases, a couple who would become their lifelong friends. Bob was a high school teacher and the camp's director, and Jean was a nurse and the camp's dietitian.[11]

Shortly after the summer camp ended, Celina and Bini got married. The intimate ceremony was held at the International House on September 12; far different, Celina chuckled, than the huge celebrity wedding of Senator John Kennedy and Jacqueline Bouvier that took place the same day. Since neither Bini nor Celina were at all religious—Bini referred to their union as a "mixed marriage" because it represented "an agnostic marrying an atheist"—they had Hank Herman, the leader of the New York Society for Ethical Culture officiate. Celina had first met him a few years earlier at the Encampment for Citizenship, where he had been an instructor.[12]

Most of the thirty or so people attending the wedding were friends the couple knew from International House, Columbia, or NYU. Celina's parents were also there as were Dottie Isaacson and her twelve-year-old son Richard, who played some of Frédéric Chopin's nocturnes on the piano at the wedding. Following the ceremony and reception, the newlyweds headed to Canada in a borrowed car for their honeymoon, where they spent six days in Montreal and Quebec.[13]

Neither the Karps nor the Biniazes were originally happy with the idea of their children marrying outside their faiths. But Celina's parents realized there was nothing they could do about their independent daughter's decision, and once they met Bini, they rapidly warmed to him. Bini's mother and siblings had a similar reaction and accepted the marriage. Eventually, both Bini's brother and sister would come to the United States, and Celina became close to both. His mother remained in Iran but would soon come for several extended visits, and she and Celina developed an affectionate relationship as well. Bini's father, however, was another story. Once he left Iran, Bini never returned, and the break between father and son became permanent; Celina never met him.[14]

Meanwhile, Celina and Bini returned from their honeymoon and set up housekeeping in a small, studio apartment near the NYU's College of Dentistry in Midtown Manhattan where Bini began his last year of the program. To support the couple, Celina took a job as a statistician for the Junior League, located in the Waldorf Astoria Hotel. The couple lived frugally. They enjoyed the city's cultural highlights when time allowed, and although as freethinkers they had no interest in religious services, they often attended or listened to radio broadcasts of the New York Society for Ethical Culture's Sunday meetings. These lectures and discussions generally stressed the importance of ethical principles and pushed for the building of a more equitable and just society.[15]

Bini completed dental school that spring and then passed the dental board exams. That March, Celina was thrilled to obtain her long awaited American citizenship; Bini had already become a citizen five years earlier. In June, the couple returned to Camp Ramapo one last time; Bini continued as head counselor, and Celina started a sewing program for the youngsters. When camp ended, they went back to their apartment in the city. Bini started working at a nearby dental clinic, and Celina gave birth to son Robert "Rob" in September 1954. Late that fall, the couple bought a used, pistachio green Chevrolet coupe and began using it on weekends for house hunting in places where they thought Bini could establish and develop his own dental practice.[16]

They soon narrowed their search to Long Island and eventually Wantagh—a hamlet within the Nassau County town of Hempstead on the southwestern portion of the island—partially because their good friends the Thomases lived there. Here Celina and Bini found a three-bedroom, ranch-style house in the twelve hundred block of Wantagh Avenue, recently built in 1950. The home and yard seemed perfect for their growing family. Plus, Bini envisioned converting the attached garage into a dental office and working from there. He again relied on his military service benefits, and the couple bought the $16,500 home with a low interest, fixed-rate GI loan.[17]

Although Celina and Bini soon made many other friends in Wantagh, they remained closest to the Thomases. The couples regularly babysat for each other, and the families enjoyed frequent holiday meals such as Thanksgiving together. They were together so often, in fact, that Linda Lafourcade, the Thomases daughter recalled that she and Rob Biniaz, three years her junior, "grew up as cousins." And when they were not together, Celina kept in close touch with Jean by telephone "pretty much every day."[18]

In buying the home and moving to the suburbs in the summer of 1955, Celina and Bini joined many others riding the wave of postwar prosperity to the American dream. This new economic abundance had been fueled by pent-up consumer demand, the baby boom, and the rise of new industries. It was also aided by the GI Bill, which had provided educational opportunities to Bini and many other veterans and provided them a path to higher paying jobs and more disposable income. Indeed, nearly half the fifteen million eligible veterans took advantage of the program, attending colleges and universities, graduate and professional schools, or vocational institutions. Together, these factors led to the development of a broad middle class and the good life for many Americans, the centerpiece of which was the rapid rise of suburbia and single-family homes.[19]

The couple easily connected with the generation of Americans that, having come of age during the Great Depression and fought in World War II, were eager to settle down in one of the many new suburbs, begin careers, start families, and partake of their newfound affluence. "Acquisitiveness, mass consumption, and then conspicuous consumption, fueled by the $100 billion Americans had saved during the war and newly available credit cards, ruled the day." This was an era when the gross national product rose by more than 75 percent over the decade, while the median family income increased 70 percent over the period. As productivity increased, work hours decreased, and many now enjoyed the five-day work week.[20]

Fourteen million new homes were added to the American landscape between 1945 and 1960, with most of them being built in the suburbs. Residents soon filled these homes with the latest appliances and gadgets, furniture, baby equipment, and toys. Pulitzer Prize-winning historian Doris Kearns Goodwin—who grew up in the 1950s on Long Island in Rockville Centre, an incorporated Nassau County village ten miles west of Wantagh—captured the mood of the time: "Excitement infested the entire block when someone got a new refrigerator with a built-in freezer, an automatic washing machine, or a television with a larger screen," and for those "who had lived through the Depression, the ever-expanding economy seemed like a cornucopia."[21]

Long Island was right in the middle of this national makeover in the 1950s. "The dam burst at the Nassau-Queens border [on the western edge of Long Island], pouring out torrents of new people, housing developments, and freshly-paved ribbons of roadway," wrote Jonathan Ruff, curator of the Long Island Museum. "The great eastward stampede out of New York City transformed Long Island from a sleepy strip of sandy shoreline and potato farms to a bustling region with more people than 18 entire states." Nassau County, which included the mass-produced suburb of Levittown, in fact, was the fastest growing county in the nation in the early 1950s.[22]

Hollywood depicted this brave new world in popular television shows such as *The Adventures of Ozzie and Harriet, Father Knows Best,* or *Leave it to Beaver.* Whether in suburbs in the Northeast, South, Midwest, or West, the romanticized narrative remained the same. Happy, nuclear families held sway in these neighborhoods: breadwinning husbands headed off to their well-paying jobs each weekday and fulfilled, fulltime homemaker wives raised two or three children in their well-ordered communities. Here behind manicured front lawns a sameness prevailed; family life was celebrated, togetherness was emphasized, and religion was a part of everyone's life. When not otherwise occupied, adults often joined clubs, civic organizations, or service groups. These upbeat sitcoms featured all white families in middle-class communities; serious problems did not exist. Author David Halberstam explained, "Mid-fifties television portrayed a wonderfully antiseptic world of idealized homes in an idealized, unflawed America." Indeed, the storylines almost never included people of color and completely glossed over the era's troubling issue of racism and the mounting anxiety over the Cold War.[23]

Still, these television programs contained kernels of truth about suburban living and to a certain extent reflected the experience in Wantagh in the 1950s and 1960s. Celina recalled her early years in Wantagh as wonderful and appreciated that she and most of her neighbors were about the same age in similar circumstances. "It was a very exciting and forward-looking time. We were all getting started, all having children, and our husbands were all just beginning their careers."[24]

During the couple's first couple of years in Wantagh, Bini took part in the morning ritual, repeated throughout much of Long Island, joining the throng of husbands heading to their local train stations for the commute to Penn Station and their jobs in the city. Celina, for her part, remained at home like most other Wantagh mothers, and in 1958, she gave birth to the couple's second child, Susan "Sue." She also learned to drive, and some of her earliest trips were to hardware and home furnishing stores as she busied herself painting and adding personal touches to the house. Over the years, she and Bini would reconfigure the home with several additions, including two bedrooms and a second story.[25]

As Bini's fledgling dental practice in Wantagh picked up, he gradually decreased his days working at a New York labor union dental clinic in the city, but he was still spending considerable time there when Celina met Rita Post, her first good friend in the area besides the Thomases. The Posts had just moved to the neighboring town of Seaford in 1956, and her husband Ralph, an oral surgeon, immediately began introducing himself to local dentists hoping to drum up business. The first few times he stopped by the Biniazes, Bini was not home, but Ralph visited with Celina, who was still working on the home and often had a paintbrush in her hand. Ralph thought Celina and his wife Rita would hit it off, and he connected the two.[26]

He was right; the two became fast friends. They shared an affiliation with Democratic politics in an area awash with Republicans, and both were young, college-educated mothers. This soon led the two to join a local chapter of the American Association of University Women (AAUW) and its book club, which met in nearby Levittown. The group was important to Celina because it "got us out of the house" and interacting with "other people who talked our language." Specifically, she remembered, "It was hard in those days if you were [a] well educated [woman] and your mind was moving in circles absorbing what was going on in the world not to be able to talk about it." The Levittown AAUW proved a welcome respite from this problem.[27]

Although Bini and Ralph were friendly, the two women "were mostly girlfriends," Rita said. Still, the families began spending a lot of time together, and the adults enjoyed visiting in each other's homes. Celina delighted in hosting such gatherings, and she especially loved holding dinner parties, generally for several couples at a time. She made everything for these dinners—including the tablecloths and matching napkins—and was an excellent cook. Celina especially enjoyed using fruits, herbs, and vegetables Bini grew in his garden and often used such ingredients in new and sometimes exotic recipes. Son Rob described her as adventurous in the kitchen.[28]

Most of all, Bini and Celina were exceptional hosts, and the evenings at their home were lively. Bini was well known for his sense of humor and kept the guests laughing with his latest jokes. Celina was more reserved and serious but very articulate and well read; she engaged her guests in conversations on a wide variety of subjects. The one matter that Celina would not address, however, was her Holocaust experience. She had remained mum on the topic after people in Des Moines seemed uninterested or unable to comprehend the handful of details she revealed during her first six months in the city. After that, only a few people besides Bini knew anything of her story, and Bini, in fact, knew very little.[29]

From the beginning, he had been patient with Celina about her past and never pressed her on the subject. Initially, she had told him she was from Poland, was Jewish, and had survived the Holocaust, but little else. As he recalled, "Celina never really delved into these things in any detail. It was a gradual thing; [the specifics] came out in dribs and drabs as time went on." But that was over decades.[30]

The only others privy to the broad outlines of Celina's Holocaust experience at the time were evidently the Thomases, although they understood that the information was not to be shared. For some reason, however, Jean Thomases did tell her daughter Linda that Celina had been in a concentration camp, but cautioned her, "it was something we should never talk about." She did not, and it was never mentioned again until Celina told Linda about it decades later in a Christmas card.[31]

Even Celina's children knew nothing of her World War II past, which she had intentionally kept from them. She told them she was Polish but that was all. "They had no idea I was a [Holocaust] survivor," Celina informed an interviewer in 1996, and that was intentional. She did not want to burden them with her horrific history: "I didn't want them to feel guilty; I didn't want them to hate; I wanted them to have a happy childhood." Rob and Sue would only begin to learn parts of their mother's traumatic experience in the late 1960s.[32]

Outside of the Thomases, those in Wantagh only knew she was from Poland and had been a displaced person because of World War II. Celina's unwillingness to talk about her background made her "a bit of an enigma in town" according to friend Anita Roll, who originally met Celina in 1961 at their daughters' dance class. Celina volunteered little about herself, and because she was clearly so tight-lipped on the issue, no one asked. Her religious activity gave nothing away either. After she lost her faith in God and Judaism during the war, she had no interest in organized religion. Nor did Bini, and they steered clear of any religious organizations. But once Rob and Sue reached early childhood, they reconsidered. They both wanted the children to have a moral grounding that religion offered, so like almost all suburbanites in Wantagh, Celina, Bini, seven-year-old Rob, and four-year-old Sue began attending religious services on weekends. The couple took the children to the Unitarian church—the South Nassau Unitarian Universalist Congregation—six miles southwest in the village of Freeport—and while Celina and Bini sat through the fellowship service, Rob and Sue went to Sunday school. There, as the couple had hoped, the children learned about ethics, morality, and several different religions.[33]

Like their suburban counterparts in Wantagh and around the country, the Biniazes' life revolved around the home. Shari Roll, one of Sue's oldest friends, recalled that Celina took great pride in her homemaking and had "an incredible sense of color and design." Years later, she wondered if Celina's penchant for bright colors was a reaction to her dark Holocaust past and the gray hues that seemed to predominate in postwar Europe. She also remembered how beautifully Celina decorated the house for Christmas, which the family celebrated in secular fashion with a tree, presents, and Santa Claus as they did Easter with decorated eggs, candy, and the Easter Bunny.[34]

By the mid-1950s, the home became even more central to the family. Bini's Wantagh dental practice had grown to the point that he no longer needed to work in the city, and he now devoted all his time to his local patients in his converted garage office. Son Rob recalled often hearing the high-pitched whine of his father's dental drill from his nearby bedroom as Bini completed various procedures on his patients in the office. Here Bini was essentially a one-man operation, scheduling appointments, cleaning teeth, doing a variety of dental work, and running the business by himself.[35]

Bini kept his patients at ease with a ready joke and built a highly successful practice. "He was a dentist of note in town," observed Anita Roll, "Everybody who was anybody went to Dr. Biniaz." Besides working in his own practice, Bini became active in both the Nassau County and New York state dental societies and served in a variety of capacities over the years. Later, he did volunteer dental work at the Cerebral Palsy Association of Nassau County and taught courses on providing dental care for those with disabilities at Meadowbrook Hospital (now Nassau University Medical Center).[36]

But for the most part, he worked from his home office, and because of this, he was a much more engaged parent than most other family men in Wantagh who worked miles away from their homes. It was the extroverted, social Bini, for instance, rather than the more reticent Celina who usually checked on the children and visited when they had friends over.[37]

Bini tended to be playful with Rob and Sue; Celina more serious, and together, they were "the most marvelous parents." Anita Roll continued, "The kids were offered everything and more, and they were the kind of kids who had the ability to be successful in everything," and they were.[38]

Celina focused much of her attention on her children's education. She understood its value better than most, especially because much of her early schooling had been stolen by the Nazis, and she was determined that Rob and Sue take full advantage of their educational opportunities in Wantagh. She enrolled her children in piano lessons early and insured they had the best instruction possible. Both would become accomplished pianists. Music remained important to them, and both spent hours practicing. Rob later played the clarinet in band, and Sue became an exceptional violinist. Both excelled in the classroom as well, where they were outstanding students, exceeding Celina's high expectations.[39]

When the children were not in school, the Biniazes joined many others in the town's burgeoning, upwardly mobile, middle class in taking one or two vacations a year. During spring break, for example, the four often headed south, driving to Miami for some warmer weather. They rarely, however, went to Iowa to see Celina's parents; rather, it was Phyllis and Irvin who came to Wantagh at least once, but usually several times a year. They loved seeing the grandchildren and were incredibly proud of Celina's independence and the life she had built. Years later while visiting with Celina, Phyllis explained, "I look around here and see the big, beautiful house and beautiful grandchildren, and I just think to myself that she was able to live her life the way she chose to do it and that gives me so much pleasure."[40]

Celina relished this time with her parents. She had always been particularly close to her mother, notably after their bond that had developed during the Holocaust and remained so throughout her life. Celina especially appreciated that her mother and father were both "forward looking and resilient." They lived in the present and were clearly role models for her. But it was her mother, who held no bitterness or anger about her World War II experience, that was particularly important. "My mother's mantra was that the world owes you nothing. You are where you are, and you make the best of it."[41]

She followed Phyllis's lead, and this became Celina's refrain as well. Her mother and Mater Leontine, the nun in Mindelheim, had played significant roles in helping Celina deal with her past. Indeed, in the 1950s, she poured her energy into the present and future. Like millions of other young women at the time, she had married and with her husband vigorously pursued the American dream. Celina quit her job once her children were born and worked hard to make the family's house a home, concentrating on ensuring a better childhood and life for Rob and Sue than she had.

All was going well for Celina; the family was prospering, she and Bini had many friends and had integrated into the Wantagh community, and Rob and Sue were thriving at school. But she still faced some demons from her past. One was a persistent fear of authority. Celina became anxious during the McCarthy era and the second Red Scare of the early 1950s, for instance, when the fear of communism led to many unwarranted accusations of subversion and treason. This atmosphere of suspicion led Celina to worry about signing anything or saying anything that could be misconstrued as disloyalty and result in her losing her citizenship and being deported.[42]

This particular concern gradually died down over the decade, but Celina would remain apprehensive about authority for the rest of her life. Worse, her years under Nazi control had crushed her self-esteem. "Once you are marginalized," she later remarked, "you don't think much of yourself. I never thought…I could do anything of value."[43]

She quietly struggled with this issue for years up until the mid-1960s, when by chance she found her true vocation in the classroom. "I hadn't thought about going back to work," she reminisced, "and went…in[to] teaching by accident." The move would prove restorative for Celina. She was a natural teacher, and even as she enriched the lives of hundreds of Wantagh children over her twenty-five-year career, she recovered her self-confidence and self-worth, shattered years earlier by the Holocaust.[44]

Eight

Finding Her Calling

Sometime in the early 1960s, Celina and friend Anita Roll joined a Great Books Foundation discussion group. Adding this second book club was completely in character for Celina since she loved the intellectual exchanges in her other one tied to the American Association of University Women (AAUW). And the Great Books group seemed an even better fit for Celina. By stressing civic and social engagement through discussions of important texts in the Western canon, Great Books appeared related to other programs from Celina's past—the Encampment for Civic Engagement or International House—which had emphasized similar ideals.

Celina and Roll soon began the program's readings, which started with selections from prominent thinkers like Plato, Thucydides, Aristotle, Homer, St. Augustine, William Shakespeare, and Adam Smith. As she had hoped, thought-provoking discussions ensued when the group met. But her participation here may not have led to anything beyond stimulating conversations were it not for the foundation's nascent Junior Great Books program.[1]

Junior Great Books had been launched in 1962 to expand the organization's reach to youngsters. To do so, it developed paperback book sets for ten to fifteen-year-olds and started afterschool clubs for fifth to nineth graders across the country. Adult volunteers who had gone through the Junior Great Books training course led the clubs.[2]

Celina was intrigued by the idea of Junior Great Books. She was enjoying the foundation's adult program and since she "was not doing anything," she enrolled in a Junior Great Books leader training class in summer 1965, thinking it might be fun to share her interest in literature with children.

The decision was pivotal for Celina. Although she did not know it at the time, it put the stay-at-home mother on a life-changing path, leading her to find her calling in teaching.[3]

That fall, Betty Wilson, Rob Biniaz's sixth-grade teacher at Wantagh's Sunrise Park Elementary School, was thinking about starting a Junior Great Books club for some of her students. Wilson contacted Great Books about finding a discussion leader in the area and was given Celina's name. She then called Celina, who expressed immediate interest. But when Wilson told her she wanted to include Rob in the club, Celina said she would have to ask him how he would feel about her leading the group. He expressed no concerns, and Celina started the extracurricular group in January 1966.[4]

Besides Rob, the Junior Great Books club included about eight other students who met Celina after school several times a month. The wide-ranging reading package included selections from children's classics by Hans Christian Andersen, adventures such as *Robinson Crusoe*, and *The Thousand and One Nights*, as well as pieces from Geoffrey Chaucer, Charles Dickens, and Rudyard Kipling.[5]

Celina was a natural teacher, and her Junior Great Books group went well from the very beginning. She loved engaging the students, and Wilson, who had observed several of the early sessions was struck by the instant rapport Celina had developed with the youngsters. So she asked Celina if she were willing help her in the classroom. Specifically, Wilson had a young boy who struggled with learning and frequently disrupted the class; she hoped Celina would take him out of the classroom and tutor him. Since she was having such a good experience with the children in the afterschool program, Celina readily volunteered.[6]

She started working with the challenging student later that winter, meeting with him several times a week in the small audiovisual room adjacent to Wilson's classroom. During their initial conversations, Celina learned of the child's fascination with automobiles and played to his interest by buying him every car magazine she could find. He loved the gifts and quickly looked through them, evidently only focusing on the photographs. That was when Celina realized the sixth grader could not read. In an era before the federal government passed PL-94-142, the Education for All Handicapped Children's Act in 1975 (later amended and renamed as the Individuals with Disabilities Education Act), children like this young boy often fell through the cracks and were promoted from grade to grade without meeting any academic standards and without individual assessment or assistance.[7]

Fortunately, Celina pinpointed the child's problem and began working with him by starting with the magazines' pictures and then associating words in the accompanying stories with them. Over the next few months, she gradually taught him to read. Betty Wilson was amazed by the progress Celina made with the student. And as he started to read, he grew more interested in classroom activities and less disruptive.[8]

The success got Wilson thinking; what if they could develop a program, which systematically identified students who were struggling in reading or math, take them out of their classrooms several times a week, and provide them with tutoring? Wilson talked with the Sunrise Park's principal, Ferdinand Hoefner, Jr., who liked the idea. She then fleshed it out, conceiving of a center in the school where academically challenged students would receive remedial assistance.[9]

Hoefner took the proposal to the school district's administrators, Walter Suess, the assistant superintendent of curriculum and instruction, and the superintendent, Charles St. Clair. They both supported the idea as did the Wantagh Board of Education. With their backing, Wilson and Hoefner wrote a three-year grant to the New York State Education Department to establish and operate a learning center for struggling fifth and sixth graders at Sunrise Park. The education department awarded the grant, and the Learning Laboratory as it was to be called, would open the following fall.[10]

As the grant was being drafted and considered, Celina was asked back as a Junior Great Books discussion leader for the 1966-1967 school year. She was busier this time around, however. Others had heard good things about Celina's work with the book club for Wilson's class the previous spring, and Celina was invited to head three book groups, two sixth grade clubs and one for fifth graders. She agreed and again thoroughly enjoyed her afternoons with the children.[11]

With the grant in hand, Wilson began preparing to launch the Learning Laboratory, which would be located in her reconfigured sixth grade classroom. She would head the new entity and serve as its fulltime teacher. Carol Taylor, the district psychologist, would assist Wilson in the room, and its instruction team would be rounded out with a part-time teacher's aide. Wilson looked to Celina to fill this role.[12]

Celina had found her efforts with Junior Great Books and tutoring so rewarding that she jumped at the chance to continue working with children, and took the job, which she recalled paid $2,000 (roughly $16,000 today). At the same time, she moved to make her work in the classroom permanent by enrolling in requisite education courses at nearby Hofstra University, eight miles west in the town of Hempstead, to get her New York teaching certificate. A student teaching assignment was required as well, but given the nature of her upcoming job, the Hofstra education department agreed to count her time working under Wilson's supervision as her student teaching assignment.[13]

The Learning Laboratory opened at Sunrise Park in September 1967. Thirty fifth and sixth graders were initially identified as "underachievers" in math or reading by teachers based on observation of their daily work, standardized test scores, or the recommendation of the school psychologist. The students came to the Lab daily, in small groups of eight to ten, for sessions that lasted about an hour. Teaching in the lab consisted of both one-to-one instruction, small group work, and independent activities at learning centers. Wilson, Taylor, and Celina prepared individual assignments for each subject and tailored the learning for each individual child.[14]

Celina thrived in this environment. With empathy and understanding, she took "children at the point they were and tried to build on that." Just as she had done with the first youngster she tutored, she worked hard to identify her students' interests and used those to connect with them. Former colleague Jeanne Bonnici recalled, "Celina was wonderful with kids, and the children loved her." She and the other team members in the Learning Lab evidently had an immediate impact. In February 1968, the parents of one of their students thanked the district superintendent for their work. "We feel that Mrs. Collins [a teacher who also helped in the Learning Lab], Mrs. Biniaz, and Mrs. Taylor have done more for Mary in five months than we thought possible. Mary is a lovely, helpful child but a slow learner. She is of average intelligence, but afraid to compete. These dedicated women have given Mary more confidence in herself, and they are trying to find the reason for her lack of assurance, and given the time, we feel they will. They are truly interested, and we feel sure they will help Mary immeasurably."[15]

That summer, Celina completed the Hofstra education program and received her permanent teaching certificate in September 1968. She stayed on as a part-time instructor in the Learning Lab for the next two years. Over that period, the lab team worked with an additional twenty-eight "underachievers," and when the grant ran out, Hoefner wrote a final report that included an evaluation of the program's success.[16]

To measure the lab's effectiveness, control groups of children experiencing similar learning difficulties as those in the Sunrise Park Learning Lab were monitored over the same period. Instead of having the same individualized educational programs as those in the lab, these children continued in their regular classrooms with the standard instruction.[17]

Although there were clearly individual successes at the Learning Lab, as the letter from Mary's parents suggested, an analysis of the data gathered at the end of each of the three years "did not indicate that the special treatment [in the Learning Lab] had any significantly positive effect on achievement as measured by the instruments used. Conclusions drawn suggest that the experimental approach employed came too late in the students' school experience."[18]

Wilson, Taylor, and Celina agreed with Hoefner's assessment and felt that the intervention came too late in the students' education to make a significant difference. They wholeheartedly supported the district's next move, which called for discontinuing the Learning Laboratory, and replacing it with a "demonstration program involving seven and eight-year-old students who evidence learning problems." Specifically, the district established two learning centers, one at Sunrise Park and one at Forest Lake. There school officials employed many of the same elements used in the Learning Lab, but they hoped the earlier intervention would yield positive results.[19]

Celina was selected to head the new learning center at Sunrise Park, which was initially a halftime position until 1972, when she became a fulltime teacher. And it was at this work, instructing early elementary students who were struggling academically, that Celina particularly excelled. "I enjoyed it so much," she recalled, "because I was reliving my childhood." Indeed, she delighted in the experience working with these children because it brought back fond memories of her own beginnings in elementary school and the wonders of learning before her education was abruptly taken away when Nazis invaded Poland before she could start third grade.[20]

Except for three years in the middle of the 1970s when Celina spent half her time in the district's other learning center at Forest Lake, she taught exclusively at Sunrise Park until the aging building was closed in 1980. Here her learning center was in the basement, and much like the Learning Lab before, it featured several distinct learning stations, which allowed students to work independently at times when Celina was helping other children.[21]

First-grade students who were having trouble with reading and/or writing were initially sent to Celina, who administered a screening exam called the Slingerland Test. It identified the children with "potential language difficulties, as well as those already exhibiting specific language disabilities" who, it was believed, would benefit from special, individualized attention.[22]

Those selected for extra help went to the learning center as second and third graders. There in groups of four to six at a time, they met with Celina every day in hour-long sessions. Public school programs like the learning center, which pulled students out of their regular classrooms for remedial assistance, were still in their infancy. Much of what Celina did was experimental. Many of her teaching strategies were gleaned from in-service courses and conferences, seminars, and workshops she began attending several years earlier when she started at the Learning Lab. These included programs sponsored by the Orton Society (now the International Dyslexia Association), which emphasized a multidisciplinary approach to helping those with dyslexia; the Association for Children with Learning Disabilities (now the Learning Disabilities Association of America); the Slingerland Institute, which focused on students having problems reading and writing and was started by educator Beth Slingerland, the creator of the screening test bearing her name; and the American Institute for Developmental Education.[23]

Celina also credited her brief time decades earlier at Smith College's social work program for helping her address the special needs of the children in the learning center. She explained in 1974 that the coursework there aided her "immeasurably in dealing with the many emotional overlays that learning disabled children exhibit in their behavior as well as bring with them to the learning process."[24]

This background and her continuing effort to increase her knowledge in perceptual disabilities and skills to address them allowed Celina to develop effective individualized learning plans for each of her students. School psychologist Carol Taylor lauded her as "a dedicated and creative educator" who "viewed each youngster as unique and…has been adept at finding his strengths and adapting instruction to overcome his weakness. I consider her an expert in enabling children to organize and express their thought and ideas, and then translating them to paper."[25]

Besides addressing her students' learning problems, Celina empathized with them and showed them great compassion. "I could understand where they were coming from," Celina once said, referring to her own educational challenges after missing years of school. "We connected, the kids and I." James Smith, the principal at Forest Lake Elementary School where Celina had worked half-time for several years, saw this firsthand: "Her feeling for children with problems is superior, and she can instill in them a degree of confidence and self-esteem."[26]

Celina recognized that some considered attending the learning centers as humiliating and degrading, and she worked especially hard to make the experience positive. Here again, Carol Taylor sang her praises: "The children like her and recognize that she likes them and will help them. They are eager to attend the Resource Room." Former student Dan Connolly, now a screenwriter in Los Angeles, agreed, "There was something unique and special about Mrs. Biniaz. The level of reassurance and care she provided, the confidence building. Actually, I think a lot of the work that she was doing was helping kids become more confident that they could overcome whatever their particular issues were."[27]

Chris Daniggelis, another former learning center student was a "worried and nervous child," who remembered that Celina came to his rescue when he was afraid to walk home from school one afternoon. She eased his fears by having him lie down on the carpeted classroom floor, put her hand gently on his head, and told him repeatedly that everything would be fine. Daniggelis also noted that Celina taught him to read "and more importantly to comprehend and understand context." Equally important in his case, Celina encouraged his artistic talent. She often had her students draw in class to help them express their ideas, and Daniggelis usually drew complex, Rube Goldberg-like contraptions.[28]

Daniggelis said "it was a gift to be educated" by Celina and credits her with his ability to go on to college and graduate school and become a successful artist and printmaker. Today, he teaches at the University of Missouri-Columbia and directs its Master of Fine Arts program.[29]

Pat Connolly, Dan Connolly's mother, concurred with Daniggelis's assessment and thought Celina was instrumental in her son's education.

"Dan was having a lot of trouble [in first grade], and a very hard time with reading. Mrs. Biniaz's class changed him. It gave him confidence, and we saw such a change in his scholastic abilities." After a year in the learning center, in fact, Dan had made such progress that both Celina and school administrators decided he no longer needed the special attention and planned to return him to his regular classroom fulltime for third grade.[30]

But the idea worried Pat. She was thrilled with Dan's progress but feared pulling him out of the learning center might set him back again. "I went to the school and asked them to please let Danny stay in there because he was doing so well." School officials and Celina agreed to keep Dan in the center another year, which Pat believed made all the difference. "It completely turned him around....The first year in it was helpful, but the second year was when I noticed the most change. His reading and ability to understand things greatly improved....I can't praise Mrs. Biniaz enough...she was a lovely looking woman with a lovely soul and heart."[31]

A highlight that Celina reserved for Fridays was the peanut game. It stressed the importance of following instructions and helped her children with directionality, something that still confused many of them. For the second and third graders though, it was just fun. Celina would hide a peanut somewhere in the room and tell her youngsters, for example, to take three steps forward, jump to the left, hop twice to the right, and so forth, moving them toward the peanut until someone found it. Her students loved the contest and considered finding the peanut and getting to eat it quite a prize.[32]

While she was working in the learning center in 1974, Celina asked the state department of education for a provisional teaching certificate in special education based on her experience. She evidently received the license, but five years later she took the required courses in the afternoons and evenings at Hofstra University and got her permanent special education certificate late in summer 1979.[33]

If Celina excelled in the classroom, she was also exceptional in collaborating with parents. "Parents sense that she cares about their children, and they respect and follow through on her suggestions for educational planning and for helping and working with their children at home," Carol Taylor explained. Over the years, many parents sent Celina letters of gratitude. One, for example, read, "'Everyone is replaceable.' Not always true. Mike could not have done this without you. You were the right person at the right time."[34]

Colleagues similarly liked and respected her. She was generous with her time and happy to share ideas and teaching strategies with coworkers. They also appreciated the old-world sophistication she exuded. Unlike most, whose casual attire seemed well suited for teaching elementary children, Celina was an elegant dresser, who sewed the clothing herself. Her outfits "were always in bright colors in really nice fabrics and designs, not like the store-bought clothing the rest of us wore," remembered fellow teacher Jeanne Bonnici. And she always wore heels, accessorized the outfits with jewelry, and had "perfectly combed hair. It was part of her persona," added friend Anita Roll.[35]

Celina also always helped when needed. Such was the case in the fall of 1979, the beginning of the last year of instruction at Sunrise Park before the old building was torn down. Leona Gouthreau, one of two sixth-grade teachers had retired the previous spring, and the school needed a replacement for her. Celina had enjoyed her earlier work with sixth graders, so she volunteered for the job. School officials happily took her up on the offer.[36]

Teaching sixth grade was "interesting and fun" for Celina, but "very different" from her previous experience because she was now teaching all the academic subjects to the youngsters. She also felt an added responsibility to make the year special since her students would be the last graduating class from Sunrise Park. According to former student Kerry Brennan, Celina pulled it all off. "No matter what we were doing, we were engaged…she found ways to channel us." She was "riveting in the way she spoke…and her accent gave her a special aura."[37]

Celina experimented in the classroom, trying a variety of tactics to hold her sixth graders' attention and making learning enjoyable. When they were studying Greco-Roman culture, for instance, she took a cue from the 1978 movie *Animal House* and hosted a toga party dinner for her students. She also had her youngsters do reports of various aspects of Greek or Roman life. When it came time for Ami Athanasoulis, a first-generation Greek student, to read her report, Celina surprised the class by having her do the presentation in Greek, so they could hear the language.[38]

Besides teaching the academic subjects, she constantly emphasized the importance of reading and the social skills of accepting personal responsibility, completing projects on time, and caring for each other. "Mrs. Biniaz ran a tight ship" and "was always challenging us to use our brains… but I didn't know anyone who didn't like her," Brennan recalled. "She was warm, sincere, and full of energy with a radiant smile and an infectious laugh." Brennan loved her laugh so much that she worked hard to elicit it as often as possible. Once, for instance, she snuck back into the classroom just before lunch period ended and put the class gerbil in Celina's desk drawer. When everyone had returned to the room, Brennan asked for a rubber band, which she knew would require Celina to open the drawer. The gerbil popped out, and Celina screamed before laughing. Brennan got a much bigger reaction than she anticipated and remembered getting into trouble for the prank, but, she concluded, "it was in a merry sort of way."[39]

After the sixth graders graduated that spring, Sunrise Park was torn down, and Celina was transferred to Wantagh Elementary School, where she would spend the rest of her career. There Celina was back in a learning center as a resource teacher, but she also spent a couple days a week at the learning centers in the district's other elementary schools. And one year, she volunteered to teach a first-grade class.[40]

For friend and colleague Anita Roll, Celina was "an outstanding teacher" who cared. "The fact that she didn't have an education impacted her," and she did "everything she could to give the kids all the advantages of education and get them to the maximum level….The kids loved her." Glowing comments from other teachers as well as parents, students, and strong evaluations suggest Roll's remarks were spot on. Celina's success in the classroom made perfect sense to her son Rob, who believed, "She has always been a teacher."⁴¹

For all the positive impacts Celina had in the Wantagh schools, her career in elementary education had a much greater effect on her. Teaching, and Celina's realization that she excelled at it, restored her self-esteem, something she had struggled with since being traumatized by the Nazis. "I learned an awful lot, and truly enjoyed it....For me as a person, it was very gratifying to learn that I was appreciated as a good teacher, and I was doing a good job."⁴²

Yet, no matter how positive the experience and regardless of the number of close friendships Celina developed over her career, she was still unwilling to discuss her past, and it remained a mystery. For some reason, however, she made one exception, and according to Anita Roll, Celina told her the very broad outlines of her Holocaust experience. "It was very shocking," Roll recalled, "and years before she opened up. I think it was when [Celina's daughter] Sue was in my fourth-grade class because I have a memory of looking for books of how to deal with children of Holocaust survivors.... Celina finished the conversation by saying she hadn't told anyone else and didn't want me to say anything." Roll was astonished by the secret but agreed not to share it.⁴³

Celina's children also knew nothing of her Holocaust history and were only introduced to it when they were in junior high. Rob first heard of it when he was twelve or thirteen years old, and Bini inadvertently mentioned her past to his son. Rob had done something or said something to Celina that Bini thought inappropriate, and he pulled his son aside and said, "You really should be nicer to your mother because she suffered in a concentration camp during World War II." Bini then gave his son a few more details. Rob was not sure what to make of the information, but the topic did not come up again, and he got on with his life.⁴⁴

Sue, likewise, was about twelve or thirteen when she initially learned the broad outlines of her mother's Holocaust experience, but it was her grandmother Phyllis not her father who told her. Like Rob, Sue did not get many specifics and would not hear much more about it for years.[45]

As they grew up, both continued to excel academically. Rob graduated from Wantagh High School second in his class; Sue was her class's valedictorian. Rob went to Yale, where he graduated in 1975, before attending Stanford Law School. After passing the bar, Rob spent nearly three years as an Assistant United States Attorney in Los Angeles. He then completely changed careers and moved into the entertainment industry, where he started at CBS Records (now Sony Records). From there, he eventually moved to Universal Studios. Sue initially followed a similar path. She also went to Yale but began as a premed student before changing course and majoring in Russian studies. She graduated in 1980 and went on to Columbia Law School. There Sue became interested in international law, and after clerking for Judge Dorothy W. Nelson on the U.S. Ninth Circuit Court of Appeals for a year, she returned to international law and joined the U.S. State Department in Washington, D.C.[46]

Meanwhile, in 1980, thousands of miles away on another continent, Australian author Thomas Keneally was looking for a new project. He soon found one by happenstance while in Southern California promoting his book *Confederates*, a novel about the American Civil War. That fall, his book tour took him to Beverly Hills, where he found himself in need of a new briefcase. He walked around the corner from his hotel and located a leather goods store and repair shop. When the owner, Holocaust survivor Leopold "Paul" Page (previously known as Leopold "Poldek" Pfefferberg; his name was changed when he arrived in the United States in 1947) learned Keneally was a writer, he told the author he had an amazing story for him to write and began telling him the tale of Oskar Schindler.[47]

Page had been on "Schindler's List" and had been working for years to get his savior's story published. Keneally was intrigued, especially after Page showed him the two file cabinets of material, which he and several screenwriters had complied on Schindler in hopes of making a movie, but nothing came of it. Now Page had Keneally, who soon decided to tackle the project; two years later, the book came out.[48]

Celina, of course, knew nothing of this. Then one crisp and sunny Sunday morning in October 1982, Celina was flipping through the *New York Times* when she came across a review of Thomas Keneally's new book, *Schindler's List*, on the front page of the paper's book review supplement. She was stunned, then quickly read and reread the review: "I couldn't believe it; I couldn't believe a book was written about our experiences." She ran out, bought the book, and was "amazed by how accurate it was" but wondered why anyone would be interested in the story.[49]

But people were very interested, and the fact-based novel went on to become a bestseller and win England's Booker Prize and the Los Angeles Times Book Prize for fiction. Shortly after it was reviewed, Celina's son Rob was among the many to pick up the book. While reading it, he was reminded of what his father had said of his mother's time in a concentration camp. Then as he reached the end of the book, he thought he saw a connection to his mother. Keneally wrote that toward the end of the war, Schindler acquired truckloads of items—bolts of cloth, thread, shoes, vodka, etc.—that his workers could use to make clothes and/or barter for needed items once they were freed. The passage made Rob think about the pairs of scissors his mother kept in her sewing corner of the basement. She had two pairs he recalled: one was a regular, modern, shiny silver pair; but the other, was an old, odd, iron, blunt-nosed pair of shears. He wondered.[50]

He called his mother immediately, told her he had just finished reading *Schindler's List*, and asked, "Mom, the scissors, are they from the camp?" "Yes," she replied, although she did not elaborate. But her response was significant and the first time she had shared anything about her World War II experiences with either child.[51]

Publication of *Schindler's List* and then the telephone conversation with Rob nudged Celina to begin talking about her Holocaust years, but only with her family, and she remained unwilling to share her story more widely. A side conversation at a party Celina and Bini threw in May 1991 was suggestive of just how quiet she continued to be about her personal history. That spring, friends and family, including Celina's parents Irvin and Phyllis, gathered to hear Rob and his wife Lucy Hood (a television executive he had married in 1990) announce they were expecting their first child. Bini had secretly arranged that the event also serve as a surprise party for Celina's sixtieth birthday and impending retirement the following year.[52]

Celina was truly surprised when the cake for her was wheeled out, but it was her father who was overcome with emotion and broke down in tears. Anita Roll happened to be standing by fellow teacher Jeanne Bonnici during the festivities and asked her if she knew why Irvin was so shaken up. Bonnici had no idea, and Roll told her that Celina and her parents had been in a concentration camp during World War II, and Irvin never expected to see his daughter's sixtieth birthday. Bonnici was shocked at the news, recalling, "None of us knew anything of Celina's past." Indeed, beyond her good friends Bob and Jean Thomases and Roll, no one in Wantagh knew that Celina was a Holocaust survivor.[53]

But her silence would eventually come to an end. Just as Junior Great Books put her on a new trajectory, pointing to her vocation in teaching, so too would Steven Spielberg's award-winning, 1993 film *Schindler's List* prove life-altering for her. With the widely viewed motion picture providing context, Celina came to believe that people could finally understand her Holocaust experience, and she ultimately decided to take her story public.

Celina's North High School
graduation photograph, Des Moines,
1948. Courtesy of Celina Biniaz.

Celina and parents in Des Moines,
circa 1950. Courtesy of Celina Biniaz.

160

Celina and Bini on their wedding day in New York City, 1953. Courtesy of Celina Biniaz.

Celina, second from the left, and colleagues talking in the Learning Lab at Sunrise Park Elementary School, Wantagh, New York, circa 1969. Courtesy of Celina Biniaz.

Celina visiting with Leopold "Paul" Page (previously known as Leopold "Poldek" Pfefferberg), in front of his leather goods store and repair shop in Beverly Hills, circa 1984. Page was also a Holocaust survivor and member of "Schindler's List." It was Page who convinced author Thomas Keneally to write *Schindler's List*. Courtesy of Celina Biniaz.

Phyllis, Irvin, and Celina in front of a tree planted in Schindler's honor on the Avenue of the Righteous Among the Nations at Yad Vashem (The World Holocaust Remembrance Center), Jerusalem, Israel, 1989. Courtesy of Celina Biniaz.

Celina and daughter Sue visiting Emilie Schindler, Oskar Schindler's widow in a suburb of Buenos Aires, Argentina, 1998. Courtesy of Celina Biniaz.

The Biniaz family, circa 2012-13. Left to right: Rob Biniaz, Bini, Bob Harris, Alex Biniaz-Harris, Sue Biniaz, Nicholas Biniaz-Harris, Lucy Hood, Celina, Rachel Biniaz, and Benjamin Biniaz. Courtesy of Celina Biniaz.

Academy Award-winning filmmaker and founder of the Shoah Foundation, Steven Spielberg with five *Schindlerjuden* at the tenth anniversary of the foundation and the release party for the DVD version of the film, *Schindler's List*. Left to right: Celina Biniaz, Rena Fagen, Steven Spielberg, Lewis Fagen, Leon Leyson, and Helen Jonas-Rosenzweig, Universal Studios lot, Los Angeles, California, March 3, 2004. Steve Granitz/WireImage via Getty Images.

Celina and President Barack Obama visit at the USC Shoah Foundation's twentieth anniversary celebration, Hyatt Regency Century Plaza, Century City, California, May 7, 2014. Michael Buckner/Getty Images Entertainment via Getty Images.

Bini, Celina, and grandson Alex Biniaz-Harris visit with Conan O'Brien, who hosted the evening's festivities at the USC Shoah Foundation's twentieth anniversary, 2014. Courtesy of the USC Shoah Foundation.

Celina speaking at the USC Shoah Foundation's twentieth anniversary, 2014. Courtesy of the USC Shoah Foundation.

Over one hundred Holocaust survivors at a reception in their honor in Kraków on the eve of the seventieth anniversary of the liberation of Auschwitz, January 26, 2015. Here they posed for a photograph with Steven Spielberg and other dignitaries. Spielberg is in the center, just below the top row; Celina is in the second row, four seats in from the right. The gathering was sponsored by the Shoah Foundation and the World Jewish Congress. Courtesy of the USC Shoah Foundation.

Celina speaking at a Shoah Foundation event at the University of Southern California, Los Angeles, 2016. Courtesy of the USC Shoah Foundation.

Celina and Robbie Winick, a past president of the Iowa Jewish Historical Society, 2017. Courtesy of the Iowa Jewish Historical Society.

Celina holding the Schindler scissors the day she donated them to the Iowa Jewish Historical Society, Tifereth Israel Synagogue, Des Moines, Iowa, 2019. Courtesy of the Iowa Jewish Historical Society.

Celina speaking to a full house at Des Moines Area Community College (DMACC) Boone, Iowa, campus, 2019. Courtesy of Sean Taylor.

Alex Biniaz-Harris, right, and Ambrose Soehn performing their "Melodies of Auschwitz" composition at the Tifereth Israel Synagogue in Des Moines, Iowa, 2019. Courtesy of the Iowa Jewish Historical Society.

Celina holding her mother's Schindler cup, 2017. Courtesy of the Iowa Jewish Historical Society.

NINE

FINDING HER VOICE

THOMAS KENEALLY'S 1982 BOOK did not persuade Celina to speak about the Holocaust, but it reminded her that much of Schindler's story was hers, and it stirred an interest in this personal history she had long suppressed. As she gradually began exploring this past, Steven Spielberg's 1993 adaptation of *Schindler's List* premiered. Celina was amazed at the movie's accuracy and thought Spielberg "did a masterful job with a difficult subject." The film brought the reality of the Holocaust to millions in a way nothing had before, and it became the catalyst for Celina to start talking about her Holocaust experience, albeit somewhat grudgingly at first. Over the next decade, however, this hesitancy slowly faded away as Celina came to terms with her past and grew comfortable sharing her story. Doing so would become her second vocation.[1]

Celina's lengthy silence on the subject was hardly unique. Many survivors refused to talk about the Holocaust for decades, but an increasing number had begun opening up earlier as American awareness of the Holocaust had undergone a transformation. Initially downplayed after World War II—when former enemy West Germany became an important ally in the Cold War and the global struggle against the Soviet Union and communism—the genocide returned to the public consciousness in 1961.

That year, former Nazi official Adolf Eichmann, who was a key figure in sending thousands of Jews to the death camps, was put on trial for war crimes in Israel. The trial was broadcast internationally and resulted in Eichmann's conviction and hanging. But equally important, historian Peter Novick explained, "The Eichmann trial was the first time that what we now call the Holocaust was an entity in its own right, distinct from

Nazi barbarism in general. In the United States the word 'Holocaust' first became attached to the murder of European Jewry as a result of the trial."[2]

German playwright Rolf Hochhuth kept the public aware of the Holocaust with *The Deputy*, which condemned Pope Pius XII for his World War II failure to speak out against the genocide. After premiering in West Berlin in 1963, the play opened on Broadway the following year with the *New York Times* calling it, "one of the most explosively controversial plays in modern theatrical history."[3]

Then in a somewhat similar vein, investigative journalist and television producer Thomas Morse claimed the U.S. government and Franklin Roosevelt refused to act when the country could have saved large numbers of European Jews from the Holocaust. The best-selling work was first serialized in *Look* magazine in 1967 before being released as *While Six Million Died*.[4]

About the same time, tensions between Israel and its Arab neighbors mounted in the Middle East, leading to two conflicts over the next six years. The Six Day War in 1967 and the Yom Kippur War in 1973 both resulted in Israeli victories but led many American Jews to become more concerned about Israel's isolation and its future security. For Americans more broadly, the fighting and comments from Arab spokesmen suggesting they would "wipe Israel off the map" stoked memories of the Holocaust.[5]

In the spring 1978, television executives at NBC weighed in on the issue with *Holocaust*, their four-part, nine-and-a-half-hour miniseries in response to ABC's *Roots*, which aired the previous year. Although the drama focused on two fictional families, it included much of the history from the Nuremberg Laws through the creation of the ghettos, the concentration camps, and the extermination of the Jews. Nearly one hundred million Americans watched all or part of the program. Historian Novick believed the miniseries was central to embedding "the Holocaust into the general American consciousness." He observed, "More information about the Holocaust was imparted to more Americans over those four nights than over the preceding thirty years."[6]

Four years later, another television program added to the public memory of the Holocaust, when CBS aired a three-hour adaptation of John Hersey's compelling 1950 novel *The Wall*, which explored Jewish resistance to the Holocaust by focusing on the Warsaw ghetto uprising in 1943. Popular media would continue to build on this foundation with Keneally's book and then Spielberg's film playing leading roles.[7]

This changing environment and increasing understanding of the Holocaust led more and more survivors to begin talking about their experiences. Celina's parents were among those to do so, breaking their decades-long silence. The two had talked briefly about living though the Holocaust shortly after arriving in Iowa in the spring of 1947, but when it was clear those who were listening could not comprehend the horrors they had encountered, the couple stopped discussing it and went about making a life in Des Moines. At that time, Irvin had worked as a bookkeeper and accountant for his brother's auto parts store, staying there eleven years before David Karp liquidated the firm. He then started a job at H. E. Sorenson, a furniture and appliance distributor. Irvin remained there as the firm's office and credit manager until 1975, when he retired.[8]

Phyllis, on the other hand, had continued as a bookkeeper at the wholesaler Roycroft until 1955, when it was shuttered. She then took a job in the business office at the downtown Kirkwood Hotel for five years before moving to the accounting firm of Peat Marwick, Mitchell and Company (now KMPG). She worked there until 1970, when mandatory retirement forced her to leave the firm. But Phyllis wanted to work a few more years and was soon hired by Louis Nussbaum, a former partner at Peat Marwick, joining him at the Iowa Phoenix Corporation, a finance firm, where she stayed until retiring in 1976.[9]

Once retired, the couple became increasingly involved in the community. Both remained regulars at the Tifereth Israel Synagogue, where Phyllis devoted more of her time to its Women's League and served as treasurer. She also was active in the Des Moines chapter of Hadassah, the women's Zionist organization of America, and served as its treasurer as well. Irvin, meanwhile, spent more time with his fraternal and service organizations. He was, for example, a longtime board member of the Des Moines lodge of B'nai B'rth, became a master mason of the Home Masonic Lodge, and was involved in the Za-Ga-Zig Shrine. And like many retired couples, the Karps soon decided to downsize, and they sold their Beaverdale home and moved into a West Des Moines condominium in 1982.[10]

It was during the first few years of their retirement and shortly before their move that Irvin and Phyllis began discussing their Holocaust experience. They probably first raised the issue with close friends, most likely Fred (a survivor himself) and Ann Badower before going public with their story. Irvin said that he and Phyllis were finally ready to talk about their experiences because the cultural climate had opened people's eyes to the genocide and programs like *Holocaust*, *The Wall*, and the film *Sophie's Choice* put the events before the public. He explained, "I think that now people can understand that something happened…and as survivors we have an obligation to tell people…so these things don't happen again."[11]

From that point on, the Karps began sharing their Holocaust memories with interviewers and reporters whenever they were asked. Phyllis, however, always remained somewhat restrained when the topic came up, noting that she would much prefer that she and Irvin be remembered as good, conscientious people rather than survivors. But from time to time, she surprised those around her with comments about her past. This happened, for example, one day when the Karps were enjoying a Sabbath luncheon with Rabbi Barry Cytron and his wife Phyllis. Completely unaware that the Karps were Schindler survivors, Phyllis Cytron mentioned that she had just read Keneally's new book and was amazed that Schindler had saved so many Jews in his factory. Phyllis responded with only, "He wasn't such a nice guy." Mouths dropped and the conversation stopped until someone changed the subject and nothing else was said of Schindler or World War II. It was not until later that the Cytrons learned of the Karps connection to the businessman.[12]

Unlike Irvin and Phyllis, however, Celina was among those still not prepared to discuss their Holocaust experiences. Irvin understood his daughter's reluctance, and neither he nor Phyllis ever raised the issue with her. He remarked in 1981, "Celina doesn't want to talk about it and has closed this chapter of her life." While that was true, reading *Schindler's List* the following year piqued her curiosity about this history.[13]

Like Celina and many others across the country, Sidney Sheinberg, the head of MCA and Universal Studios had also read *Schindler's List* and sent a copy to Steven Spielberg, who was then basking in the glow of his recent blockbuster, *E. T. The Extra-Terrestrial*. Spielberg was intrigued by the story, so Sheinberg acquired the rights, hoping the filmmaker would adapt it into a movie. Celina learned the news before it was widely known, when her son Rob, who then worked at Universal and had heard of the plans, called her. Celina's reaction was one of disbelief, "Are you kidding? How can they make a movie about a concentration camp?"[14]

The startling news kept Schindler's story in her mind, and it slowly awakened an interest in her own past. A year later in 1984, when she and Bini were planning a trip to see their son Rob in Los Angeles, they arranged to visit the Beverly Hills leather goods store owner Leopold "Paul" Page, who had been mentioned by Keneally as the person who convinced him to write *Schindler's List*. Page had known Celina's parents well from their years in Kraków, Płaszów, and in Schindler's factory, and remembered Celina. "He was famous by the time I saw him, and he was quite a character," she recalled. After talking briefly about their past, Celina asked for the details of how the book came about, and Page happily regaled her with the tale.[15]

Celina found the conversation so interesting she took her parents to see him the following year. It was a good experience. Celina largely listened this time, while Irvin, Phyllis, and Page shared many memories.[16]

In 1986, Celina delved into her past again. This time, she and Bini were on a month-long trip driving through Germany with friends Ed and Ann Abrahamsen, a couple they had met on an earlier trip to Kenya. Although Celina and her husband had been to Europe several times before, and she had returned to Kraków and even the front gate at Auschwitz—she and her tour group did not enter the former camp—she had not been back to Mindelheim. Thus, while touring with the Abrahamsens, Celina took the couple and Bini to the German town where she and her parents had stayed for a year-and-a-half before coming to the United States.[17]

Memories came flooding back for Celina as she walked the streets of the town and saw the old bank building where she and her parents had lived in an apartment on the third floor. But seeing the *Englisches Institut Mindelheim* convent was most important to her. It was there that the nun Mater Leontine spent hours tutoring her as a young teenager. Celina especially appreciated revisiting the convent's garden, where years earlier, she used to walk with Mater Leontine. During this visit, she walked and talked in the garden with a nun who still remembered her long deceased teacher and friend.[18]

Three years later, Celina took her parents to Israel for their sixtieth wedding anniversary. Celina's parents had been there twice before; she had not. Besides taking some general tours, the three saw old friends they knew from their time in Mindelheim, and they visited with the family of Irvin's deceased brother Felix. Celina and her parents also went to a couple of gravesites; first was that of her grandfather and her father's father Leon, who had lived in Israel since the 1930s. The three likewise went to the Catholic Cemetery at Mount Zion in Jerusalem to the grave of their savior, Oskar Schindler, who died in 1974. There they paused over his marker, inscribed with a cross, his name, the dates of his life, and the phrases "Righteous Among the Nations," in Hebrew and "The Unforgettable Lifesaver of 1,200 Persecuted Jews." They also honored Schindler by going to see the Carob tree planted in his honor on the Avenue of the Righteous Among the Nations at Yad Vashem, the World Holocaust Remembrance Center located in Jerusalem.[19]

In the meantime, Spielberg had been making more movies, including among others, *Indiana Jones and the Temple of Doom*, *The Color Purple*, *Empire of the Sun*, *Indiana Jones and the Last Crusade*, and *Hook*, but he had not yet attempted to bring *Schindler's List* to the screen. He would later explain that he did not feel ready to work on such an important project, and over the decade, he tried to entice others to do it. But Roman Polanski, a Holocaust survivor himself, and Brian De Palma both turned the project down. Martin Scorsese was eventually signed to direct it. But by 1991, Spielberg had changed his mind and was ready to do the film. He and Scorsese traded projects—Spielberg gave him the rights to remake *Cape Fear*, and Scorsese turned *Schindler's List* over to Spielberg.[20]

Eleven years after Keneally's book appeared, Steven Spielberg's adaptation of *Schindler's List* hit the big screen and further solidified the place of the Holocaust "on the American cultural map."[21]

Time magazine film critic Richard Schickel instantly saw the film's release as "a consequential event." Up to that time, he wrote, the Holocaust had only been dealt with "gingerly, and only occasionally" by American movies and "mostly left to documentarians and to Europeans," which reached only small audiences. *Schindler's List*, on the other hand, "is a high-profile, big-studio film, produced and directed by the most popular filmmaker of our era, possible of all time... These factors alone would grant it access to the mainstream public consciousness that no other movie on this subject has enjoyed. The fact that it is a very good movie means it has the chance to lodge there instructively, and perhaps permanently."[22]

The film premiered on November 30, 1993, at the new United States Holocaust Memorial Museum in Washington, D.C., which had opened several months earlier. That afternoon, the museum gave its highest honor, the Medal of Remembrance, posthumously to Oskar Schindler, with Supreme Court Justice Ruth Bader Ginsberg presenting the award to his widow, Emilie Schindler.[23]

A second, larger benefit premiere was held a week later in Los Angeles at the Cineplex Odeon in the ABC Entertainment Center in Century City. Rob was able to get his parents tickets to this special showing. Celina found the movie "very emotional" and was shocked by its realism, but she had been able to hold it together until the scene with the train carrying

the three hundred Schindler women pulling into Auschwitz. "That was
the first time I'd seen that reproduced; it was heartbreaking...and I started
crying." She was not alone in shedding tears. "There was not a dry eye in
the house," she recalled.[24]

Schindler's List went nationwide later that month, and *Miami Herald*
reporter Elinor Brecher was among the many Americans to see it. Brecher
was so transfixed by the film she felt compelled to dig deeper into the
survivors' side of the story. She soon located a number of *Schindlerjuden*
residing near her in Florida and profiled eight of them in a lengthy feature
that ran in the paper a few weeks later in January 1994. The piece led to a
bigger project and book deal, which led her to Celina.[25]

When Brecher contacted Celina, she and Bini had recently retired
and moved to Camarillo, California, a Ventura County city fifty miles
northwest of Los Angeles, the previous year, to be close to their son,
daughter-in-law, and Rachel, their first grandchild, born in 1991. A second
grandchild, Benjamin, followed in 1996. The reporter asked if she could
come to Southern California with a photographer and interview Celina
for the book. In a real change of heart, Celina agreed; it would be the first
time she had discussed her Holocaust experience publicly in over forty
years. The interview marked the beginning of a real turning point for her,
but she initially did so reluctantly. As she ultimately explained to Brecher,
"I can't wait for [the Schindler phenomenon] to be over, because of the
memories. Why not have a pleasant life. These are not pleasant thoughts."[26]

A year after the interview, however, Celina was again reminded of this
past, when her father Irvin died in June 1995. His health had been steadily
declining the previous few years because of multiple myeloma or cancer of
the plasma cells, and he required home care for much of that time. He was
eventually moved to the Iowa Jewish Senior Living Center in Des Moines,
where he finally succumbed to pneumonia. Celina mourned his loss. She
had been "fond and respectful" of her father and was incredibly grateful
for all he had done for her. But the two had never been especially close,
largely because, during her formative years, they had not spent much time

together. Before the war, Irvin worked long hours outside the home, and the Holocaust resulted in a lengthy separation between the two.[27]

Seven months later, Celina was asked to do an interview for the Shoah Foundation. Originally called the Survivors of the Shoah (Hebrew for Holocaust) Visual History Foundation, the nonprofit had been founded by Steven Spielberg in 1994 and initially housed in several trailers on the Universal Studios lot. Its goal was to preserve the memories of Holocaust survivors by videotaping their testimonies and creating the largest such archive in the world. Inspiration for the organization came to Spielberg while filming *Schindler's List*. He explained, "I felt a much more important contribution to remembering the Shoah would be aural-visual history." There was also a sense of urgency to the undertaking. It was a "race against time," Spielberg said, almost all the survivors were elderly. "My whole dream is to take as many testimonies as is humanly possible and make their stories available for no fee for those who want it."[28]

A representative of the Shoah Foundation contacted Celina and her mother in early 1996 about participation in the project. Both agreed, and Carol Stulberg, then the director of major gifts at the foundation, drove to Camarillo with a videographer to interview Celina and her mother, who was out visiting her daughter and Bini, late that January. This was only Celina's second major interview about her Holocaust experience, but it proved important. She was clearly becoming more comfortable telling her story, and it was the beginning of a long and significant relationship with the Shoah Foundation.[29]

A little over a year after sitting for the Shoah interview, Phyllis died of heart failure in February 1997. Ironically, she passed away just hours after *Schindler's List* premiered on network television. She did not see the movie that time around, but shortly before she did in January 1994, she said of Schindler, "For us, he was our angel." Phyllis's rabbi, Neil Sandler of the Tifereth Israel Synagogue noted the film's significance for her: "It was very important for her to have this movie out. It opened up the subject for many people who were not knowledgeable about the Holocaust. It was personally important, too; she was able to open up and talk more about her experience."[30]

The loss hit Celina hard. The two had been very close, and it was Phyllis's love, strength, and support—particularly for the lengthy period the two were separated from Irvin—that had gotten Celina through the darkest days of the Holocaust. After the war, Celina forever admired her mother's resolve and resilience and recalled that she constantly focused on the present and future: "She did not dwell on things that already happened. There was no point. They happened," and she was always ready to move on.[31]

Celina was now the only one left of her family, and thus the only one with firsthand knowledge of their Holocaust years. This surely further encouraged her to share the story. She soon had another opportunity to do so, when, in late 1997 or early 1998, she received a phone call about including what had been her mother's "Schindler cup" in a museum exhibit on Jewish women in Iowa. This cup, along with many other similar ones, and metal bowls had been made in either Schindler's enamelware factory in Kraków or at his operation in Płaszów. They were provided to his Brünnlitz armaments factory workers—including Phyllis, Irvin, and Celina—for use during meals. Phyllis kept the cup after liberation and brought it to the United States, to "remind me, every day," she once said, "that there is a better tomorrow."[32]

In the fall 1996, the Minnesota Historical Society debuted an exhibit called "Unpacking on the Prairie: Jewish Women in the Upper Midwest Since 1855" at its facility in St. Paul, before it went out on a five-year-tour, traveled to museums across the Midwest as well as Washington, D.C., and Canada. The exhibit was scheduled for Des Moines in 1998. Before its arrival, the Iowa Jewish Historical Society (IJHS) worked with the State Historical Society of Iowa (SHSI) to put together a companion exhibit with artifacts focusing on Jewish women's experience in Iowa. Robbie Winick and Roselind Rabinowitz of the IJHS headed the effort to collect local objects for the exhibit.[33]

Winick had been well acquainted with Celina's parents and had seen Phyllis's enamelware cup many times over the years. More importantly, she knew the story behind it. It was Winick who called Celina to ask if she would lend the cup to IJHS for the exhibit. Celina agreed, and the cup became one of the most talked about items in the Iowa portion of the exhibit, which was at the State Historical Building in Des Moines from May through July 27, 1998. When the main exhibit moved on to the next stop on its tour, the SHSI and IJHS agreed to keep the Iowa artifacts on display through the rest of the year.[34]

Shortly before the exhibit was to close, Winick, then president of the IJHS, called Celina again and asked if she might donate the cup to IJHS permanently. Celina was already in talks with the United States Holocaust Memorial Museum about donating it there. But Winick suggested it would have more meaning in the local collection in Des Moines because of her parents' long and close ties to the community. Celina said she would discuss it with her children and called back almost immediately, giving the cup to IJHS. This would be Celina's introduction to IJHS; her relationship with the group would grow closer down the road.[35]

Meanwhile, Celina's daughter had remained at the U.S. State Department, where she met and began dating colleague Robert "Bob" Harris in the late 1980s. They married several years later and had two children, Alex Biniaz-Harris in 1993 and Nicholas Biniaz-Harris in 1996. At that point, Sue worked in State Department's Assistant Legal Adviser's office for Oceans and International Environmental and Scientific Affairs. Here, she had become the lead climate lawyer and was regularly attending the annual United Nations Climate Change conferences, begun in 1995. The November 1998 meeting was to be held in Buenos Aires, and Sue invited her mother to accompany her on the trip.[36]

Several members of Congress from agricultural states went along as well. Their trip was sponsored by Monsanto, which arranged for the group to tour large farms, ranches, and local agribusinesses. Linda Strachan, Monsanto's director of federal government affairs and the person leading the congressional tour, was a former State Department official and good friend of Sue's. Strachan wanted to include Celina on the tours and asked Carlos Popek, the president of Monsanto for Argentina if she could join the group. For some reason, Strachan mentioned that Celina was a Holocaust survivor who had been on "Schindler's List." Popek, an important figure in the city's Jewish community, could not get over the news. He responded that Oskar Schindler's widow, Emilie, lived in San Vincente, a town thirty miles southwest of Bueno Aires, in a house built for her by his local B'nai B'rith group in the 1960s. He insisted on arranging a visit for Celina to see Emilie Schindler.[37]

Subsequently, on a day Sue did not have responsibilities at the conference, she, Strachan, an interpreter, and Celina drove down to Schindler's home. Celina had no idea Schindler's widow was even alive and had not seen her since May 1945, when the Schindlers fled Brünnlitz shortly before Russian troops liberated the factory camp. The visit naturally triggered a host of recollections, and Celina found it "very emotional."[38]

Celina brought Mrs. Schindler a large bouquet of flowers and reminded her that she had nursed her back to health with bowls of her homemade farina while Celina was ill in the camp infirmary. Mrs. Schindler replied that she had not done anything special. But Celina shook her head and with tears in her eyes, she thanked the ninety-one-year-old for keeping her alive. Celina finished by telling Mrs. Schindler that she would not have had a chance to have a family without her kindness and care.[39]

This unexpected reconnection with Emilie Schindler was another step in Celina's growing willingness to confront and discuss her Holocaust past. The next one came in late 2003, when Celina received a telephone call from Amblin Entertainment, Steven Spielberg's production company. The person explained that they were making a documentary about Oskar Schindler told through the words of some *Schindlerjuden*—gleaned from their testimonies collected by the Shoah Foundation—and wanted permission to include portions the 1996 videotaped interview Celina had done for the organization. She agreed, and sent along a few photographs, which would also be used in the film. *Voices from the List*, the seventy-seven-minute documentary was completed in 2004. It was made to accompany that year's debut DVD release of *Schindler's List* and coincided with the ten-year anniversary of the Shoah Foundation. By that time, the organization had collected over 120,000 hours of interviews from 52,000 Holocaust survivors and witnesses.[40]

To kick off the release, Spielberg and the foundation hosted an event in March under large tents at the Universal Studios lot. Celina and four others whose testimonies were among those used in the documentary—Rena Fagen, Lewis Fagen, Leon Leyson, and Helen Jonas-Rosenzweig—attended the affair along with cast members from *Schindler's List*, including Ralph Fiennes and Ben Kingsley. It began with a tour of the Shoah Foundation headquarters, followed by a screening of several clips of *Schindler's List* and *Voices from the List*. Celina became "overwhelmed" by the images, and as people were filing out, she walked over to Spielberg and said, "You are my second Schindler. He gave me my life, but you gave me my voice."[41]

Afterward, he and the five survivors visited privately before everyone headed to the press conference where it became apparent that Celina's heartfelt comment to Spielberg had stuck a chord. Several speakers addressed the crowd, but David Greenberg, the foundation's president and chief executive focused on the impact that *Schindler's List* had on the survivors. Then in an unscripted move, likely prompted by Celina's remark to Spielberg, Greenberg surprised Celina by inviting her to the podium to speak. Caught off guard, she nevertheless complied. In a "voice cracking with emotion," she tweaked her earlier comment, but the meaning remained the same: "I was thirteen years old when I was liberated from Schindler's camp. And I told Mr. Spielberg that Schindler saved my life. But this picture, *Schindler's List*, gave me a second life." David Germain of the Associated Press noted that "Spielberg was visibly moved" by her words, while Celina went on to explain how the movie eventually liberated her to talk about her Holocaust experience.[42]

It had been a long process for Celina to come to grips with this past. The publication of Keneally's book in 1982 had first sparked her interest, but as she told Spielberg in early 2004, it was his film that finally pushed her to embrace it. Her watershed moment came at the DVD release party, when Celina realized that her long repressed Holocaust memories were important, people could now understand them, and she was soon ready to share them.

This brought an unexpected change in Celina's life, and the seventy-two-year-old eventually returned to her familiar role as an educator. Instead of teaching elementary students in a classroom, however, she would now fill auditoriums with people of all ages, recounting her Holocaust story and bearing witness to its horrors.

TEN

SHARING HER STORY

STEVEN SPIELBERG'S 1993 FILM gave Celina a voice by introducing "people to the Holocaust in a way that had not happened before," she explained, and providing "a frame of reference that would allow them to relate to my experience." But the actual impetus for publicly speaking about the Holocaust did not come for another ten years, when people began learning of Celina's story with the 2004 DVD release party of *Schindler's List*. The occasion was closely covered by the press, and Celina's elegant comment about the role Oskar Schindler and Steven Spielberg had played in her life was prominently featured in many of the next morning's newspapers. At the same time, the movie's special DVD package included the new *Voices from the List* documentary, which featured portions of Celina's 1996 foundation testimony.[1]

Together, these events made Celina and her past known to a wide audience, and she soon began getting letters and emails expressing interest in her story. Then, daughter Sue explained, "People started finding her and asking her to speak here and there. She got more used to it and started saying yes to all these invitations." Indeed, this opened "a whole [new] era" for Celina. Sharing her Holocaust experience became her new mission, especially since fewer and fewer survivors remained. "I speak for our generation," she once said, believing that it was critical to provide a "correct picture of what happened [during the Holocaust]" and denounce hatred to ensure that it does not occur again.[2]

Just months after the DVD's release, Celina was surprised by the first of what became many letters from strangers who had been inspired by her observations in *Voices from the List*. That June 2004, a Jane Bohon from

Olympia, Washington, wrote that she had watched the documentary four times, and "didn't think that anything could move me more than the movie [*Schindler's List*], but I was wrong. I saw a group of wonderful people sharing stories that were so horrific it was hard to believe that anyone could survive." Then she focused on Celina: "I found myself in awe of you—here is a beautiful, gracious, and lovely woman, who has lived through some of the worst situations in the entire history of our planet, and yet if someone met you on the street, they would probably never guess what you experienced. I don't know how you manage to do it, but you have my utmost respect and admiration." Bohon closed with, "I want to thank you for sharing your story and allowing me into your life. I feel my life has been made richer just knowing about you."[3]

Celina was "overwhelmed" by the letter and wrote Bohon, saying she had been "really touched" by her thoughts. She added that she planned to share it with Spielberg and Douglas Greenberg, then head of the Shoah Foundation. The two would continue corresponding.[4]

Similar letters and emails ensued, as people saw the documentary or found Celina's testimony on the internet. Most were from strangers, but some were from acquaintances who had no idea of her Holocaust experience. Maybe the most interesting were from former students, who years later saw her Shoah interview and felt compelled to write. In 2012, for instance, Kerry Brennan, who was a sixth grader in Celina's class thirty-two years earlier, was "flabbergasted" to learn her former teacher was a survivor. She searched Celina on the internet, found and watched her testimony, and then wrote: "I had no idea you were a Holocaust survivor; I don't even think I knew you were Jewish....I watched the video three times, trying to wrap my head around the stark contrast of the upbeat, energetic woman I remember and the horrific life experience you were describing." Brennan added that she would "never forget what a wonderful teacher you were and what an incredible human being you are. Your suffering, your loss, and your ultimate victory over evil will remain with me the rest of my life."[5]

Chris Daniggelis another former student of Celina's from the mid-1970s, was also shocked to discover her Holocaust past and wrote that it was "truly beyond comprehension" what she had experienced. He then said what a privilege it was to have had her as a teacher.[6]

Celina also began hearing from current middle and high school students seeking assistance on National History Day projects. The requests reawakened the teacher in Celina, and she was happy to help. One, for instance, came from a Bernice Robles, who was putting together a project on Oskar Schindler. Celina invited the student to her home, submitted to an interview, answered questions, and loaned the youngster documents, which were included in her trifold, posterboard display. In thanking Celina, Robles wrote, "Though I did not win at [the] state level, your documents were extremely helpful to me. I learned a lot about Oskar Schindler and his Jews, and I consider myself more than lucky to have had a chance to interview you."[7]

At the same time, Celina had been lured to the stage to speak publicly about her Holocaust experience. Not surprisingly, it was the Shoah Foundation that first got her to do so. The institute was hosting a special screening of *Voices from the List* in November 2006 and wanted Celina to be part of a panel to comment on the film. Her great admiration for the foundation and all that it had done overcame her reluctance to discuss these horrific years, and she agreed. Others on the panel would include foundation director Greenberg, Leon Leyson, another *Schindlerjude* featured in the documentary, and the filmmaker, Mike Mayhew.[8]

The panel discussion went well that night, but Celina had quite a shock earlier during the showing of the film. Although she had watched a few segments of the documentary previously, she had not seen the entire film before that evening. She had been sitting next to Mayhew watching the film when an archival image of her father walking into Płaszów appeared on the screen. Celina "literally jumped" out of her seat and said to Mayhew "that is my father!" Mayhew was completely unaware of the connection and "was also stunned."[9]

A few months earlier that year, Celina had begun talking with her family about her past. That summer, she and Bini took Sue, her husband Bob, and their children, Alex and Nicholas, on a trip to Poland. Sue had already told her sons a little of her mother's Holocaust experience, but once in Kraków, Celina talked to her grandchildren about it for the first time while touring sites of her childhood. Together, they went past her family's prewar apartment, saw her elementary school, and the park where she used to play. They also went to the Oskar Schindler memorial, located at his original factory in the city. Bob and the boys went on a tour of Auschwitz. Celina, however, could not bear going inside the camp, and she, Bini, and Sue stayed behind. Although she and Bini had seen it from the outside on their 1970s' trip to Poland, they did not enter the camp then either, and Celina had not been inside its gates since she left it for Brünnlitz and Schindler's factory in 1944. When ten-year-old Nicholas returned from seeing the camp, he told Celina, "Grandma, it was horrible, but everyone should see it."[10]

In 2008, Celina repeated the trip, this time taking her son Rob, wife Lucy, and their children, Rachel and Benjamin to Kraków. Again, she shared her experiences with Rob and his family as they toured the city. But as before on her 2006 visit, when it came to Auschwitz, Celina again chose not to go. She remained at the hotel with grandson Benjamin as Rob, Lucy, and Rachel went to see the former concentration camp.[11]

Later that year, Jackie Hartling Stolze, then the editor of *The Grinnell Magazine*, became aware of Celina's Holocaust past and included her story in a lengthy article called, "Defying Darkness: Three Children Who Survived the Holocaust," which also featured two others from the college community; alumnus, Sam Harris, and emeritus professor of religious studies, Harold Kasimow. The piece appeared in the magazine's September 2008 issue and covered several of the traumas Celina overcame. Many at the college were moved by Celina's story and wanted more.[12]

One of them was sophomore Rebecca Heller, the leader of Chalutzim, (Hebrew for pioneers), the college's Jewish student organization. Heller contacted Celina the following February, inviting her to speak at Grinnell on April 21, that year's Holocaust Remembrance Day. Celina was still not committed to making public presentations about her experience, and she was not completely comfortable with the idea. But her fondness for her alma mater won out, and she agreed to give the lecture that spring. This would be her first formal speaking engagement, and the seventy-seven-year-old prepared a PowerPoint slideshow to accompany her talk.[13]

After meeting with students in a Holocaust literature class earlier that day, Celina delivered her lecture, "Second Chance: Memories of a Holocaust Survivor," to over three hundred Grinnell students and community members. She was both astonished and gratified by the large turnout. Daveen Litwin, the campus rabbi and community service coordinator, had difficulty finding words to describe Celina's program and the connection she had with the audience. "I believe you created a sacred time and space and memory for those you touched here." She continued, "It takes a rare individual, the honesty and grace and truth they offer, and the openness of others to receive and respond. I witnessed that happen between you and the students, faculty, staff and community members…when you shared your story at the *Yom HaShoah* commemoration."[14]

On the heels of this success, Celina was asked to speak locally at her American Association of University Women (AAUW) chapter. She agreed, although she was unsure her conservative, "WASPy," hometown was ready to hear such memories. But her early summer 2009 presentation was well received. Norma Maidel, a former president of the chapter, wrote Celina after the program to thank her: "Your talk to your AAUW is still drawing raves and appreciation. People stop me in the stores to say how much they were moved by hearing your story."[15]

These two public presentations and the warm receptions they garnered convinced Celina that people were prepared for her story and sharing it became her second calling. Her new direction made sense to longtime friend Anita Roll because Celina always felt she should "be doing something purposeful." But the move was also somewhat surprising because Celina was reserved by nature and uneasy with public speaking. Still, she went forward. It was probably the educator in her who saw such presentations as "offering teachable moments," in son Rob's words, to warn that "hatred is corrosive" and emphasize "you can go through something horrible and make a meaningful life out of it."[16]

Word of Celina's story quickly spread through Camarillo. More invitations to speak ensued after her AAUW talk, and she was soon making presentations at local churches and area schools. The latter talks were among her favorites, taking her back to her years of teaching, and she readily connected with the youngsters. All the while, she refined her talk and PowerPoint slide show, but she always highlighted a lesson she gleaned from the Holocaust: "Evil can happen anywhere, with any human being, if you give it a chance," adding the admonition, "Don't hate, try to see the good in people. Nobody is better than anyone else."[17]

Celina continued to speak throughout Southern California over the next few years until the spring of 2013, when the Shoah Foundation widened her horizons and arranged for her and her grandson Alex to give two talks in Philadelphia. By that time, Alex was a sophomore at the University of Southern California, double majoring in music and business. Earlier that fall, he had decided to intern at the Shoah Foundation, which had merged with the university and relocated to the school's downtown Los Angeles campus in January 2006. There Alex worked in the institute's social media and marketing department, and it was there he learned much more about his grandmother's Holocaust experience. He explained, "I never got the entire story out of her," and "I felt that the best way to learn her story was to watch her video online [her Shoah Foundation testimony given in 1996]."[18]

Sometime in late 2012 or early 2013, the Har Zion Temple in Penn Valley, an affluent, Main Line suburb of Philadelphia, Pennsylvania, began planning its annual Yom Hashoah commemoration, scheduled for that April. Harry Sauer, the synagogue board member who had funded the temple's Yom Hashoah programming, asked congregant Jayne Perilstein—

then the executive director of advancement for the Shoah Foundation, but based in Philadelphia and New York—if she could schedule a speaker for the event. Perilstein agreed and decided to base the program on the twentieth anniversary of the film *Schindler's List*, which also fell in 2013.[19]

People at the foundation understood Celina had been active speaking about her Holocaust experience and Oskar Schindler. Perilstein thought Celina would be perfect for the temple's program. She also invited Celina's grandson Alex, who could talk about keeping his grandmother's story and that of other survivors alive through the work of the Shoah Foundation.[20]

The Sunday evening program drew a large audience and was followed the next day with a second program Perilstein had arranged, with Celina and Alex speaking at the Barrack Hebrew Academy in nearby Bryn Mawr. Here over two hundred students, staff, and parents were captivated by Celina's story. As usual, Celina ended her harrowing tale on an upbeat note: "Please never give up hope. There are good people out there who want to do good for other people." And as usually happened, she received a standing ovation.[21]

The following year, the foundation invited Celina to a much bigger stage at the fundraising gala celebrating its twentieth anniversary. Thirteen hundred attended the exclusive, glitzy, Hollywood affair including such stars as Barbra Streisand and Samuel L. Jackson. It took place in May 2014 at the Century Plaza Hotel in Century City, an upscale neighborhood and business district ten miles west of downtown Los Angeles. Actor Liam Neeson, who played Oskar Schindler in *Schindler's List*, made the evening's opening remarks, comedian Conan O'Brien served as the emcee, and rocker Bruce Springsteen provided the musical entertainment. Event organizers expected the high point of the evening to be Steven Spielberg giving President Barack Obama the foundation's prestigious Ambassador of Humanity Award.[22]

Spielberg highlighted the foundation during his remarks, explaining, "As long as we fail to learn, our work will be urgent work. This institute exists because we know that the future can always be rewritten." Then he focused on Obama and presented him the award for his work on human rights, his efforts to fight genocides worldwide, and his creation of the first ever Special Envoy for U.S. Holocaust Survivor Services.[23]

In accepting the award, Obama concentrated on storytelling and memory. He lauded the Holocaust survivors who told their stories to the foundation and praised it "for setting alight an eternal flame of testimony that can't be extinguished." Obama continued, "The testimonies of survivors like those with us tonight also remind us that the purpose of memory is not simply to preserve the past, it is to protect the future. We only need to look at today's headlines—the devastation of Syria, the murders and kidnappings in Nigeria, the sectarian conflict, the tribal conflicts, to see that we have not yet extinguished man's darkest impulses." Then he challenged the audience: "And it's up to us, each of us, every one of us, to forcefully condemn any denial of the Holocaust. It's up to us to combat not only anti-Semitism, but racism and bigotry and intolerance in all their forms, here and around the world."[24]

But according to the PBS *NewsHour*, it was two "non-famous women" who "most inspired" the audience. One was Michelle Sadrena Clark, a San Diego high school teacher, who read a poem about how the Shoah Foundation's work improved her instruction and was instrumental in her students to this history.[25]

The other was Celina, who briefly recounted her Holocaust experience, talked about the importance of the Shoah Foundation, and delivered her powerful statement with aplomb, "Oskar Schindler gave me my life, but Steven Spielberg gave me my voice." The remark carried more significance now than when she first uttered a derivation of it a decade earlier at the foundation's ten-year anniversary, for over the previous eight years, she had begun using her voice and telling the public her story.[26]

Son Rob agreed with the *NewsHour*'s assessment, thinking that his mother had indeed upstaged Obama that night, but he also noted the irony of it, because she was "very shy." His sister Sue agreed, finding it hard to believe her mother seemed so at ease and spoke so eloquently before such a large crowd: "If someone would have told her twenty years ago, she would get up and speak to hundreds or thousands of people, including the president of the United States, she would have said what are you talking about?" Indeed, Celina had developed into a powerful, passionate speaker, and would continue sharing her past with audiences large and small.[27]

That fall, the Shoah Foundation again played an important role in Celina's life, inviting her and a guest to Auschwitz for the seventieth anniversary commemoration of its liberation. The Auschwitz-Birkenau State Museum and the International Auschwitz Council partnered with the Shoah Foundation and the World Jewish Congress to organize the anniversary program. The latter two groups spent months working together to bring more than one hundred camp survivors and their guests from around the world back to Auschwitz for the commemoration. Celina knew it would be difficult to be back at the camp but wanted to attend. She asked Sue to accompany her to the January 2015 program.[28]

Meanwhile, Stephen Smith, the executive director of the Shoah Foundation, who regularly hosted Sabbath dinners at his home, invited Alex to one that October. Ambrose Soehn, another foundation intern—who Alex had gotten to know a couple of years earlier in a four-hands piano class—was invited as well. While there, Smith told the two a bit about the upcoming commemoration and suggested they research the foundation's archives for music associated with concentration camps and Auschwitz. Then Smith went further, encouraging the two to compose a piece based on those songs, even hinting that the foundation might be able to use it at some point.[29]

The two interns left the evening excited and dove into the foundation's videotaped testimony collection. There they learned that traditional Jewish folk melodies had been important to many camp inmates, helping many get through their darkest days. The two soon consulted Nick Strimple, an expert on music of the Holocaust and a faculty member at USC Thornton School of Music, and as the semester wound down, they composed a score inspired by the music of Holocaust survivors. The two sent a recording of their piece to Smith who was impressed but unsure how or where he might use it. Then, a week before the commemoration, violinist Itzhak Perlman, who was scheduled to perform at the special reception for survivors the evening before the official anniversary, had to cancel. Organizers scrambled to find a replacement, and that was when Smith turned to the two USC seniors.[30]

Smith invited them to perform their composition, "Melodies of Auschwitz," but cautioned them that they would have to rewrite the score for one piano because the program's stage would not support two. Both were thrilled, accepted immediately, and began revising their piece for a piano duet.[31]

Thus, Alex and Ambrose, along with Celina and Sue flew to Kraków, where as planned the two college seniors opened the January 26, 2015, evening gathering for Auschwitz survivors, and other guests, including Steven Spielberg, who would deliver the reception's closing comments. Alex recalled that it was a "powerful event," and he and Ambrose were initially nervous playing before the solemn audience but soon settled into the music. However, shortly after they began, the pianists noticed that several audience members stood up before soon sitting back down again. The two musicians were unclear why some people rose but continued playing and finished their piece. Celina, meanwhile, was beaming with pride during her grandson's performance. Alex described the moment as "surreal" because it was a distinctive opportunity to honor his grandmother and the memory of his great-grandparents. Only later would he learn that the first few notes of their composition were similar to the opening of the Israeli national anthem, which had led some to stand before realizing their error.[32]

The official anniversary ceremony began the following day on a cold, gray, wintry afternoon at the former Auschwitz-Birkenau camp. Celina and Sue, Alex and Ambrose were among the three thousand gathered under a large, white tent, erected at the camp's distinctive front gate. Bisecting the huge temporary structure were the railroad tracks—illuminated for the event—over which cattle cars had once carried Celina, her mother, and hundreds of thousands of other prisoners into the camp. Under this canopy, world leaders, dignitaries, special guests, and nearly three hundred Auschwitz survivors from nineteen countries came to remember its liberation and honor the more than one million murdered there.[33]

The president of Poland welcomed guests and then several survivors spoke. Most moving may have been Israeli writer and Holocaust survivor Halina Birenbaum, who recalled Auschwitz as "a bottomless pit of hell I couldn't get out of." New Yorker Roman Kent, another survivor who then headed the International Auschwitz Committee, grew emotional when he said, "We do not want our past to be our children's future."[34]

A short documentary, *Auschwitz*, produced by Steven Spielberg then aired. Narrated by Meryl Streep and others, it provided a brief history of the camp. When the film concluded, many of the survivors, heads of state and their delegations, and other officials walked from the main gate through the snow-covered camp to place candles at the site's memorial. The rest of the audience watched the solemn procession on large television screens inside the tent. It was likely the last such anniversary many survivors would be able to attend.[35]

For Celina, however, being back at Auschwitz was painful enough, and she decided to remain in the tent and forgo walking the grounds to the memorial. But as Celina sat with other audience members and listened to the various speakers, she had what she described as "an out of body experience." In her mind's eye, she was a young teenager again, struggling to get through her trying days at the concentration camp. "There I was, the eighty-three-year-old woman, looking down onto the thirteen-year-old girl and her experiences in Auschwitz." The episode brought back a flood of long repressed memories, which would be the focus of a poem she would write later that year.[36]

Celina had never written poetry, or anything about herself for that matter, and did not have any inclination to do so. Regardless, she had remained a very active lifelong learner and regularly took Osher Lifelong Learning Institute (OLLI) courses available at the nearby California State

University Channel Islands (CSUCI) campus. The institute offered older adults a wide variety of university-level courses without the stress of exams or grades. Shortly after returning from Europe that winter, Celina saw an OLLI course with the word tapestry in the title, assumed it was a history of tapestries, and enrolled.[37]

On the first day of class, however, Celina was surprised to learn that "Tapestries: A Life Journey," was not about textiles at all, but a poetry course; the title was a reference to weaving together the threads of one's life into poetry. Celina considered leaving, but the class was already small, so she decided to stay.[38]

The instructor, Mary Kay Rummel taught part-time at CSUCI and was the current poet laureate of Ventura County. One of her goals in that latter capacity was the "do more with poetry for seniors," hence, the OLLI course. Rummel began with some basics about poetry, explaining, as Celina recalled, that poems did not have to rhyme but were about emotion. After the brief introduction, Rummel wanted to get her students writing, so she then gave them a prompt—think about a place—and asked that they use their sensory memory to incorporate the sights, sounds, and smells associated with that location.[39]

Anita Roll also took OLLI classes and registered for the course because she had written some poetry and was interested in improving her style. But she was stumped by the prompt. Celina, however, was writing away furiously. When the class ended, Rummel told her students to continuing working on their poems over the next few days, and volunteers would share their poetry at the next session.[40]

The following week, Celina read her poem without identifying the location and withheld the one-word title until the very end:

Night, So Dark, So Cold

The Wagon sways

The rhythmic pounding
Of the wheels repeating

Sends a message to
My frightened heart
"Do not stop beating!"

The Sudden Lurch,
Screech of Steel on Steel
The door slides open

"Raus, Raus"
Angry voices shouting
A multitude of dogs barking!

Plumes of fire
Illuminate the night sky.
The smoke drifts over
The gathered people.

The Smell, The awful Smell
It is the smell of fear!

We have arrived in Hell!

Auschwitz

When she finished, the room was silent. "We were all blown away," Rummel remembered, "People in the class couldn't talk....It wasn't just the memory that was powerful, it was poetry."[41]

For that second class, Rummel asked students to use their sensory memory to describe a person or people. Celina thought of Mater Leontine and again started writing immediately. Over the course of the next few weeks, she would turn out a handful of poems, all dealing with her Holocaust experience and the aftermath. She was invited to do a poetry reading at the E.P. Foster Library in Ventura that spring and had five of her poems published—a rare achievement for a first-time poet—in *Askew*, a local literary journal.[42]

Celina's family could not believe she was writing, but Rummel reported that the stanzas "just poured out of her." Roll was "stunned" by what her friend had been able to do and was certain Celina surprised herself. For her part, Celina gave all the credit to Rummel: "She had a way of pulling things out of me." Specifically, Celina felt it was the focused prompts and being freed from worrying about rhyming that were key to her success.[43]

In the end, Celina wrote eight poems, five during the class, two shortly thereafter, and her last one, "My Life as 'The Other,'" the following year. She then stopped, saying that her "muse refuses to supply me with ideas," and she became busy with other things. But Rummel maintained that poetry provided Celina "a vehicle for excavating her experience." Indeed, the process of brainstorming and putting her thoughts into verse gave Celina a new window to understanding her past. She felt it sharpened her memories, particularly how she had felt during the Holocaust and made this period increasingly tangible to her. "I knew we always walked around in groups of five [in the camps], for example, but writing it down made it more real."[44]

Her successful stab at poetry was part of the conversion Celina had undergone over the past decade. Now speaking out about her Holocaust experience, Celina again became transformative, much as she had been for many of her students years earlier. She never dwelled on the change or her new public self, but she put it in the framework of what she called "people power." Schindler, she told an audience in 2014, saved her and her parents by including their names on his list. Then Mater Leontine, the German nun who tutored her after the war, restored her self-esteem, showed her the power of forgiveness, and got her life back on track. Finally, it was Spielberg and his film that made the Holocaust understandable. Such context made it possible for Celina to tell her story. "It is because of my belief in the power of the individual to affect lives that I now devote time to speaking about the Holocaust. I hope that by sharing my experiences I can convince others to treat all human beings with respect."[45]

EPILOGUE

IN 2015, DR. RUTH WESTHEIMER, the renowned sex therapist, television personality, and Holocaust survivor told *The Hollywood Reporter*, "People like me need to stand up and be counted to repair the world." Celina could not have agreed more and remained busy telling audiences of her Holocaust experience and sharing her message of forgiveness, compassion, and hope.[1]

Interestingly, Celina appeared in the same magazine story that had quoted Dr. Ruth, which was prompted by the seventieth anniversary of the ending of the Holocaust. The lengthy print essay referred to those it profiled as "the entertainment world's eleven remaining survivors" and was accompanied by videotaped interviews of those figures, accessible on *The Hollywood Reporter*'s website. Besides Dr. Ruth and Celina, others featured in the article included, for instance, Roman Polanski, the award-winning but controversial Polish French film director; Branko Lustig, the Oscar-winning producer of *Schindler's List* and *Gladiator*; actor Robert Clary, who starred as Corporal Louis LeBeau in the television sitcom, *Hogan's Heroes*; actor Curt Lowens, who ironically often played Nazis on stage and in film; and actress, dancer, and chorographer Ruth Posner, a former member of the Royal Shakespeare Company.[2]

Celina's presence in the article was curious. She was not a media figure, nor did she have ties to Hollywood, save for her son's work at Universal and her link to Spielberg and the Shoah Foundation. Maybe it was a conversation she had with son Rob in late 1992 or early 1993 that landed her in the article. Although he was not at all involved in the *Schindler's List* film, he knew Sidney Sheinberg, the head of Universal Studios, and Sheinberg had once introduced him to Steven Spielberg at a company function, explaining that Rob's mother was a Holocaust survivor who had been on "Schindler's List." Before Spielberg began shooting the film,

Sheinberg gave Rob a copy of the script and told him he could share it with his mother.[3]

While she was reading it, Rob told her that the studio and Spielberg had cast Liam Neeson for the role of Schindler but there was concern that he was too handsome for the role. "Oh, no," replied his mother, "Schindler was very suave and very good looking." Rob passed her comment on to Sheinberg. The tale evidently made the rounds in Hollywood circles, but it became altered a bit to imply that Celina's comment led to Neeson getting the part. That apparently caught the magazine's attention. Whether or not this led to her inclusion in the article is unclear, but the story became the lead in its essay on Celina.[4]

The same year the article came out, Sandi Yoder, the executive director of the Iowa Jewish Historical Society (IJHS), and the organization's board were working to increase the group's visibility and expand its educational outreach. Yoder started thinking about the Schindler enamelware cup Celina had given the society several years earlier and wondered if she might come back to Iowa to speak. Surely a real-life member of "Schindler's List" would draw a lot of attention. The IJHS board liked the idea, and Yoder asked Robbie Winick, a past president of the group who had earlier worked with Celina to secure the cup, to broach the subject with her.[5]

Celina was receptive and came to Iowa in September 2017. There she gave several lectures, including a large public event at Valley High School in West Des Moines and a fundraiser at the Caspe Terrace, home to the IJHS and the Jewish Federation of Greater Des Moines in Waukee, a suburb fifteen miles west of Des Moines. She also returned to both her alma maters, speaking at Des Moines's North High School, where she had been inducted into its alumni hall of fame in 1994, and once again at Grinnell College, fifty-five miles to the east.[6]

As she did in all her talks, Celina emphasized the importance of the Shoah Foundation's vast collection of videotaped survivor testimonies, which, she believed, personalized the Holocaust, making it that much more real. She explained, "You can read about the Holocaust, you can go to a museum and look at artifacts, but nothing connects like the human voice."[7]

And Celina did just that in all her presentations—she connected with people. One Iowan, for example, said of Celina, "My heart was touched for her compassion for humanity and for the world. How can that be after all that she has been through?" Another thought, "That was an amazing experience…the inspiring/moving/graceful presentation by Celina…I will never forget her stories and the message of hope I took from them." A similar comment came from a woman who heard her speak later in Las Vegas and felt Celina made the past come alive: "When I grew up, history was a textbook, and you learned dates and places and a few names here and there. You can only truly know the history if you hear it from the personal stories of the people who live it."[8]

Yoder and the IJHS board were grateful that Celina came to speak and thrilled with the large crowds she drew. As they had hoped, the programs enhanced the organization's profile and increased awareness of its educational mission. Celina, likewise, appreciated the invitation, especially because her Iowa trip raised her visibility and led to many more speaking engagements.[9]

For her presentations in Des Moines and elsewhere, Celina continued using a PowerPoint slideshow and personal keepsakes to supplement her remarks. One of the objects she frequently brought was the pair of blunt-nosed iron scissors she still had from the items Schindler gave her and her family to use or barter for things they needed once they were liberated. But those scissors were almost lost on her 2017 trip to Iowa. Celina had packed them in her carry-on, not thinking about the security screening it would go through at the airport. Sure enough, TSA personnel at Los Angeles International Airport flagged her bag and removed the priceless scissors, which could serve as a potential weapon, and were going to confiscate them. Fortunately, Celina's daughter Sue was traveling with her that day and convinced the agent in charge that the scissors were, in fact, a priceless historic artifact from the Holocaust, and they were part of her mother's upcoming presentations in Iowa. Celina and Sue then proceeded with the scissors to Des Moines without incident.[10]

After these Iowa programs, Celina talked with Yoder about getting the scissors back to Southern California. They tried contacting TSA about the procedures for flying with such objects but were unable to reach anyone. Celina then said she could mail them to herself, but Yoder advised against that because they were irreplaceable. They then discussed shipping them as museums send rare pieces, but Yoder estimated the cost of that with insurance would be well over $1,000. With no good option, Celina left the scissors with Yoder until she could arrange for their safe transport back to California.[11]

While thinking about how to do so, Yoder happened to mention the scissors to a technician servicing the building's air conditioning system. During their conversation, he said that his brother flew a corporate jet for Pioneer Hi-Bred International, an agribusiness based in Johnston, a suburb ten miles northwest of Des Moines, but he only flew the eastern routes out of the city. But then the two began talking about other local firms that had company planes, as Yoder wondered if she might find a business willing to carry the scissors with them on one of their flights to Los Angeles. Flying them on a corporate jet would avoid certain TSA regulations.[12]

Des Moines-based MidAmerican Energy came up in the conversation about local firms with their own planes, and a light bulb went on in Yoder's head. She knew its senior managing attorney, Chuck Montgomery. She asked him about the possibility, he made some inquiries, and on Valentine's Day, 2018, two MidAmerican pilots, who said they were honored to carry the Holocaust relic, flew the scissors to Los Angeles, where they were then picked up by a private courier and hand delivered to Celina in Camarillo.[13]

More talks for Celina followed, but she was careful in bringing the scissors with her, and Yoder helped make special arrangements with the TSA when Celina flew. Maybe Celina's most noteworthy trips were two additional ones she made to Iowa. In May 2018, Celina returned to Grinnell College, this time to deliver the commencement address, where she stressed the power of people to change the lives of others just as figures such as Julius Madritsch and Oskar Schindler changed hers. And she was elated to receive an honorary Doctor of Humane Letters degree from the college that had meant so much to her.[14]

The next April, she was back in Des Moines, again at the invitation of the IJHS. While there, she spoke at three Des Moines Area Community College (DMACC) campuses, but her most moving program took place at Tifereth Israel Synagogue, which had been her parents' house of worship. Instead of her standard "second chance," presentation, this program opened with her grandson Alex Biniaz-Harris and composer/pianist Ambrose Soehn discussing and later playing their "Melodies of Auschwitz" composition. Then Alex gave his grandmother a heartfelt introduction.[15]

For this presentation, Celina told her story using the poetry she had written to accentuate key moments and people of her past. As she recounted her experiences, she recited her poems "Auschwitz," about the camp; "Selection," about facing Josef Menegele; "May 9, 1945—Liberation," about the end of the war and freedom; "Mater Leontine," about the nun who tutored her and helped her recover emotionally from the Holocaust; "*Silent Night 1945*," about Christmas Eve and her first winter after the war; and "SS *Marine Marlin*," about the ship that ferried her and her family to the United States and her future. She ended the program with "Tree," her ode to Oskar Schindler and a reference to the tree planted in his honor in Israel:

In Jerusalem
In Yad Vashem
The Holocaust Museum.
In the Street of the
"Righteous Gentiles"
In a designated third spot
From the start,
A man plants a tree!

Womanizer, Cheater
Black market profiteer,

Risk taker, Gambler,
Takes on the
Biggest Gamble
Of his life.

He puts eleven hundred
Names on a list,
Lies, bribes authorities,

Wrenches a group of
Human Beings from
The Jaws of Evil.

This group under
His protection will
Survive the War!

Magnificent, this tree
Dedicated to
Oskar Schindler

As it grows and
Spreads it limbs,
Roots and branches
Proliferate,
So do the descendants,
The saved group's
New generations!

I bear witness!
Evil can be harnessed!
People of good will
Can make a difference!

Forever I shall be, in
Debt and grateful
To Oskar Schindler
For giving me a Life![16]

When she finished the poem, applause broke the room's silence. It had been an especially riveting program and another successful visit for Celina and the IJHS. But there was more good news for the society. As the evening ended, Celina pulled out her Schindler scissors, and with Sandi Yoder and Sarah Carlson, the IJHS curator and collections manager, standing by her side, she donated the scissors to the historical society, where they would join the Schindler cup she had given them several years earlier.[17]

Celina's calendar remained full of scheduled speaking engagements over the next year until her routine, and that of everyone else, was completely upended by COVID-19 in 2020. The global pandemic disrupted all aspects of life. Stores and businesses closed, public events were cancelled, and with schools shuttered, students were moved to virtual, online learning. People socially distanced, wore facemasks, and whenever possible, isolated in their homes. Even though effective vaccines were developed with breakneck speed and made available across the United States early the following year, vaccine hesitancy and the Delta variant, a new, highly contagious strain of the virus, kept COVID-19 from being brought under control. As of late 2021, life remained far from normal.

At first, Celina appreciated the changes and shutdowns because she could take some time to relax and not worry about her next appearances. She initially liked the idea of not having any commitments and kept the feelings of isolation at bay by staying in touch with friends and family by telephone. Celina was especially proud of her children and grandchildren and delighted in keeping up with their lives through weekly Zoom video teleconferencing.

Son Rob was now living in Northern California doing pro bono legal work for the nonprofit, Bay Area Legal Aid. He had been a top manager at Universal Studios—first in its concert division, then in its record company, and finally starting and then running its first video gaming division—before retiring in the late 1990s when new ownership led to numerous changes in company leadership. He then became a stay-at-home dad for years when sadly his wife Lucy Hood, a longtime executive in media and television, who had just been named president and chief operating officer of the Academy of Television Arts & Sciences in 2013, died of cancer the following spring.[18]

Granddaughter Rachel, meanwhile, had gone on to the Olin School of Engineering and was a senior software engineer at Google, while her husband Jeff Bryson owned and operated Next-Gen Games, a Los Angeles shop specializing in board games, video games, trading cards, and collectibles. Rachel's brother Ben had received his bachelor's degree from Yale, and like his cousin, Alex Biniaz-Harris, he also interned at the Shoah Foundation. He was now a manager at Caples Jefferson Architects in New York.[19]

Celina's daughter Sue remained at the State Department for over thirty years as a Deputy Legal Adviser and its top climate attorney. She played an important role in several major international climate accords, including the Paris Agreement in 2015. Two years later, she became a senior fellow for climate change at the United Nations Foundation before recently returning to the federal government and joining Special Presidential Envoy for Climate John Kerry's staff. Her husband, Bob Harris, continued at the State Department as the Assistant Legal Adviser for East Asian and Pacific Affairs.[20]

Grandson Alex, who played the piano at the seventy-fifth anniversary of the liberation of Auschwitz, became a professional musician and composer, while his brother Nicholas, like several other family members, had been an undergraduate at Yale and now attended medical school at Columbia University's Vagelos College of Physicians and Surgeons.[21]

Her regular Zoom visits with these family members helped Celina get through the first few months of the pandemic, but she soon became antsy. Fortunately, some of her former activities became available virtually. Book clubs that she had been active in for years resumed online as did her Osher Lifelong Learning Institute (OLLI) courses at California State University Channel Islands.[22]

However, lecturing about her Holocaust experience had become "part of her," according to friend Anita Roll, and Celina missed telling her story. To fill the void, she gave several Holocaust talks via Zoom. They went well. People watching her Zoom program for Des Moines University's Women at Noon series in April 2021, for instance, were effusive in their praise. Angela Franklin, the president of DMU, thanked her for sharing her "amazing message of positivity." Others offered similar sentiments: "I could listen all day," one wrote, while another said of her talk, "So powerful and inspirational; [I] cannot thank you enough for your time."[23]

While it was clear her virtual presentations had an impact, Celina much preferred doing them in person, but she wondered if or when she might be able to return to an actual podium and share her story before a live audience again. She missed making those individual connections, which undoubtedly had been compelling. Monica Chavez-Silva, then the assistant vice president of community enhancement at Grinnell College, described Celina's 2017 visit to the school: "I was so impressed with her grace and good spirits as she stayed to personally greet so many people who stayed after the event to get the chance to speak with her. It was clear that there was one young man in particular who was truly affected by her experience…. Just as Celina spoke about the nun who had changed her life…she was herself changing the lives of those in the room."[24]

The comparison to Mater Leontine—the German nun who not only tutored her after the war, but renewed her spirit and restored her soul, allowing Celina to put the Holocaust behind her and move on with her life—would have humbled Celina. Nothing could have pleased her more than the knowledge that she may have helped others the way Mater Leontine had helped her.

APPENDIX

Like her two poems in the text, all of Celina's poetry addressed aspects of her experience during the Holocaust, the immediate postwar years, and their lasting impact on her life. Her six other poems follow. They are taken from Celina's private papers and reprinted here with her permission.

Selection

There He Stands
Resplendent in his Uniform,
Shiny black boots,
Insignia on His Chest,
Swastika armband on
His Sleeve, and in His
Hand a Pencil!

Unusual this pencil,
For with one flick to
Either Left or right,
It has the power to
Give you Life or Death!

In Front of Him a Line
Of Naked Women,
All Shapes and Sizes.

This is my Second time
Confronting the Pencil.
First time was not lucky
but the Pencil beckons
The group back into the Line.

My body is skinny,
undeveloped, but clean.
Don't know how or why,
The will to live forces me
To utter three words
"Lassen Sie Mich!"

This time the Pencil slowly
Leans towards Life!

I grab my pile of clothes
Hugging them, run out
Into the snowy outdoors.

My pent-up emotions
Burst forth,
Hysterically crying start
to put on my clothes.

I am only thirteen and
Have gotten a reprieve
From Death,
From Dr. Mengele,
The Butcher of Auschwitz!

May 9, 1945—Liberation

We Are Survivors
To exit barbed wire gates,
Two days we are waiting
Not safe on outside with
Black Shirts still marauding!

A Soldier on a horse
Appears in the distance
Behind him a small
Bedraggled group of soldiers
They have come to liberate us.

We Are Survivors
The barbed wire gates open
We are free, hesitant to
Venture beyond!
How can one walk alone
Not in a row of five
Not overseen by guards
Armed ready to shoot.

We Are Survivors
How after five years
Following orders can we
Think and act on our own!
Will we be able to
Restore our humanity,
Or will we always be
Held suspect in society?

Will there be a rejoining
With the rest of family,
Or will we encounter their Loss,
Forever gone into eternity?

We Are Survivors
Freedom is ours,
Comes with problems!
Can we retrieve former lives?
Can we go back to homes we lost?
Having experienced horrific events
Starving, fearful we start
Our Journey.

Eleven days walking, hitching
Emaciated scarecrows reach
Krakow.

There is no welcome
We are not wanted!
Four months later
We are back on the road.

Leaving Europe, seeking
New existence in more
Welcoming countries.

We Are Survivors
We shall succeed!

Silent Night 1945

Every time I hear *Silent Night*
It brings me back to a snowy night
In Mindelheim, Germany.

First winter after the war
The night sky is illuminated
By a myriad of blinking stars!
The church bells are
Ringing out *Stille Nacht*!

No bombs falling
No loud noises of shooting,
Or soldiers' boots marching.
No commandants shouting
Into rows of five pushing,
No more in fright cowering,
We have survived!

It is Christmas Eve and I am free!
I feel the peace and tranquility,
And hope for "Good Will"
To all mankind to take hold!

Mater Leontine

In a small town
in Southern Bavaria
In a semi-cloistered convent
Home of the "English Sisters"

An 80-year-old retired nun
Entered the convent at age 16,
Never left it in all these years!

She is German and Catholic,
She will teach a 14-year-old girl
Traumatized by years of
Ghettoes and Camps
German and English!

She does not know
She is supposed to hate her,
Hitler's ideas and propaganda
Are not part of her knowledge.

Her outlook on life, gentle manner,
And total acceptance,
slowly work the magic
of transformation!

    The realization:
    Not all Germans are ogres!
    Hatred is corrosive
    Have to work through
    Anger and hate
    To move forward in life!

We bond for 2 years!

Leaving for America,
Our letters criss-cross the oceans
For the next 2 years.

Mater Leontine loves to hear
About America,
She is so very happy
To hear about my new life!

The letter arrives from
Mother Superior,
At 84, Mater Leontine
is no longer with us!

That is absurd! That cannot be!
For I have all her letters still,
For she will always be
A part of me
In my heart and memories
For she was my salvation!

SS *Marine Marlin*

The fog horns sound
The engines begin to chug!

Today is my Birthday
I am 16 years old
The SS *Marine Marlin* is
A vessel of hope
For my new life!

I turn and look East
See the continent
slowly disappearing!

It is a place I know
And understand!
It is a place that
Does not want me,

Maybe the West will
Be more welcoming!

The SS *Marine Marlin*
Is a troop ship
It ferried soldiers
To fight "Nazism!"

Now it ferries
Europe's "Discards"
Immigrants with
Guarded hope!

Will this new place
Grant them an "Identity?"
Will it restore and
Protect their "Humanity?"

Only the Future will tell
For now, they are happy
They have escaped
Europe's Hell!

My Life as "The Other"

George Herbert Mead
An American philosopher
Introduced the sociological
Construct of the "Generalized Other."
My life has been a proof
Of that concept.

In the country where I was born
I was the "Other" because
My religion was different!

During World War II,
To the Germans I was
The "Other" because I did
Not fit the Aryan profile.

Living in Germany I was
The "Other" because I was
A displaced person, a foreigner.

Coming to America I was
The "Other" because I was not
Native born, an immigrant
Speaking with an Accent.

People of faith view me as
The "Other" for I am not
Religious and don't belong
To any organized group!

When society marks a group
Of people as the "Other"
It tends to marginalize and
Stigmatize the members
Of that group.

The "Other" often becomes
The "scapegoat" for a variety
Of societal ills. It creates
Enormous pressure and desire
To find a way to fit in!

Now that I have reached that
Certain age, I feel that I belong,
For I will not allow society to
Define me or put me in a
Certain category, for I am
A Survivor!

A NOTE ON SOURCES

This book is based on a wide variety of public and private sources, which are listed throughout the notes. Most prominent among the former was material from the Iowa Jewish Historical Society and the United States Holocaust Memorial Museum. Several books proved especially helpful including Thomas Keneally, *Schindler's List* (1982); David Crowe, *Oskar Schindler: The Untold Account of His Life, His Wartime Activities, and the True Story Behind the List* (2004); Elinor Brecher, *Schindler's Legacy: True Stories of the List Survivors* (1994); Evgeny Finkel, *Ordinary Jews: Choice and Survival During the Holocaust* (2017); and Peter Novick, *The Holocaust in American Life* (1999). But most important were the individuals who agreed to interviews, corresponded with me, or gave me access to their personal papers. A list of these people and their contributions follow:

INTERVIEWS, TELEPHONE CONVERSATIONS, ZOOM VIDEO CONFERENCES, AND CORRESPONDENCE

Mike Badower, telephone conversation with author, 10 December 2020.

Amir Biniaz, telephone conversation with author, 21 April 2020. Correspondence with author, 24 April 2020; 18 March, 14 April 2021.

Celina Biniaz, telephone conversation with author, 7, 16 March, 3, 21 April, 17 August, 16, December 2020; 16 March, 5 May, 17 August 2021. Zoom video conference with author, 29 June 2021. Conversation with author, Camarillo, California, 31 July 2021. Correspondence with author, 13, 16, 19, 20, 25, 31 March, 4, 7, 9, 21, 22, 24, 30 April, 1 May, 4, 13, 27 June, 1, 24 July, 7 August, 2, 24 September, 1 October, 29 November, 14, 17, 18, 19, 23, 29 December 2020; 8, 30, 31 January, 11, 24 February, 8, 17 March, 14, 24 April, 21 May, 16, 30 June, 5, 7, 15 July, 17, 18 August, 13, 15, 19 September, 6 October, 4, 10 November 2021.

Rob Biniaz, telephone conversation with author, 25 March 2021. Correspondence with author, 25 August 2021.

Sue Biniaz, telephone conversation with author, 21 August 2021.

Alex Biniaz-Harris, telephone conversation with author, 26 August 2021. Correspondence with author. 9 September, 11 November 2021.

Nicholas Biniaz-Harris, telephone conversation with author, 6 November 2021.

Ann Blumberg, telephone conversation with author, 29 March 2021.

Jeanne Bonnici, telephone conversation with author, 26 April 2021.

Kerry Brennan, telephone conversation with author, 23 April 2021. Correspondence with author 5 May 2021; 4 April 2022.

Carolyn "Kay" Bucksbaum, telephone conversation with author, 26 March 2020.

Olga Burkhardt-Vetter, correspondence with author, 2 September 2020; 17 January 2022.

Sarah Carlson, correspondence with author, 24 September 2019; 30 March, 13 July 2020.

Dan Connolly, telephone conversation with author, 28 April 2021.

Pat Connolly, telephone conversation with author, 6 May 2021.

Barry Cytron, Zoom video conference with author, 29 October 2020.

Phyllis Cytron, Zoom video conference with author, 29 October 2020.

Moses Gaynor, telephone conversation with author, 25 April 2020. Correspondence with author, 25, 26 April 2020; 19, 29, 30 January, 1, 20 February 2021.

Rebecca Heller, correspondence with author, 21 October 2021.

Lou Hurwitz, telephone conversation with author, 27 January 2020; 7 April 2020

Richard Isaacson, telephone conversation with author, 1 April 2020.

Basil Karp, telephone conversation with author, 27 April 2020.

Linda Lafourcade, correspondence with author, 16 May 2021.

Jean Lory, telephone conversation with author, 25 March 2020. Correspondence with author, 25, 26 March 2020; 15, 16, 17 February 2021.

Marcus Pearce, correspondence with author, 20 July 2021.

Jayne Perilstein, correspondence with author, 26, 27 August, 16 December 2021.

Nick Piediscalzi, telephone conversation with author, 28 April 2020. Correspondence with author, 28 April 2020.

Zona Pigeon, telephone conversation with author, 12 December 2020.

Rita Post, telephone conversation with author, 2 July 2020.

Brigitte Reynolds, correspondence with author, 16 March, 5 April 2020; 13 November 2021.

Anita Roll, telephone conversation with author, 8 July 2020.

Shari Roll, telephone conversation with author, 4 April 2021.

Mary Kay Rummel, telephone conversation with author 23 August 2021 Correspondence with author, 23, 24 August 2021.

Ken Sayre, telephone conversation with author, 4 May 2020.

Eleanor Schumacher, interview by author, Clive, Iowa, 9 August 2021.

Sarah Smith, correspondence with author, 12 August 2021.

Jackie Hartling Stolze, correspondence with author, 31 August 2021.

Rachel Temple, telephone conversation with author, 20 April 2020.

Scott Temple, telephone conversation with author, 20 April 2020.

Jerome Thompson, correspondence with author, 9 July 2021.

Robbie Winick, correspondence with author, 6, 8, 9 July 2021.

Sandi Yoder, telephone conversation with author, 24 June 2021. Correspondence with author, 21 August 2017; 28 June 2018; 6, 10, 13, 16, 17, 24 September 2019; 6 January, 13 March, 20 November 2020; 24 March, 17 June, 20 July, 24, 27 September, 5, 12 October, 4 November 2021.

PAPERS

Celina Biniaz Papers, private collection, Camarillo, California.
Jeremy Gaynor Papers, private collection, Coral Gables, Florida.
Moses Gaynor Papers, private collection, Chicago, Illinois.
Rebecca Heller Papers, private collection, Astoria, New York.
Jean Lory Papers, private collection, Ames, Iowa.
Marcus Pearce Papers, private collection, Bryon Bay, New South Wales, Australia.
Mary Kay Rummel Papers, private collection, Minneapolis, Minnesota.

Notes

Introduction

1. Celina Biniaz, conversation with author, 31 July 2021, Camarillo, California.

2. Quote is from Celina's opening statement at Valley High School, West Des Moines, Iowa, 10 September 2017. For video of presentation, see https://www.jewishdesmoines. org/our-pillars/iowa-jewish-historical-society/our-collection/celina-karp-biniaz/.

3. https://www.amestrib.com/news/20190331/i-dont-know-whether-it-was-chance-luck-or-fate-but-it-saved-me, accessed on 25 September 2021.

4. For Moshe Taube's quote, see *New York Times*, 13 February 1994; for Celina's quote, see Celina Biniaz, Zoom video conference with author, 29 June 2021.

5. *Los Angeles Times*, 5 December 2018. For Siskel quote, see https://www.chicagotribune.com/news/ct-xpm-1993-12-17-9312170245-story.html, accessed on 12 September 2021.

6. For Lipstadt quote, see *Los Angeles Times*, 5 December 2018; for Crowe quote, see https://time.com/5470613/schindlers-list-true-story/, accessed on 10 August 2021.

7. Ibid.

8. First quote from Rena Finder with Joshua Greene, *My Survival: A Girl on Schindler's List* (New York: Scholastic Press, 2019), 100; second quote Leon Leyson with Marilyn Harran and Elisabeth Leyson, *The Boy on the Wooden Box: How the Impossible Became Possible… on Schindler's List* (New York: Antheneum Books for Young Readers, 2013), 186.

9. http://www.thesandb.com/article/holocaust-survivor-celia-biniz-52-spoke-to-students-about-resilience-survival.html?print=print, accessed on 12 September 2021.

10. https://www.amestrib.com/news/20190331/i-dont-know-whether-it-was-chance-luck-or-fate-but-it-saved-me, accessed on 25 September 2021.

11. Celina frequently speaks of being given second chances by both Schindler and Spielberg, although she often phrases these statements in various ways. These second chance phrases are third person versions of her commonly used wording.

Chapter One

1. Celina Biniaz, telephone conversation with author, 7 March 2020. On Kraków's population, see https://encyclopedia.ushmm.org/content/en/article/Kraków-cracow, accessed on 25 May 2020. For Phyllis's quotation, see Phyllis Karp, interview by Robert Mannheimer, Des Moines, Iowa, 1 April 1981, Des Moines Oral History Project, Iowa Jewish Historical Society, Waukee, Iowa.

2. Quotation from Nathan Glazer, foreword to Celia Heller, *On the Edge of Destruction: Jews of Poland between the Two World Wars* (Detroit: Wayne State University Press, 1977), xi. For the history of Poland and its relationship with Jews, see pp. 13-46.

3. Irvin Karp, interview by Robert Mannheimer, Des Moines, Iowa, 12 May 1981, Des Moines Oral History Project, Iowa Jewish Historical Society, Waukee, Iowa. On Radomsko, see https://www.jewishgen.org/yizkor/Radomsko/rado43.html#HISTORY,

accessed on 15 April 2020.

4. Irvin Karp, interview, 12 May 1981.

5. Ibid.; and Moses Gaynor, telephone conversation with author, 24 April 2020.

6. Moses Gaynor, telephone conversation; and Basil Karp, telephone conversation with author, 27 April 2020. For concerns about Jews in New York, see Gary Dean Best, "Jacob H. Schiff's Galveston Movement: An Experiment in Immigrant Deflection, 1907-1914," *American Jewish Archives* (April 1978), 47-48.

7. On the Galveston Movement, see Best, "Jacob H. Schiff's Galveston Movement," 43-79.

8. See Moses Gaynor, telephone conversation; Basil Karp, telephone conversation; Celina Biniaz, telephone conversation, 16 March 2020; Ship Manifest, SS Chemnitz, 1913, included in Moses Gaynor, correspondence with author, 26 April 2020; Irvin Karp, interview by Moses Gaynor, 12 February 1989, Hallandale, Florida, Jeremy Gaynor Papers, private collection held by Jeremy Gaynor, Coral Springs, Florida; and *R. L. Polk & Co.'s Des Moines City Directory, 1914* (Des Moines: R. L. Polk & Co, 1914), 672.

9. Irvin Karp, interview, 12 May 1981. On decree and parliament's choice not to support it, see *The New International Yearbook: A Compendium of the World's Progress for the Year 1923* (New York: Dodd, Mead and Company, 1924), 394.

10. See Irvin Karp, interviews, 12 May 1981, and 12 February 1989. On ORTs, see Nathan Eck, "The Educational Institutions of Polish Jewry, 1921-1939," Jewish Social Studies 9 (January 1947), 28-30; and https://www.ort.org/en/about-ort/history/, accessed on 16 April 2020.

11. Phyllis Karp, interview,1 April 1981. Quotation is from Phyllis Karp, interview by Carol Stulberg, 25 January 1996, tape one, Camarillo, California, USC Shoah Foundation, Los Angeles, California.

12. Phyllis Karp, interview, 1 April 1981.

13. Ibid. For Scott Temple's quotation, see Scott Temple, telephone conversation with author, 20 April 2020.

14. Phyllis Karp, interview, 25 January 1996; and Irvin Karp, interview, 12 February 1989.

15. Ibid.

16. Phyllis Karp, interview, 1 April 1981; and Celina Biniaz, correspondence with author, 30 April 2020.

17. Phyllis Karp, interview, 1 April 1981.

18. Ibid. On the economy, see https://poland-today.pl/1929-1938/, accessed on 29 April 2020.

19. Phyllis Karp, interview, 1 April 1981; and Celina Biniaz, telephone conversation, 7 March 2020.

20. Celina Biniaz, telephone conversation, 7 March 2020.

21. Ibid. See also Phyllis Karp, interview, 1 April 1981.

22. Ibid.

23. Celina Biniaz, telephone conversation, 7 March 2020. See also Rena Finder with Joshua Greene, *My Survival: A Girl on Schindler's List* (New York: Scholastic Press, 2019), 27.

24. Celina Biniaz, telephone conversation, 7 March 2020. See also Mietek Pemper, *The*

Road to Rescue: The Untold Story of Schindler's List (New York: Other Press, 2005), 5.

25. See Pemper, *Road to Rescue*, 5-6; and Celina Biniaz, telephone conversation, 7 March 2020.

26. Ibid. See also Celina Biniaz, interview by Carol Stulberg, 25 January 1996, Camarillo, California, USC Shoah Foundation, Los Angeles, California; Irvin Karp, interview, 12 May 1981; and Phyllis Karp, interview, tape one, 25 January 1996.

27. Celina Biniaz, telephone conversation, 7 March 2020; Phyllis Karp, interview, tape two, 25 January 1996. See also Elinor Brecher, *Schindler's Legacy: True Stories of the List Survivors* (New York: Dutton, 1994), 6-8.

28. Celina Biniaz, telephone conversation, 7 March 2020.

29. Irvin Karp, interviews, 12 May 1981, and 12 February 1989; Celina Biniaz, telephone conversation, 7 March 2020; Scott Temple, telephone conversation; and Basil Karp, telephone conversation. See also https://www.jewishgen.org/Yizkor/radomsko/rad538.html, accessed on 14 May 2020.

30. See Irvin Karp, interview, 12 February 1989.

31. On Nuremberg Laws, see Henry Friedlander, *The Origins of Nazi Genocide: From Euthanasia to the Final Solution* (Chapel Hill: University of North Carolina Press, 1995), 23-24.

32. Phyllis Karp, interview, 25 January 1996.

33. See David Faber, *Munich: 1938: Appeasement and World War II* (New York: Simon and Schuster, 2009); and Giles MacDonogh, *1938: Hitler's Gamble* (New York: Basic Books, 2009). See Evgeny Finkel, *Ordinary Jews: Choice and Survival during the Holocaust* (Princeton and Oxford: Princeton University Press, 2017), 41-42; and Irvin Karp, Yom HaShoah interview, Rock Island, Illinois, 11 April 1983, Iowa Jewish Historical Society, Waukee, Iowa; and Pemper, *Road to Rescue*, 10-11.

34. Phyllis Karp, interview, 25 January 1996, tape one.

35. First quote is from Phyllis Karp, interview, 1 April 1981. Second quote is from Brecher, *Schindler's Legacy*, 111. See also Celina Biniaz, telephone conversations, 7, 16 March 2020.

36. Phyllis Karp, interview, 25 January 1996, tape one; and Irvin Karp, interview, 12 May 1981.

37. Ibid.

38. For first quotation. see Irvin Karp, interview, 12 May 1981. On her puppy Leda, see Celina Biniaz, interview, 25 January 1996; and Celina Biniaz, telephone conversation, 7 March 2020. Second quotation from Brecher, *Schindler's Legacy*, 112. See also Malvina Graf, *The Kraków Ghetto and the Płaszów Camp Remembered* (Tallahassee: Florida State University Press), 8.

CHAPTER TWO

1. Phyllis Karp, interview by Robert Mannheimer, Des Moines, Iowa, 1 April 1981, Des Moines Oral History Project, Iowa Jewish Historical Society, Waukee, Iowa. Quotation from Celina Biniaz, telephone conversation with author, 16 March 2020.

2. Irvin Karp, interview by Robert Mannheimer, Des Moines, Iowa, 12 May 1981, Des Moines Oral History Project, Iowa Jewish Historical Society, Waukee, Iowa. See also Evgeny Finkel, *Ordinary Jews: Choices and Survival during the Holocaust* (Princeton and Oxford: Princeton University Press, 2017), 58. See also Rena Finder with Joshua Greene, *My Survival: A Girl on Schindler's List* (New York: Scholastic Press, 2019), 15.

3. Phyllis Karp, interview, 1 April 1981; Irvin Karp, interview, 12 May 1981; Celina Biniaz,

telephone conversation, 16 March 2020.

4. For quotation, see Finder, *My Survival,* 14.

5. Celina Biniaz, telephone conversation, 7 March 2020.

6. On food rationing and early decrees against Jews in Kraków, see Bernard Offen with Norman Jacobs, *My Hometown Concentration Camp: A Survivor's Account of Life in the Kraków Ghetto and Płaszów Concentration Camp* (London: Vallentine Mitchell, 2008), 5, 122. Quote is from Finkel, *Ordinary Jews,* 31. On schools, see Celina Biniaz, interview by Carol Stulberg, 25 January 1996, Camarillo, California, USC Shoah Foundation, Los Angeles, California; Celina Biniaz, telephone conversation, 16 March 2020; and David Crowe, *Oskar Schindler: The Untold Account of His Life, Wartime Activities, and the True Story Behind The List* (Boulder: Westview Press, 2004), 90.

7. Phyllis Karp, interview, 1 April 1981; and Celina Biniaz, telephone conversation, 7 March 2020.

8. On Saul Karp, see Celina Biniaz, telephone conversations, 7 March, 21 April 2020.

9. Irvin Karp, interview, 12 May 1981; Phyllis Karp, interview, 1 April 1981.

10. Crowe, *Oskar Schindler,* 72-77.

11. On restricting media, confiscating radios, and jamming signals, see Mietek Pemper, *The Road to Rescue: The Untold Story of Schindler's List* (New York: Other Press, 2005), 14; see also Malvina Graf, *The Kraków Ghetto and the Płaszów Camp Remembered* (Tallahassee: Florida State University Press), 13. For first quote, see Irvin Karp, interview, 12 May 1981. Second quote from Finkel, *Ordinary Jews,* 60.

12. Offen, *Hometown Concentration Camp,* 122; and Irvin Karp, interview, 12 May 1981.

13. Ibid.; Graf, *Kraków Ghetto,* 16-17; and Crowe, *Oskar Schindler,* 93-94.

14. Crowe, *Oskar Schindler,* 94.

15. Crowe, *Oskar Schindler,* 95. On trustee Lukas, see Julius Madritsch, *People in Distress* (Vienna: V. Roth), 1962), 10; and on Phyllis staying on at Hogo, see Phyllis Karp, interview, 1 April 1981.

16. Quote from Crowe, *Oskar Schindler,* 157. On factory work, see Irvin Karp, interview, 12 May 1981.

17. For new restrictions, see Offen, *Hometown Concentration Camp,* 122; and for Irvin quote, see Irvin Karp, interview, 12 May 1981.

18. David Crowe, *The Holocaust: Roots, History, and Aftermath* (Boulder: Westview Press, 2008), 178.

19. Ibid.

20. Ibid., 179.

21. The best book on Schindler is David Crowe, *Oskar Schindler.* See also Robin O'Neil, *Oskar Schindler: Stepping Stone to Life; A Reconstruction of the Schindler Story* (League City, Tex.: Susaneking.com, 2010; online in pdf format available at https://www.jewishgen.org/yizkor/schindler/files/SchindlerPart1.pdf; https://www.jewishgen.org/yizkor/schindler/files/SchindlerPart2.pdf; and https://www.jewishgen.org/yizkor/schindler/files/SchindlerAddendum.pdf; accessed on 12 June 2020); and Thomas Keneally, *Schindler's List* (New York: Touchstone, 1982).

22. Crowe, *Oskar Schindler,* 7-54.

23. Ibid., 88-97.

24. Ibid., 106-112.

25. Madritsch, *People in Distress*, 6. See also Rod Gregg, *My Brother's Keeper: Christians Who Risked All to Protect Jewish Targets in the Nazi Holocaust* (New York: Center Street, 2016), 82-83; Martin Gilbert, *The Righteous: The Unsung Heroes of the Holocaust* (New York: Henry Holt and Company, 2003), 219-224; and O'Neil, *Stepping Stone to Life* (online pdf format, part 1), 59.

26. Madritsch, *People in Distress*, 6. For more on Madritsch and first quote, see Crowe, *Oskar Schindler*, 155; and for second quote, see Celina Biniaz, telephone conversation, 7 March 2020.

27. See Crowe, *Holocaust*, 179-80.

28. On rumors, see Crowe, *Oskar Schindler*, 145; and Graf, *Kraków Ghetto*, 35. For more on this and her mother selling furniture, see Celina Biniaz, interview, 25 January 1996.

29. Crowe, *Oskar Schindler*, 144-45; O'Neil, *Stepping Stone*, (online pdf, format part 1) 55; and for newspaper quote, see Pemper, *Road to Rescue*, 24.

30. Crowe, *Oskar Schindler*, 145; and Pemper, *Road to Rescue*, 24-25.

31. See Christine Liu, "Mapping and Visualizing Testimonies of Spaces of Confinement: A Digital Analysis of the Kraków Ghetto" (MA thesis, Duke University, 2019), 10; and http://www.holocaustresearchproject.org/ghettos/Kraków/Kraków.html, accessed on 18 June 2020. First quote of furniture from Celina Biniaz, telephone conversations, 16 March 2020; second quote from Celina Biniaz, interview, 25 January 1996.

32. Celina Biniaz, telephone conversations, 7, 16 March 2020; Irvin Karp, interview, 12 May 1981; Phyllis Karp, interview by Carol Stulberg, 25 January 1996, tape two, Camarillo, California, USC Shoah Foundation, Los Angeles, California; Crowe, *Oskar Schindler*, 147; Stella Müller-Madej, *A Girl from Schindler's List* (London: Polish Cultural Foundation, 1997), 12-13. For a short, black and white film of Jews moving to the Kraków ghetto, see https://collections.ushmm.org/search/catalog/irn1002726, accessed on 19 June 2020.

33. For allotting space in the ghetto apartments, see Finkel, *Ordinary Jews*, 32; and Pemper, *Road to Rescue*, 24. On the Karps's apartment, see Celina Biniaz, telephone conversation, 16 March 2020; Irvin Karp, interview, 12 May 1981; Phyllis Karp, interview, 25 January 1996, tape two.

34. Crowe, *Oskar Schindler*, 148.

35. Ibid.; http://www.holocaustresearchproject.org/ghettos/Kraków/Kraków.html; and Phyllis Karp, Yom HaShoah interview, Rock Island, Illinois, 11 April 1983, Iowa Jewish Historical Society, Waukee, Iowa.

36. Crowe, *Oskar Schindler*, 148.

37. Liu, *Mapping and Visualizing Testimonies*, 10.

38. Celina Biniaz, telephone conversation, 16 March 2020. For quote, see Graf, *Kraków Ghetto*, 40.

39. Celina Biniaz, telephone conversation, 16 March 2020. Years earlier in a 1996 interview, Celina's mother identified a Fred Oberfeld as Gucia's husband, explaining that he was with the family at liberation in May 1945. Fred may have been a nickname or Phyllis misremembered his first name, but she was referring to Adolf Oberfeld, a Kraków Jew who married

Gucia Wittenberg, see Gusta Oberfeld prisoner questionnaire, Stutthof camp documents, ITS Digital file, 1.1.41.2/NOWIK-OLO/00046286/0002, accessed at the United States Holocaust Memorial Museum Digital Collection, 8 December 2021. On Oberfeld, see his form for an identification card, "To the Commissioner of the District Chief for the City of Kraków," OberfeldAdolphAARG-15.098M.0095.00000005, accessed at the United States Holocaust Memorial Museum Digital Collection, 8 December 2021. See Phyllis Karp, interview, 25 January 1996, tape three.

40. Celina Biniaz, telephone conversation, 16 March 2020, and Müller-Madej quoted in Crowe, *The Holocaust*, 183. See also Celina Biniaz, interview, 25 January 1996.

41. Liu, *Mapping and Visualizing Testimonies*, 12-13; Crowe, *The Holocaust*, 185; Finkel, *Ordinary Jews*, 111; and Irvin Karp, interview, 12 May 1981.

42. For first quote, see Finkel, *Ordinary Jews*, 32; and for second quote, see Graf, *Kraków Ghetto*, 42; and for third quote, see Celina Biniaz, telephone conversation, 17 August 2020. See also Crowe, *Oskar Schindler*, 152; and Celina Biniaz, interview, 25 January 1996.

43. Crowe, *The Holocaust*, 181-82; and Phyllis Karp, interview, 1 April 1981.

44. Celina Biniaz, telephone conversation, 7 March 2020.

45. For gates, see Crowe, *Oskar Schindler*, 148. See also Irvin Karp, interview, 12 May 1981; and Celina Biniaz, telephone conversation 7 March 2020. Because Oberfeld was on the Madritsch-Titsch list (a list of Madritsch workers later assigned to "Schindler's List"), it is clear that he worked at the Madritsch factory, although there is no way to know when he started there. There is no hard evidence that Gucia worked there, but it seems highly likely, since Gucia was always deemed an essential worker and able to remain in the ghetto. Irvin would have done everything in his power to protect his sister-in-law, and his job as a Madritsch factory manager would likely have put him in a position to get her a job there.

46. See Crowe, *Oskar Schindler*, 154; and http://www.holocaustresearchproject.org/ghettos/Kraków/Kraków.html, accessed on 22 June 2020.

47. Madritsch, *People in Distress*, 7-13; Crowe, *Oskar Schindler*, 157; https://righteous.yadvashem.org/?search=julius%20madritsch&searchType=righteous_only&language=en&itemId=4016227&ind=0, accessed on 27 June 2020; and Irvin Karp, Yom HaShoah interview, Rock Island, Illinois, 11 April 1983, Iowa Jewish Historical Society, Waukee, Iowa.

48. Ibid.

49. Ibid.

50. Ibid.; and Irvin Karp, interview, 12 May 1981.

51. Crowe, *Oskar Schindler*. 157-58, 168, 171-76.

52. Crowe, *The Holocaust*, 169-71.

53. For discussion of debate, see Christopher Browning, *Nazi Policy, Jewish Workers, and German Killers* (New York: Cambridge University Press, 2000), 26-57; quote comes from p. 28.

54. Crowe, *The Holocaust*, 196-201.

55. Ibid., 225-254; and https://encyclopedia.ushmm.org/content/en/article/final-solution-in-depth, accessed on 10 July 2020.

56. Quote is from Crowe, *The Holocaust*, 234. For more on the Wannsee Confer-

ence, see Mark Roseman, *The Wannsee Conference and the Final Solution* (New York: Metropolitan Books, 2002).

57. See Crowe, *Oskar Schindler*, 182; and http://www.holocaustresearchproject.org/ghettos/Kraków/Kraków.html, accessed on 23 June 2020. On Auschwitz I and Auschwitz II, see Charles Sydnor, "Auschwitz I Main Camp," and Franciszec Piper, "Auschwitz II-Birkenau Main Camp," in *The United States Holocaust Memorial Museum Encyclopedia of Camps and Ghettos, 1933-1945*, vol. 1, part A (Bloomington and Indianapolis: Indiana University Press, 2009), 204-214. See also https://www.yadvashem.org/odot_pdf/Microsoft%20Word%20-%206400.pdf, accessed on 4 August 2020; https://encyclopedia.ushmm.org/content/en/article/auschwitz; accessed on 8 August 2020; and Christopher Browning, *The Origins of the Final Solution: The Evolution of Nazi Jewish Policy, September 1939-March 1942* (Lincoln: University of Nebraska Press, 2007).

58. On Operation Reinhard, see Yitzhak Arad, *The Operation Reinhard Death Camps: Belzec, Sobibor, Treblinka*, second edition (Bloomington: Indiana University Press, 2018).

59. Crowe, Crowe, *Oskar Schindler*, 182-86; and http://www.holocaustresearchproject.org/ghettos/Kraków/Kraków.html, accessed on 23 June 2020.

60. See http://www.holocaustresearchproject.org/nazioccupation/zgody.html, accessed on 26 June 2020.

61. Offen, *My Hometown Concentration Camp*, 18.

62. Phyllis Karp, interview, 25 January 1996, tape two; and Phyllis Karp, Yom HaShoah interview, Rock Island, Illinois, 11 April 1983, Iowa Jewish Historical Society, Waukee, Iowa.

63. Ibid; and Celina Biniaz, telephone conversation, 17 August 2020.

64. Ibid.; see also Elinor Brecher, *Schindler's Legacy: True Stories of the List Survivors* (New York: Dutton), 113.

65. Ibid.

66. Quote is from Crowe, *Oskar Schindler*, 153. On efforts to get or keep precious work permits, see Finkel, *Ordinary Jews*, 112-13.

67. On the issuing of the *Blauschein*, see Crowe, *Oskar Schindler*, 184.

68. Ibid.; and Offen, *My Hometown Concentration Camp*, 20.

69. Celina Biniaz, telephone conversation, 7, 16 March 2020; and Phyllis Karp, interview, 9 April 1981. For quote and more on operating factory, see Madritsch, *People in Distress*, 14.

70. Celina Biniaz, telephone conversation, 16 March 2020. For more on Madritsch's treatment of his workers and Fagen quote, see Gregg, *My Brother's Keeper*, 84.

71. Celina Biniaz, correspondence with author, 1 July 2020; and Graf, *Kraków Ghetto*, 49. On Himmler's order, see https://encyclopedia.ushmm.org/content/en/article/1942-key-dates, accessed on 3 July 2020.

72. On the October *Aktion*, see https://encyclopedia.ushmm.org/content/en/article/Kraków-cracow, accessed on 13 July 2020; Crowe, *Oskar Schindler*, 187-193; and Graf, *Kraków Ghetto*, 60-61. For Celina's recollection, see Celina Biniaz, interview, 25 January 1996; and telephone conversation, 16 March 2020.

73. Ibid.; and Celina Biniaz, telephone conversation, 17 August 2020.

74. See Ryszard Kotarba, *A Historical Guide to the German Camp in Płaszów, 1942–1945*,

(Kraków: Institute of National Remembrance Commission of the Prosecution of Crimes against the Polish Nation, 2014), 14-15; Dieter Pohl, "Kraków-Płaszów Main Camp," in *The United States Holocaust Memorial Museum Encyclopedia of Camps and Ghettos, 1933–1945,* vol. 1, part B (Bloomington and Indianapolis: Indiana University Press, 2009), 862; Crowe, *Oskar Schindler,* 239; and http://www.holocaustresearchproject.org/othercamps/Płaszów/ Płaszów.html, accessed on 15 July 2020.

75. On the rumors, see Graf, *Kraków Ghetto,* 67-68. See also, Kotarba, *Historical Guide to Płaszów,* 13.

76. O'Neil, *Stepping Stone to Life,* (online pdf format, part 1) 69; and Pohl, "Kraków-Płaszów Main Camp," 862.

77. See http://www.holocaustresearchproject.org/ghettos/Kraków/Kraków.html, accessed on 17 July 2020; Kotarba, *Historical Guide to Płaszów,* 14: Crowe, Oskar Schindler, 194; and O'Neil, *Stepping Stone to Life,* (online pdf format, part 1), 77.

78. Offen, *My Hometown Concentration Camp,* 44, 46; Celina Biniaz, interview, 25 January 1996; and telephone conversation, 16 March 2020.

79. Crowe, *Oskar Schindler,* 197-201; O'Neil, *Stepping Stone* (online pdf format, part 1), 77-78; and Celina Biniaz, interview, 25 January 1996; and telephone conversation, 16 March 2020.

80. Crowe, *Oskar Schindler,* 197-201; O'Neil, *Stepping Stone* (online pdf format, part 1), 77-78.

81. Phyllis Karp, interview, 11 February 1983.

82. Pemper, *Road to Rescue,* 38.

CHAPTER THREE

1. For first and third quotes, see Elinor Brecher, *Schindler's Legacy: True Stories of the List Survivors* (New York: Dutton), 114, 210. "Pathalogical sadist," is a descriptive phrase for Göth from George Kren, foreword to Malvina Graf, *The Kraków Ghetto and the Płaszów Camp* (Tallahassee: Florida State University Press, 1989), xi. For Phyllis's quote, see Phyllis Karp, interview by Robert Mannheimer, Des Moines, Iowa, 9 April 1981, Des Moines Oral History Project, Iowa Jewish Historical Society, Waukee, Iowa.

2. On Płaszów, see Ryszard Kotarba, *A Historical Guide to the German Camp in Płaszów, 1942–1945,* (Kraków: Institute of National Remembrance Commission of the Prosecution of Crimes against the Polish Nation, 2014), 14-17; Dieter Pohl, "Kraków-Płaszów Main Camp," in *The United States Holocaust Memorial Museum Encyclopedia of Camps and Ghettos, 1933–1945,* vol. 1 (Bloomington and Indianapolis: Indiana University Press, 2009), 862; and http://www.holocaustresearchproject.net/othercamps/Płaszów/ Płaszów.html, accessed on 30 July 2020.

3. Ibid. For quote, see Graf, *Kraków Ghetto,* 87.

4. Pohl, "Kraków-Płaszów Main Camp," 862-63; Kotarba, *Historical Guide to Płaszów,* 21-22; and David Crowe, *Oskar Schindler: The Untold Account of His Life, Wartime Activities, and the True Story Behind The List* (Boulder: Westview Press, 2004), 245.

5. Ibid.

6. Pohl, "Kraków-Płaszów Main Camp," 865; and Crowe, *Oskar Schindler,* 242-43.

7. Celina Biniaz, telephone conversation with author, 20 March 2020.

8. http://www.holocaustresearchproject.net/othercamps/Płaszów/Płaszów.html, ac-

cessed on 30 July 2020; Rena Finder with Joshua Greene, *My Survival: A Girl on Schin-dler's List* (New York: Scholastic Press, 2019), 43; Graf, *Kraków Ghetto*, 90; and Celina Biniaz, interview by Carol Stulberg, 25 January 1996, Camarillo, California, USC Shoah Foundation, Los Angeles, California.

9. Celina Biniaz, telephone conversation, 16 March 2020; and Phyllis Karp, interview by Robert Mannheimer, Des Moines, Iowa, 9 April 1981, Des Moines Oral History Project, Iowa Jewish Historical Society, Waukee, Iowa.

10. http://www.deathcamps.org/occupation/Płaszów.html, accessed on 15 July 2020; and Phyllis Karp, interview, 9 April 1981.

11. For quotation, see Finder, *My Survival*, 44; for second quotation and more on food, see Bernard Offen, *My Hometown Concentration Camp: A Survivor's Account of Life in the Kraków Ghetto and Płaszów Concentration Camp* ((London: Vallentine Mitchell, 2008), 68. See also, Irvin Karp, interview by Robert Mannheimer, Des Moines, Iowa, 19 May 1981, Des Moines Oral History Project, Iowa Jewish Historical Society, Waukee, Iowa; and Kotarba, *Historical Guide to Płaszów*, 28; Crowe, *Oskar Schindler*, 286; and Celina Biniaz, telephone conversation, 7 March 2020.

12. Crowe, *Oskar Schindler*, 286.

13. Celina Biniaz, telephone conversation, 7 March 2020; and https://www.motl.org/survivor-celina-biniaz-the-youngest-of-schindlers-jews/, accessed on 7 August 2020.

14. For quote, and more on her time in the hospital, see Celina Biniaz, correspondence with author, 8 August 2020. See also Irvin Karp, interview, 19 May 1981; and Graf, *Kraków Ghetto*, 124; Pohl, "Kraków-Płaszów Main Camp," 864; and Phyllis Karp, interview, 9 April 1981. Story of Göth shooting patients is from Leon Leyson, with Marilyn Harran and Elisabeth Leyson, *The Boy on the Wooden Box: How the Impossible Became Possible... on Schindler's List* (New York: Atheneum Books for Young Readers, 2013), 119.

15. Celina Beinaz, telephone conversation, 7 March 2020; Celina Biniaz, interview, 25. January 1996; Phyllis Karp, interview, 9 April 1981; and Graf, *Kraków Ghetto*, 125. Biniaz, See also Celina Biniaz, correspondence, 8 August 2020.

16. Celina Biniaz, telephone conversation, 16 March 2020.

17. For quote, see https://www.history.co.uk/article/the-horrors-of-the-krak%C3%B3w-p%C5%82asz%C3%B3w-concentration-camp, accessed on 3 September 2020.

18. Crowe, *Oskar Schindler*, 216-218. Madritsch quote from Rod Gregg, *My Brother's Keeper: Christians Who Risked All to Protect Jewish Targets in the Nazi Holocaust* (New York: Center Street, 2016), 83.

19. Crowe, *Oskar Schindler*, 219-20.

20. Ibid., 224-25.

21. Ibid.

22. Ibid., 226-27.

23. Pfefferberg quote from Thomas Keneally, *Schindler's List* (New York: Touchstone Books, 1982), 360. On Göth's size, see Finder, *My Survival*, 45; and http://www.holocaustresearchproject.org/othercamps/Płaszów/bauPłaszów.html, accessed on 4 September 2020. On his dogs, see Mietek Pemper, *The Road to Rescue: The Untold Story of Schindler's List* (New York: Other Press, 2005), 51; and Graf, *Kraków Ghetto*, 93.

24. First quote from Robin O'Neil, *Oskar Schindler: Stepping Stone to Life; A Reconstruc-

tion of the Schindler Story (League City, Tex.: Susaneking.com, 2010), online pdf format, part 1, 69. Second quote from Graf, *Kraków Ghetto*, 93; third quote from Pemper, *Road to Rescue*, 44; and Fourth quote from Phyllis Karp, interview, 9 April 1981. On Göth shooting workers from his balcony, see Crowe, *Oskar Schindler*, 245.

25. For first quote, see Celina Biniaz, telephone conversation, 7 March 2020. See also, Irvin Karp, interview, 19 May 1981; Finder, *My Survival*, 46; and http://www.auschwitz.dk/goeth.htm, accessed on 14 September 2020.

26. Celina Biniaz, interview, 25 January 1996.

27. See Irvin Karp, interview, 19 May 1981; O'Neil, *Stepping Stone to Life* (online pdf format, part 1), 69; and Celina Biniaz, interview, 25 January 1996.

28. This hanging was recounted by *Schindlerjude* Moshe Beijski at the trial of the war criminal Adolf Eichmann. See http://www.auschwitz.dk/goeth.htm, accessed on 14 September 2020; and https://www.nizkor.org/session-021-08-eichmann-adolf/, accessed on 14 September 2020.

29. Celina Biniaz, telephone conversation, 7 March 2020. For the story of such an underground library operating in Auschwitz, see Dita Kraus, *Delayed Life: The True Story of the Librarian of Auschwitz* (New York: Feiwel & Friends, 2020).

30. Julius Madritsch, *People in Distress* (Vienna: V. Roth, 1962), 13, 17, and Crowe, *Oskar Schindler*, 230-31.

31. Crowe, *Oskar Schindler*, 278.

32. Madritsch, *People in Distress*, 20, 22; and Crowe, *Oskar Schindler*, 245.

33. First quote from Ryszard Kotarba, *Historical Guide to Płaszów*, 35. For more on the move, see Celina Biniaz, correspondence, 27 June 2020. For second quote and more on his factory in Płaszów, see Madritsch, *People in Distress*, 23.

34. Crowe, *Oskar Schindler*, 279-84; Pemper, *Road to Rescue*, 69, and O'Neil, *Stepping Stone to Life* (online pdf format, part 1), 73.

35. Crowe. *Oskar Schindler*, 279; and http://www.holocaustresearchproject.org/other-camps/Płaszów/Płaszów.html, accessed on 12 September 2020.

36. Pohl, "Kraków-Płaszów Main Camp," 865; Crowe, Oskar Schindler, 321; and Kotarba, *Historical Guide to Płaszów*, 47.

37. See Celina Biniaz, interview, 25 January 1996; Celina Biniaz, telephone conversation, 16 March 2020; and Celina Biniaz correspondence, 24 September 2020.

38. Offen, *Hometown Concentration Camp*, 82; and http://dachaukz.blogspot.com/2012/08/Płaszów-klkz-schindlers-list-part-1_6.html, accessed on 30 September 2020.

39. Crowe, *Oskar Schindler*, 316-20.

40. Two of the best books on Mengele are David Marwell, *Mengele: Unmasking the "Angel of Death"* (New York: W. W. Norton & Company, 2020; and Gerald Posner and John Ware, *Mengele: The Complete Story* (New York: McGraw Hill, 1986).

41. The roll call is described by Graf, *Kraków Ghetto*, 122-24; Pemper, 91-95; and Crowe, *Oskar Schindler*, 320-21; and http://www.holocaustresearchproject.org/othercamps/Płaszów/Płaszów.html, accessed on 12 September 2020.

42. See Graf, *Kraków Ghetto*, 123; and Phyllis Karp, interview, 9 April 1981.

43. David Crowe, *Oskar Schindler*, 321-22; Graf, *Kraków Ghetto*, 123-24; and Kotarba,

Historical Guide to Płaszów, 47.

44. Ibid. For Celina's quote, see https://www.motl.org/survivor-celina-bini-az-the-youngest-of-schindlers-jews/, accessed on 10 September 2020. See also Celina Biniaz, telephone conversation, 7 March 2020. Offen's quote from Offen, *Hometown Concentration Camp*, 82.

45. Brecher, *Schindler's Legacy*, 163.

46. Crowe, *Oskar Schindler*, 323; Celina Biniaz, interview, 25 January 1996; and Phyllis Karp, interview, 25 January 1996, tape two.

47. Irvin Karp, interview, 19 May 1981; Phyllis Karp, interview, 14 April 1981; Celina Biniaz, telephone conversation 16 March 2020; and Celina Biniaz correspondence, 24 September 2020.

48. See Graf, *Kraków Ghetto*, 160; Offen, *Hometown Concentration Camp*, 88; Phyllis Karp, interview, 14 April 1981, tape three; Irvin Karp, interview, 19 May 1981, tape two; Celina Biniaz, correspondence, 24 August 2020; Brecher, *Schindler's Legacy*, 112; and https://encyclopedia.ushmm.org/content/en/article/stutthof, accessed on 15 September 2020. See also transport list from Auschwitz to Stutthof (which included Gusta Oberfeld's name), 16 September 1944, ITS Digital file, 1.1.41/0067/0004, accessed at the United States Holocaust Memorial Museum Digital Collection, 8 December 2021.

49. Crowe, *Oskar Schindler*, 265-66.

50. https://www.yadvashem.org/odot_pdf/Microsoft%20Word%20-%205721.pdf, accessed on 25 September 2020; and https://encyclopedia.ushmm.org/content/en/article/sonderkommandos, accessed on 25 September 2020.

51. Kotarba, *Historical Guide to Płaszów*, 50; and Pohl, "Kraków-Płaszów Main Camp," 865.

52. http://www.holocaustresearchproject.org/trials/goeth1.html; http://www.holocaustresearchproject.org/trials/goeth2.html; and http://www.holocaustresearchproject.org/trials/goeth3.html, accessed on 10 September 2020.

53. Crowe, *Oskar Schindler*, 340-42.

54. Ibid.; Celina Biniaz, interview, 26 January 1996; and Celina Biniaz, correspondence, 1 October 2020.

55. Pemper, *Road to Rescue*, 132-34; and Celina Biniaz, telephone conversation, 7 March 2020; and Celina Biniaz, correspondence, 1 October 2020.

56. On rumors of camp's closing, see Crowe, *Oskar Schindler*, 324; and on Madritsch ordered to close his factory and getting an extension for six months, see Madritsch, *People in Distress*, 25.

57. Crowe, *Oskar Schindler*, 332.

58. Madritsch, *People in Distress*, 26-27; and Crowe, *Oskar Schindler*, 370-71.

59. Crowe, *Oskar Schindler*, 369, 371.

60. Madritsch, *People in Distress*, 26-27; and Crowe, *Oskar Schindler*, 370-71.

61. Pemper, *Road to Rescue*, 140.

62. Ibid., 139-45; Crowe, *Oskar Schindler*, 361-66; and O'Neil, *Stepping Stone to Life* (online pdf format, part 1), 96-100.

63. Ibid.

64. Crowe, *Oskar Schindler*, 366, 368.

65. Ibid , 368.

66. Ibid., 368; and Madritsch, *People in Distress*, 27.

67. Ibid., 368, 373. See also typed Madritsch-Titsch list, ITS Digital file, 1.1.19.1/0004/0002, accessed at the United States Holocaust Memorial Museum Digital Collection, 4 March 2020. Translation of Titsch note on list is from O'Neil, *Stepping Stone to Life* (online pdf format, part 1), 100.

68. Crowe, *Oskar Schindler*, 376; and Celina Biniaz, correspondence, 1 October 2020.

69. Pemper, *Road to Rescue*, 147; Leyson, *Boy on the Wooden Box*, 150; and Crowe, *Oskar Schindler*, 383.

CHAPTER FOUR

1. https://www.amestrib.com/news/20190331/i-dont-know-whether-it-was-chance-luck-or-fate-but-it-saved-me, accessed on 12 September 2020.

2. For the Schindler women arriving at Auschwitz, see Rena Finder with Joshua Greene, *My Survival: A Girl on Schindler's List* (New York: Scholastic Press, 2019), 62-63, and David Crowe, *Oskar Schindler: The Untold Account of His Life, Wartime Activities, and the True Story Behind The List* (Boulder: Westview Press, 2004), 88-94; Celina Biniaz, interview by Carol Stulberg, 25 January 1996, Camarillo, California, USC Shoah Foundation, Los Angeles, California; and Celina Biniaz, telephone conversation with author, 7 March 2020. For conversation about chimneys and more on arrival, see Phyllis Karp, Yom HaShoah interview, Rock Island, Illinois, 11 April 1983, Iowa Jewish Historical Society, Waukee, Iowa; and Phyllis Karp, interview by Robert Mannheimer, Des Moines, Iowa, 9 April 1981, Des Moines Oral History Project, Iowa Jewish Historical Society, Waukee, Iowa.

3. Finder, *My Survival*, 62-63. For Celina quote, see https://jewishjournal.com/culture/survivor/217308/survivor-celina-biniaz-youngest-schindlers-jews/, accessed on 2 September 2020.

4. See also Celina Biniaz, telephone conversation, 7 March 2020; and Phyllis Karp, interview, 9 April 1981.

5. Celina Biniaz, telephone conversation, 7 March 2020; and Finder, *My Survival*, 61-62. On being sent to Auschwitz instead of Gross-Rosen, see Mietek Pemper, *The Road to Rescue: The Untold Story of Schindler's List* (New York: Other Press, 2005), 151.

6. Elinor Brecher, *Schindler's Legacy: True Stories of the List Survivors* (New York: Dutton), 68-69; and Crowe, *Oskar Schindler*, 388-89.

7. Crowe, *Oskar Schindler*, 389. On Auschwitz and Auschwitz II-Birkenau, see Charles Sydnor, "Auschwitz I Main Camp," and Franciszec Piper, "Auschwitz II-Birkenau Main Camp," in *The United States Holocaust Memorial Museum Encyclopedia of Camps and Ghettos, 1933-1945*, vol. 1, part A (Bloomington and Indianapolis: Indiana University Press, 2009), 204-214.

8. Celina Biniaz, interview, 25 January 1996; Celina Biniaz, telephone conversation; 7 March 2020; Phyllis Karp, interviews, 9 April 1981; 11 April 1983; and Crowe, *Oskar Schindler*, 388, 390. Quotes are from Finder, *My Survival*, 65, 63.

9. Quotes are from Phyllis Karp, interview, 9 April 1981. On Celina's hair being cut short, see https://jewishjournal.com/culture/survivor/217308/survivor-celina-biniaz-youngest-schindlers-jews/, accessed on 2 September 2020. On disinfecting, see Crowe, *Oskar Schindler*, 390.

10. Celina Biniaz, interview, 25 January 1996. See also Celina Biniaz, telephone conver-

sation, 7 March 2020; Finder, *My Survival*, 64-65; and Evgeny Finkel, *Ordinary Jews: Choices and Survival during the Holocaust* (Princeton and Oxford: Princeton University Press, 2017), 62. For quote, see https://jewishjournal.com/culture/survivor/217308/survivor-celina-biniaz-youngest-schindlers-jews/, accessed on 2 September 2020.

11. Crowe, *Oskar Schindler*, 391; Finder, *My Survival*, 63; Celina Biniaz, telephone conversation, 7 March 2020. For more and story of woman dancing, see Phyllis Karp, interview, 9 April 1981.

12. Celina Biniaz, telephone conversation, 7 March 2020. For temporary nature of stay and rumors, see Crowe, *Oskar Schindler*, 392.

13. Crowe, *Oskar Schindler*, 392.

14. Phyllis Karp, interview, 9 April 1981. See also *Des Moines Register*, 19 June 1947; and Finder, *My Survival*, 69.

15. See Celina Biniaz, telephone conversation, 7 March 2020; Celina Biniaz, interview 25 January 1996; Phyllis Karp, interview, 9 April 1981; and Phyllis Karp, interview by Carol Stulberg, 25 January 1996, tape two, Camarillo, California, USC Shoah Foundation, Los Angeles, California.

16. Ibid. For Celina's let me go quote, see telephone conversation, 7 March 2020. For first part of last quote, see https://jewishjournal.com/culture/survivor/217308/survivor-celina-biniaz-youngest-schindlers-jews/, accessed on 2 September 2020; and for second part of quote, see Brecher, *Schindler's Legacy*, 115.

17. For Irvin's quote, see Irvin Karp, interview by Robert Mannheimer, Des Moines, Iowa, 19 May 1981, Des Moines Oral History Project, Iowa Jewish Historical Society, Waukee, Iowa. For more on train conditions and the man having a nervous breakdown, see Brecher, *Schindler's Legacy*, 210-11.

18. Leon Leyson, with Marilyn Harran and Elisabeth Leyson, *The Boy on the Wooden Box: How the Impossible Became Possible... on Schindler's List* (New York: Atheneum Books for Young Readers, 2013), 155.

19. Crowe, *Oskar Schindler*, 384-85; Irvin Karp, interview, 19 May 1981.

20. Crowe, *Oskar Schindler*, 385-87.

21. Ibid.; Robin O'Neil, *Oskar Schindler: Stepping Stone to Life; A Reconstruction of the Schindler Story* (League City, Tex.: Susaneking.com, 2010), online pdf format, part 2, 2; and Irvin Karp, interview, 19 May 1981.

22. Crowe, *Oskar Schindler*, 396.

23. See O'Neil, *Stepping Stone to Life*, online pdf format, part 2, 11-12; Crowe, 358-60; 394-404.

24. https://encyclopedia.ushmm.org/content/en/article/tattoos-and-numbers-the-system-of-identifying-prisoners-at-auschwitz, accessed on 12 September 2020.

25. Ibid.; and Crowe, *Oskar Schindler*, 403. For more on waiting to get tattoos and quote see Phyllis Karp, interview, 9 April 1981; and Celina Biniaz, interview, 25 January 1996.

26. Celina Biniaz, interview, 25 January 1996; Celina Biniaz, telephone conversation, 7 March 2020; and Crowe, *Oskar Schindler*, 405.

27. See Celina Biniaz, interview, 25 January 1996; and Phyllis Karp, interview, 9 April 1981. For story of train trip, see Stella Müller-Madej, *A Girl from Schindler's List* (London: Polish Cultural Foundation, 1997), 204-07.

28. Müller-Madej, *Girl from Schindler's List*, 206-07; Finder, *My Survival*, 72; and Celina

Biniaz, interview, 25 January 1996.

29. Ibid.; see also Phyllis Karp, interview, 25 January 1996, tape three; and Irvin Karp interview, 19 May 1981; and Celina Biniaz, telephone conversation, 7 March 2020.

30. For Schindler's address to the women, see O'Neil, *Stepping Stone to Life*, online pdf format, part 2, 14. Phyllis Karp, interview, 25 January 1996, tape three.

31. On Celina's illness and Emilie Schindler's assistance, see Celina Biniaz, telephone conversation, 7 March 2020; Celina Biniaz, interview, 25 January 1996; Phyllis Karp, interview, 25 January 1006, tape three; and Phyllis Karp, Yom HaShoah interview, Rock Island, Illinois, 11 April 1983, Iowa Jewish Historical Society, Waukee, Iowa. On Emilie Schindler's help in the infirmary in general, see Crowe, *Oskar Schindler*, 417, 427; and Finder, *My Survival*, 74, 76.

32. Celina Biniaz, interview, 25 January 1996; Phyllis Karp, interview, 25 January 1996, tape three; Leyson, *Boy on the Wooden Box*, 148; and Crowe, *Oskar Schindler*, 438-39.

33. Crowe, *Oskar Schindler*, 439; and Pemper, *Road to Rescue*, 159-62.

34. On apartment, see Crowe, *Oskar Schindler*, 404, 414, and for Schindler'squote, see Crowe, *Oskar Schindler*, 411. See also Finder, *My Survival*, 73. Schindler also thought it was important to be on site to protect his factory and property from approaching Soviet troops.

35. Crowe, *Oskar Schindler*, 437-38.

36. Ibid., 438.

37. Ibid., 428, 432; and Irvin Karp, interview, 19 May 1981.

38. Ibid.; and Leyson, *Boy on the Wooden Box*, 159.

39. Celina Biniaz, correspondence with author, 25 March 2020; Brecher, *Schindler's Legacy*, 116; and Crowe, *Oskar Schindler*, 440.

40. Celina Biniaz, interview, 25 January 1996; Celina Biniaz, telephone conversation, 7 March 2020; and Brecher, *Schindler's Legacy*, 116, 211.

41. See Crowe, *Oskar Schindler*, 434-35. For more on visit, and Schindler quote, see Pemper, *Road to Rescue*, 155-56; and for Celina story and quote, see Celina Biniaz, interview, 25 January 1996.

42. See Irvin Karp, interview, 19 May 1981; Phyllis Karp, interview, 9 April 1981; Celina Biniaz, interview, 25 January 1996; and Müller-Madej, *Girl from Schindler's List*, 243.

43. Irvin Karp, interview, 19 May 1981; Phyllis Karp, interview, 9 April 1981; and Müller-Madej, *Girl from Schindler's List*, 244.

44. Crowe, *Oskar Schindler*, 446.

45. Ibid., 447.

46. Ibid., 448-49; and Celina Biniaz, interview, 25 January 1996.

47. Crowe, *Oskar Schindler*, 453-54; Finder, *My Survival*, 83-84; and Pemper, *Road to Rescue*, 165-66.

48. Ibid.

49. Crowe, *Oskar Schindler*, 450-51; Leyson, *Boy on the Wooden Box*, 162-63; Phyllis Biniaz, interview, 9 April 1981; Celina Biniaz, telephone conversation, 7 March 2020.

50. Celina Biniaz, correspondence, 29 November 2020; Irvin Karp, interview, 19 May

1981; Phyllis Karp; interview, 9 April 1981; and Brecher, *Schindler's Legacy*, 92, 213.

51. On hanging in general, see Crowe, *Oskar Schindler*, 458. For Celina watching event and Russian soldier's reaction, see Phyllis Karp, interview, 9 April 1981; and Irvin Karp, interview, 19 May 1981.

52. Phyllis Karp, interview, 9 April 1981; and Irvin Karp, interview, 19 May 1981.

53. Ibid.

54. Brecher, *Schindler's Legacy*, 116.

55. Phyllis Karp, interview, 9 April 1981; and Irvin Karp, interview, 19 May 1981.

56. Quoted phrase is from Leyson, *Boy on the Wooden Box*, 166.

CHAPTER FIVE

1. Celina Biniaz, interview by Carol Stulberg, 25 January 1996, Camarillo, California, USC Shoah Foundation, Los Angeles, California.

2. For Celina seeing herself in mirror and quote, see Celina Biniaz, telephone conversation with author, 16 March 2020; for Nasaw quote, see David Nasaw, *The Last Million: Europe's Displaced Persons from World War to Cold War* (New York: Penguin Press, 2020), 2; and for Celina's last quote, see http://www.thesandb.com/article/holocaust-survivor-celina-biniaz-52-spoke-to-students-about-resilience-survival.html?print=print, accessed on 3 December 2020.

3. See Phyllis Karp, interview by Carol Stulberg, 25 January 1996, Camarillo, California, USC Shoah Foundation, Los Angeles, California; Phyllis Karp, interview by Robert Mannheimer, Des Moines, Iowa, 9 April 1981, Des Moines Oral History Project, Iowa Jewish Historical Society, Waukee, Iowa; Irvin Karp, interview by Robert Mannheimer, Des Moines, Iowa, 19 May 1981, Des Moines Oral History Project, Iowa Jewish Historical Society, Waukee, Iowa; Celina Biniaz, interview, 25 January 1996; and Celina Biniaz telephone conversation with author, 16 December 2020.

4. Celina Biniaz, telephone conversations, 16 March, 16 December 2020; Irvin Karp, interview, 19 May 1981; Phyllis Karp, interview, 25 January 1996.

5. Ibid.

6. Irvin's memory from Irvin Karp, interview, 19 May 1981. Years later in the late 1970s or early 1980s, Phyllis Karp told Phyllis Cytron the story of the candlesticks, see Phyllis Cytron, Zoom video conference with author, 29 October 2020.

7. Quote from Rena Finder with Joshua Greene, *My Survival: A Girl on Schindler's List* (New York: Scholastic Press, 2019), 90-91.

8. Irvin Karp, interview, 19 May 1981; and Celina Biniaz, telephone conversation, 16 December 2020.

9. See Nasaw, *Last Million*, 84-85; Finder, *My Survival*, 91, and Irvin Karp, interview, 19 May 1981.

10. See http://www.thesandb.com/article/holocaust-survivor-celina-biniaz-52-spoke-to-students-about-resilience-survival.html?print=print, accessed on 3 December 2020.

11. Celina Biniaz, telephone conversation, 16 December 2020. For a reference to the school, see http://www.aapjstudies.org/index.php?id=218, accessed on 18 December 2020.

12. Celina Biniaz, telephone conversation, 16 December 2020.

13. Ibid.

14. Ibid; and David Crowe, *Oskar Schindler: The Untold Account of His Life, Wartime Activities, and the True Story Behind The List* (Boulder: Westview Press, 2004), 371. On the denazification of Austria, see http://www.entnazifizierung.at/denazification-in-austria/, accessed on 18 December 2020.

15. Celina Biniaz, telephone conversation, 16 December 2020; Irvin Karp, interview, 19 May 1981; *Des Moines Register*, 7 November 1945; *Kansas City Star* 24 December 1945; *St. Louis Star and Times*, 13 December 1945; and the *Wisconsin Jewish Chronicle*, 7 September, 23 November 1945. For quote and more on pogroms, see Nasaw, *Last Million*, 228.

16. Irvin Karp, interview, 19 May 1981; Phyllis Karp, interview 14 April 1981; and Celina Biniaz, telephone conversation, 16 December 2020.

17. Nassaw, *Last Million*, 229. For more on Klausner, see his obituary, *New York Times*, 30 June 2007.

18. Klausner quote from *Waterloo Courier* (Waterloo, Iowa), 13 December 1945. Harrison quote is from "Harrison Report," https://www.ushmm.org/exhibition/displaced-persons/resourc1.htm, accessed on 3 January 2021.

19. *St. Louis Star and Times*, 11 December 1945.

20. Quote from http://www.thesandb.com/article/holocaust-survivor-celina-biniaz-52-spoke-to-students-about-resilience-survival.html?print=print, accessed on 3 December 2020. See also Zadjia Bauman note to Celina, 29 October 1945, Celina Biniaz Papers, private collection held by Celina Biniaz, Camarillo, California; hereafter cited as Celina Biniaz Papers; and Celina Biniaz, telephone conversations, 16 March, 16 December 2020.

21. See Adolf Oberfeld file card, listing him in Rome, Italy, as of 31 December 1945, from list compiled by the Delegation for the Assistance of Jewish Emigrants, an Italian aid organization, postwar displaced persons camp lists, ITS Digital file, o.1/image vorhanden/TD_Nachtrag_Alt/0426720/2037; and Adolf Oberfeld, United Restitution Organization card identifying his death in Jerusalem, 21 July 1950, ITS Digital file, 6.3.3.2/42000…/427200…/0427292/2 inbound/0002; both documents accessed at the United States Holocaust Memorial Museum Digital Collection, 8 December 2021.

22. Phyllis Karp, interview 14 April 1981; and Irvin Karp, interview, 19 May 1981. For more on the journey, see Celina Biniaz, interview, 25 January 1996; and telephone conversations, 16 March, 16 December 2020.

23. See Phyllis Karp, interview, 14 April 1981; and Irvin Karp, interview, 19 May 1981. For more on Prague, staying in laundry, and quote, see Celina Biniaz, 16 March 2020.

24. Irvin and Celina recalled they knew the woman from Kraków; Phyllis thought they knew her from a camp. They agreed, however, on the rest of the story. See Irvin Karp, interview, 19 May 1981; Phyllis Karp, interview, 14 April 1981; and Celina Biniaz, telephone conversation, 16 March 2020.

25. Phyllis Karp, interview, 14 April 1981; and Irvin Karp, interview, 19 May 1981.

26. Ibid; and Celina Biniaz, interview, 25 January 1996. For more on camp and quote, see Celina Biniaz, telephone conversation, 16 December 2020.

27. Phyllis Karp, interview, 14 April 1981; Celina Biniaz, telephone conversations, 16. March, 16 December 2020; and Celina Karp's A. E. F. Assembly Registration Card, ITS

Digital file, 0.1/_K/K0254/01129\\192.168.101.238\, accessed at the United States Holocaust Memorial Museum Digital Collection, 5 February 2020. For Klausner's comment of putting DPs into private German homes, see *St. Louis Star and Times*, 12 December 1945.

28. Phyllis Karp, interview 14 April 1981.

29. Ibid.

30. Ibid.; and Phyllis Karp, interview, 9 April 1981.

31. Ibid.; and Celina Biniaz, interview, 25 January 1996; and telephone conversation, 16 March 2020.

32. Phyllis Karp, interview, 14 April 1981; Celina Biniaz, interview, 25 January 1996; and Elinor Brecher, *Schindler's Legacy: True Stories of the List Survivors* (New York: Dutton), 118.

33. For first quote, see Celina Biniaz, telephone conversation, 16 December 2020; for second and third quotes, see Brecher, *Schindler's Legacy*, 118.

34. Phyllis Karp, interview, 14 April, 1981; and Celina Biniaz, telephone conversation, 16 March 2020.

35. Phyllis Karp, interview, 14 April 1981. Celina's first quote from *Des Moines Register*, 19 June 1947; second quote from Brecher, *Schindler's Legacy*, 118.

36. On Angelika and Hanelore Bloch, see Celina Biniaz, telephone conversation, 16 March 2020; and Celina Biniaz correspondence with author, 20 March 2020. On films Celina saw in Germany, see Brecher, *Schindler's Legacy*, 118.

37. Celina Biniaz, telephone conversation, 16 March 2020.

38. Ibid.

39. On Mater Leontine , see Celina Biniaz, telephone conversations, 7, 16 March, 16 December 2020; and Celina Biniaz, interview, 25 January 1996. First quote from Celina Biniaz, telephone conversation, 16 March 2020; second quote from Brecher, *Schindler's Legacy*, 117.

40. First quote from http://www.thesandb.com/article/holocaust-survivor-celina-biniaz-52-spoke-to-students-about-resilience-survival.html?print=print, accessed on 3 December 2020; second quote from https://www.vcstar.com/picture-gallery/news/local/communities/camarillo/2018/04/05/camarillo-grandmother-shares-images-of-holocaust/33574459/, accessed on 3 December 2020.

41. First quote from Celina Biniaz, telephone conversation, 16 December 2020. Second quote from https://www.vcstar.com/picture-gallery/news/local/communities/camarillo/2018/04/05/camarillo-grandmother-shares-images-of-holocaust/33574459/, accessed on 3 December 2020.

42. Celina Biniaz, telephone conversation, 16 December 2020; and Phyllis Karp, interview, 14 April 1981.

43. On Truman's directive, see Irvin Karp, interview, 19 May, 1981; https://scholarship.law.stjohns.edu/cgi/viewcontent.cgi?article=1195&context=tcl, accessed on 12 December 2020; and https://historynewsnetwork.org/article/164324, accessed on 14 December 2020. For Truman and immigration more broadly, see Roger Daniels, ed., *Immigration and the Legacy of Harry S. Truman* (Kirksville, Mo: Truman State University Press, 2010).

44. On weight gain, see *Des Moines Register*, 19 June 1947; 14 August 1952.

45. Irvin Karp, interview by Moses Gaynor, 12 February 1989, Hallandale, Florida, Jeremy Gaynor

Papers, private collection held by Jeremy Gaynor, Coral Springs, Florida. Helene Cazes Benatar to American Joint Distribution Committee, Munich, 10 April 1946, ITS Digital file, 6.3.3.2/ 300000 .../ 318300 .../0318374/2, accessed at the United States Holocaust Memorial Museum Digital Collection, 4 March 2020. See also Moses Gaynor, correspondence with author, 19, 30 January 2021.

46. Ibid. See also Phyllis Karp, interview, 9 April 1981; Celina Biniaz, conversation, 16 March 2020; and Celina Biniaz, correspondence, 17 December 2020.

47. See Irvin Karp, interview, 19 May 1981; and *Des Moines Register*, 19 June 1947.

48. Phyllis Karp, interview, 25 January 1996, tape three; Celina Biniaz, telephone conversations, 16 March, 16 December 2020; and Celina Karp's, Munich Emigrant Assembly Center card, ITS Digital file, 3.1.1.1/DP1790/0683, accessed at the United States Holocaust Memorial Museum Digital Collection, 5 February 2020.

49. For the collection of Mater Leontine's letters to Celina, see Mater Leontine letters to Celina Karp, Iowa Jewish Historical Society, Waukee, Iowa. On Mater Leontine's death, see Olga Burkhardt-Vetter, correspondence with author, 2 September 2020.

50. Celina Karp, Munich Emigrant Assembly Center card; and Celina Biniaz, correspondence, 17 December 2020.

51. On the Church World Service, see Haim Genizi, "Problems of Protestant Cooperation: The Church World Service," in Hubert Locke and Marcia Littell, *World Council of Churches and Post-War Relief in Germany," in Holocaust and Church Struggle: Religion, Power and the Politics of Resistance* (Lanham, Md.: University Press of America, 1996), 163-196. On Irvin and Phyllis not knowing English, see Irvin Karp, interview, 19 May 1981; and Phyllis Karp, interview, 14 April 1981.

52. On the SS *Marine Marlin*, see Roland Charles, *Troopships of World War II* (Washington, D.C.: The Army Transportation Association, 1947), 211; http://www.navsource. org/archives/09/22/22201.htm, accessed on 12 January 2021; and https://addiesrose. wordpress.com/2017/10/01/ss-marine-marlin/, accessed on 12 January 2021. For Celina's first quote, see Celina Biniaz, telephone conversation, 16 March 2020; second quote is from Celina Biniaz, correspondence, 17 December 2020.

53. See Passenger Manifest Form (for the SS *Marine Marlin*), 30 May 1947, ITS Digital file, 3.1.3.2/0001-0100/0018/0086 and 3.1.3.2/0001-0100/0018/0101, accessed at the United States Holocaust Memorial Museum Digital Collection 26 March 2021; Irvin Karp, interview, 19 May 1981; and Phyllis Karp, interview, 14 April 1981. For ice cream story and quote, see Celina Biniaz, telephone conversation, 16 March 2020. On Coca-Cola, see Mark Pendergrast, *For God, Country, and Coca-Cola: The Unauthorized History of the Great American Soft Drink and the Company That Makes It* (New York: Charles Scribner's Sons, 1993); and on Celina's reaction to tasting it, see Brecher, *Schindler's Legacy*, 118.

54. See Phyllis Karp, interview, 14 April 1981; and Celina Biniaz, telephone conversation, 16 March 2020.

55. For first quote, see *Des Moines Register*, 19 June 1947; second quote is from Celina Biniaz, correspondence, 29 December 2020.

CHAPTER SIX

1. For likely route, see 1947 Rand McNally United States road map, https://www. davidrumsey.com/luna/servlet/detail/RUMSEY~8~1~23824~920008:Rand-McNally-road-map-United-States, accessed on 25 January 2021. Quote is from

https://www.dmschools.org/2017/09/holocaust-survivor-north-high-alum-celi-na-karp-biniaz/, accessed on 12 January 2021.

2. *Des Moines Tribune*, 2 October 1947.

3. Celina's first quote from Celina Biniaz, interview by Moses Gaynor, 23 February 1990, Fort Lauderdale, Florida, Jeremy Gaynor Papers, private collection held by Jeremy Gaynor, Coral Springs, Florida; hereafter cited as Jeremy Gaynor Papers. Second quote from Celina Biniaz, telephone conversation with author, 16 March 2020.

4. Celina Biniaz, interview, 23 February 1990.

5. Phyllis Karp, Phyllis Karp, interview by Robert Mannheimer, Des Moines, Iowa, 14 April 1981, Des Moines Oral History Project, Iowa Jewish Historical Society, Waukee, Iowa; and Celina Biniaz, telephone conversation, 3 April 2020.

6. Richard Isaacson, telephone conversation with author, 1 April 2020. See also Celina Biniaz, telephone conversation, 3 April 2020.

7. Phyllis Karp, interview, 14 April 1981.

8. Celina Biniaz, telephone conversation, 3 April 2020. For Des Moines weather that month, see https://www.almanac.com/weather/history/IA/Des%20oines/1947-07-05, accessed on 20 January 2021. See also Celina Biniaz, interview 23 February 1990.

9. For flooding, see https://pubs.usgs.gov/of/1997/0557/report.pdf, accessed on 15 February 2021; and *Des Moines Tribune*, 13, 25 June 1947. For Mater Leontine's quote, see Mater Leontine to "Linka," 25 June 1947, Iowa Jewish Historical Society, Waukee, Iowa. Celina's letters to Mater Leontine no longer exist.

10. On location of Karp home, see *Des Moines Register*, 19 June 1947. For Celina and Reed's Ice Cream, see Celina Biniaz, interview, 23 February 1990.

11. Celina Biniaz, interview, 23 February 1990. On Reed's Ice Cream and its stands in Des Moines, see *Des Moines Register*, 28 July 1993.

12. On cousins and quote, see Celina Biniaz, interview, 23 February 1990. See also *Des Moines Register* 19 June 1947.

13. Celina Biniaz, telephone conversation, 16 March 2020; and Basil Karp, telephone conversation with author, 27 April 2020.

14. Ibid; and Celina Biniaz, correspondence with author, 1 May 2020. For a contemporary mention of the summer school classes, see Mater Leontine to "Linka," 22 August 1947.

15. Ibid; Celina Biniaz, interview, 23. February 1990; and *Des Moines Register*, 30 April 2015. Quote from Elinor Brecher, *Schindler's Legacy: True Stories of the List Survivors* (New York: Dutton), 119.

16. See https://www.ushmm.org/learn/timeline-of-events/1942-1945/truman-di-rective-on-immigrant-visas, accessed on 14 January 2021; and https://immigra-tiontounitedstates.org/464-displaced-persons-act-of-1948.html, accessed on 14 January 2021. For background of DPs and U.S. immigration policy, see Haim Genizi, *America's Fair Share: The Admission and Resettlement of Displaced Persons, 1945-1952* (Detroit: Wayne State University Press, 1993).

17. https://www.jewishdatabank.org/content/upload/bjdb/537/C-IA-Des_Moines-1956-Summary_Report.pdf, accessed on 15 January 2021.

18. Brecher, *Schindler's Legacy*, 119.

19. Phyllis Karp, interview, 14 April 1981; and Celina Biniaz, correspondence, 11 February 2021.

20. *Des Moines Register*, 19 June 1947

21. Peter Novick, *The Holocaust in American Life* (New York: Houghton Mifflin, 1999), 63-123; quote from p. 83.

22. Novick, *Holocaust in American Life*, 114.

23. For quote, see Novick, *Holocaust in American Life*, 87; and for the role of the Cold War in the deemphasizing the Holocaust, see pp. 85-102.

24. Phyllis Karp, interview 14 April 1981.

25. Ibid.

26. Irvin Karp, interview by Robert Mannheimer, 19 May 1981, Des Moines Oral History Project, Iowa Jewish Historical Society, Waukee, Iowa.

27. Phyllis Karp, interview, 14 April 1981. See also Ivin Karp, interview, 19 May 1981.

28. Ibid. See also *Des Moines Register*, 13 June 1995; 25 February 1997.

29. First quote from Celina Biniaz, telephone conversation, 16 March 2020. On North High School and class size, see two North High yearbooks, January, and June 1948, available online, https://archive.org/details/north_1948/mode/2up and https://archive.org/details/north_1948_june/mode/2up, accessed on 12 February 2021. See also *Des Moines Tribune*, 2 October 1947; and Celina Biniaz, interview, 23 February 1990.

30. For Hurwitz quote, see Lou Hurwitz, telephone conversation with author, 27 January 2020. On Celina not talking about Holocaust and Augusta story, see, Celina Biniaz, telephone conversation, 16 March 2020.

31. Quote from *Des Moines Tribune* 2 October 1947. On school activities, see North High School yearbook, June 1948, https://archive.org/details/north_1948_june/mode/2up, accessed on 12 February 2021. On buying violin, see Celina Biniaz, interview, 23 February 1990.

32. Hurwitz, telephone conversation; and Jean Lory, telephone conversation with author, 25 March 2020.

33. For Celina quote, see Celina Biniaz, telephone conversation, 3 April 2020. Lory quote from Ellsworth Lory, *Glimpses of the Past* (Ankeny, Iowa: Life Story Enterprises, 1982), 81, Jean Lory Papers, private collection held by Jean Lory, Ames Iowa, hereafter cited as Jean Lory Papers.

34. Celina's recollection from Jerold Mathews, "Some North High Teachers, 1945-1948, (unpublished manuscript, 2009), 7, Jean Lory Papers.

35. Celina Biniaz, correspondence, 11 February 2021.

36. Celina Biniaz, telephone conversation, 3 April 2020.

37. Celina Biniaz, telephone conversation, 3 April 2020. For more on the Encampment for Citizenship, see Algernon D. Black, *The Young Citizens: The Story of the Encampment for Citizenship* (New York: Frederick Ungar Publishing Co., 1962).

38. Lou Hurwitz, telephone conversation, 7 April 2020; and Celina Biniaz, telephone conversation, 3 April 2020.

39. Ibid.

40. Celina Biniaz, telephone conversation, 23 April 2020; see also ticket for day four of the 1948 Democratic National Convention, Celina Biniaz Papers, private collection held by Celina Biniaz, Camarillo, California, hereafter cited as Celina Biniaz Papers.

41. Celina Biniaz, telephone conversation, 3 April 2020.

42. Ibid. See also Black, *Young Citizens,* 49, 66.

43. For Harnack quote and information on Grinnell, see https://www.grinnell.edu/news/historic-figures, accessed on 15 February 2021.

44. First quote from http://www.thesandb.com/article/holocaust-survivor-celina-biniaz-52-spoke-to-students-about-resilience-survival.html?print=print, accessed on 3 December 2020. For other quotes and story about dormitory, see Celina Biniaz, correspondence, 6 April 2020. Piediscalzi quote from Nick Piediscalzi, telephone conversation with author, 28 April 2020.

45. For Bucksbaum quote, see Carolyn "Kay" Bucksbaum, telephone conversation with author, 26 March 2020. For Celina's attitudes and quotes, see Celina Biniaz, interview by Carol Stulberg, 25 January 1996, Camarillo, California, USC Shoah Foundation, Los Angeles, California.

46. Celina Biniaz, 3 April 2020; and https://www.latimes.com/archives/la-xpm-1992-09-13-mn-1265-story.html, accessed on 17 February 20201.

47. Celina Biniaz, telephone conversation, 3 April 2020. For quote see David Balducchi, "Talk Stalks and Plain Talk: Truman's 1948 Whistle-Stop Tour in Iowa," *Iowa Heritage Illustrated* (Winter 2007), 152. On Grinnell population, see https://www2.census.gov/library/publications/decennial/1950/pc-02/pc-2-30.pdf, accessed on 16 February 2021.

48. Truman quote and story of girl giving him an ear of corn from Balducchi, "Tall Stalks and Plain Talk," 152. Celina quote from Celina Biniaz, correspondence 24 February 2021.

49. Quotes from https://magazine.grinnell.edu/news/defying-darkness, accessed on 12 December 2020.

50. Celina Biniaz, telephone conversation, 3 April 2020.

51. Celina Biniaz, correspondence, 6, 9 April 2020.

52. Ibid. On the exchange program's beginnings, see *Des Moines Register,* 25 May 1947.

53. Celina Biniaz, correspondence, 6, April 2020; 24 February 2021.

54. Ibid., and Celina Biniaz, telephone conversation, 3 April 2020. On Stroessinger, see https://www.grinnell.edu/news/one-mans-odyssey, accessed on 10 February 2021.

55. Ibid.

56. Celina Biniaz, telephone conversation, 3 April 2020.

57. Ibid. First quote from https://magazine.grinnell.edu/news/defying-darkness, accessed on 12 December 2020. Second quote from http://www.thesandb.com/article/holocaust-survivor-celina-biniaz-52-spoke-to-students-about-resilience-survival.html?print=print, accessed on 3 December 2020.

58. Celina Biniaz, telephone conversation, 3 April 2020. For Harrison and Piediscalzi quotes, see Nick Piediscalzi, telephone conversation. Ken Sayre quote from Ken Sayre, telephone conversation with author, 4 May 2020.

59. Ken Sayre, telephone conversation; and Celina Biniaz, telephone conversation, 3 April 2020.

60. Celina Biniaz, telephone conversation, 3 April 2020; Irvin Karp, interview, 19 May 1981; and *Des Moines Register,* 14 August 1952. Quote from http://www.thesandb.com/

article/holocaust-survivor-celina-biniaz-52-spoke-to-students-about-resilience-surviv-al.html?print=print, accessed on 3 December 2000.

61. Celina Biniaz, telephone conversation, 3 April 2020.

62. *Des Moines Register*, 14 August 1952.

63. Celina Biniaz, telephone conversation, 3 April 2020.

64. *Des Moines Register*, 14 August 1952; and http://content.time.com/time/subscriber/article/0,33009,889509,00.html, accessed on 14 February 2021.

65. Phyllis Karp, interview, 14 April 1981; and Irvin Karp, 19 May 1981. Quote is from *Des Moines Register*, 14 August 1952.

CHAPTER SEVEN

1. Celina's first quote from Celina Biniaz, interview by Moses Gaynor, 23 February 1990, Fort Lauderdale, Florida, Jeremy Gaynor Papers, private collection held by Jeremy Gaynor, Coral Springs, Florida; hereafter cited as Jeremy Gaynor Papers. For Prestley quote, see https://www.pbs.org/wgbh/americanexperience/features/newyork-postwar/, accessed on 8 March 2021.

2. E. B. White quote from https://www.pbs.org/wgbh/americanexperience/features/newyork-postwar/, accessed on 8 March 2021.

3. Celina Biniaz, telephone conversation with author, 3 April 2020. For International House, see https://www.ihouse-nyc.org/about-student-housing-in-ny/our-history/, accessed on 2 March 2021.

4. Celina Biniaz, telephone conversation, 3 April 2020. On Lawrence Cremin, see https://www.anb.org/view/10.1093/anb/9780198606697.001.0001/anb-9780198606697-e-0901033, accessed on 3 March 2021.

5. Celina Biniaz, telephone conversation, 3 April 2020.

6. Amir Biniaz, correspondence with author, 18 March 2021; Celina Biniaz, telephone conversation, 19 April 2021.

7. Ibid; and Amir Biniaz, telephone conversation with author, 21 April 2020.

8. Ibid.

9. Amir Biniaz, telephone conversation. For Celina quote, see Celina Biniaz, telephone conversation, 3 April 2020.

10. Ibid. For Necchi Fellowship renewal, see Teachers College to Celina Karp, 10 April 1953, Celina Biniaz Papers, private collection held by Celina Biniaz, hereafter cited as Celina Biniaz Papers; and *Des Moines Tribune*, 16 April 1953. For wedding announcement see *Des Moines Register*, 2 August 1953.

11. Amir Biniaz, telephone conversation; and Celina Biniaz, telephone conversation, 21 April 2020.

12. Ibid. For Bini's quote and more on wedding, see Celina Biniaz, telephone conversation, 16 March 2021.

13. Celina Biniaz, telephone conversations, 3 April 2020, 16 March 2021; and Richard Issacson, telephone conversation with author, 1 April 2020.

14. Celina Biniaz, telephone conversation, 16 March 2021.

15. Celina Biniaz, correspondence with author, 6 April 2020; and Amir Biniaz, tele-

phone conversation, 21 April 2020.

16. Ibid; see also Celina Biniaz, correspondence, 4 June 2020.

17. Ibid.

18. Linda Lafourcade, correspondence with author, 16 May 2021.

19. Quote from John Diggins, *The Proud Decades: Ameircan in War and Peace, 1941–1960* (New York and London: W.W. Norton & Company, 1988), 181. See also Lizabeth Cohen, *A Consumer's Republic: The Politics of Mass Consumption in Postwar America* (New York: Vintage Books, 2003), 112-165.

20. William Friedricks, *The Real Deal: The Life of Bill Knapp* (Des Moines: Business Publications Corporation, 2013), 54.

21. Doris Kearns Goodwin, *Wait Till Next Year* (New York: Touchstone Book, 1998), 76-77.

22. Ruff quote from https://patch.com/new-york/threevillage/bp--boom-town-usa-long-island-in-the-1950s, accessed on 24 March 2021. On growth in Nassau County, see *New York Times*, 3 August 2012.

23. For Halberstam quote, see David Halberstam, *The Fifties* (New York: Fawcett Columbine 1993), 508.

24. Celina Biniaz, telephone conversation, 16 March 2021.

25. On morning ritual of men commuting from Long Island to Penn Station, see Goodwin, *Wait Till Next Year*, 52. See also Linda Lafourcade, correspondence. On home additions, see Celina Biniaz, telephone conversation, 5 May 2021.

26. Rita Post, telephone conversation with author, 2 July 2020; and Celina Biniaz, telephone conversation, 16 March 2021.

27. First quote from Celina Biniaz, telephone conversation, 16 March 2021; second quote from Celina Biniaz, telephone conversation, 17 August 2020. See also Rita Post, telephone conversation.

28. Rita Post, telephone conversation. See also Anita Roll, telephone conversation; Amir Biniaz, telephone conversation; Linda Lafourcade correspondence; and Rob Biniaz, telephone conversation with author, 25 March 2021.

29. Ibid.

30. See Amir Biniaz, telephone conversation.

31. Linda Lafourcade, correspondence.

32. Celina Biniaz, interview by Carol Stulberg, 25 January 1996, Camarillo, California, USC Shoah Foundation, Los Angeles, California.

33. Amir Biniaz, telephone conversation; and Celina Biniaz, telephone conversation, 21 April 2020.

34. Shari Roll, telephone conversation with author, 4 April 2021. See also Amir Biniaz, telephone conversation; and Celina Biniaz, telephone conversation, 21 April 2020.

35. Rob Biniaz, telephone conversation; Shari Roll, telephone conversation; Amir Biniaz, telephone conversation; and Celina Biniaz, telephone conversation, 16 March 2021.

36. Quote is from Anita Roll, telephone conversation. For Bini's dental work outside his practice and activity in dental associations, see Amir Biniaz, telephone conversation; Amir Biniaz, correspondence, 14 April 2021; and Celina Biniaz, correspondence, 14 April 2021.

37. Shari Roll, telephone conversation.

38. Anita Roll, telephone conversation.

39. Ibid. See also Shari Roll, telephone conversation; Rita Post, telephone conversation; and Celina Biniaz, telephone conversation, 17 August 2020.

40. See Amir Biniaz, telephone conversation; Rob Biniaz, telephone conversation; and Celina Biniaz, telephone conversation 21 April 2020. For more and quote, see Anita Roll, telephone conversation.

41. Celina Biniaz, telephone conversation, 21 April 2020.

42. Ibid., 17 August 2020.

43. Ibid.

44. Ibid.

CHAPTER EIGHT

1. Celina Biniaz, telephone conversation with author, 17 August 2020; and Anita Roll, telephone conversation with author, 8 July 2020. On Great Books and Junior Great Books, see *Chicago Tribune*, 15 June 1947; 23 October 1949; 2 October 1962.

2. *Chicago Tribune*, 2 October 1962.

3. Celina Biniaz, telephone conversation, 17 August 2020. See also her "Junior Great Books Leadership and Training Record," and "Junior Great Books Co-Leader Certificate," Celina Biniaz Papers, private collection held by Celina Biniaz, Camarillo, California; hereafter cited as Celina Biniaz Papers. Celina Biniaz, telephone conversation, 17 August 2020.

5. Ibid.; and Celina Biniaz, telephone conversation, 5 May 2021. See also *Chicago Tribune*, 2 October 1962.

6. Celina Biniaz, telephone conversations, 17 August 2020; 5 May 2021.

7. On the law and the history of special education in the United States, see, for example, Ernest Boyer, "Public Law 94-142:A Promising Start?" *Educational Leadership* (February 1979), 298-301; and Robert Osgood, *The History of Special Education: A Struggle for Equality in American Public Schools* (Westport, Conn.: Praeger,2008); and https://www2.ed.gov/policy/speced/leg/idea/history.html, accessed on 11 May 2021.

8. Celina Biniaz, telephone conversations, 17 August 2020; 5 May 2021.

9. Ibid.

10. Ibid; and Ferdinand Hoefner, Jr., "An Experiment to Evaluate the Effectiveness of a Learning Laboratory Approach for Fifth and Sixth Grade Underachievers in Language Arts and Arithmetic," Union Free School District # 23, Wantagh, New York, August 1970, https://files.eric.ed.gov/fulltext/ED044304.pdf, accessed on 4 May 2021.

11. Celina Biniaz, telephone conversation, 5 May 2021; and "Junior Great Books Leadership and Training Record," Celina Biniaz Papers.

12. See Hoefner, "An Experiment," 4-5; and Celina Biniaz, telephone conversation, 5 May 2021.

13. Celina Biniaz, telephone conversation, 17 August 2020.

14. Ibid.; and Hoefner, "An Experiment," 3-4.

15. First quote from Celina Biniaz, 17 August 2020; second quote from Jeanne Bonnici,

telephone conversation with author, 26 April 2021; and third quote from Mr. and Mrs. H. J. Englehart to Dr. Sinclair, 5 February 1968, Celina Biniaz Papers.

16. Celina Biniaz, 17 August 2020; and Hoefner, "An Experiment," 3.

17. Hoefner, "An Experiment," 23-24.

18. Ibid., document resume abstract.

19. Ibid., 23.

20. Celina Biniaz, telephone conversation, 17 August 2020.

21. Ibid.

22. Ibid., and Celina Biniaz, telephone conversation, 5 May 2021. Quote from Beth H. Slingerland, *Screening Tests For Identifying Children with Specific Language Disability*, rev.ed. (Cambridge, Mass.: Educators Publication Service, 1970), xx.

23. Ibid., and Celina Biniaz, telephone conversation, 17 August 2020. See also Celina Biniaz to Charles Mackey, Jr., 16 December 1974, Celina Biniaz Papers.

24. Quotes from Celina Biniaz to Charles Mackey, Jr., 16 December 1974. See also Celina Biniaz, telephone conversation, 3 April 2020.

25. Quote from Carol Taylor to Graduate Admission Committee, Hofstra University, 10 November 1978, Celina Biniaz Papers.

26. For first quote, see https://www.vcstar.com/story/news/local/2018/04/05/camarillo-grandmother-holocaust-survivor-schindlers-list-share-her-story/484029002/, accessed on 4 April 2021; second quote is from James Smith to Director of Graduate Admission, Hofstra University, 27 October 1978, Celina Biniaz Papers.

27. First quote from Carol Taylor to Graduate Admissions Committee; second quote from Dan Connolly, telephone conversation with author, 28 April 2021.

28. Chris Daniggelis to Celina Biniaz, 4 January 2020, Celina Biniaz Papers.

29. Ibid.

30. Pat Connolly, telephone conversation with author, 6 May 2021.

31. Ibid.

32. Celina Biniaz, telephone conversation, 5 May 2021.

33. Celina Biniaz to Mr. Charles Mackey 16 December 1974; and Celina Biniaz, correspondence with author, 23 May 2021.

34. First quote from Carol Taylor to Graduate Admissions Committee; second quote from The Mazeika family to Mrs. Biniaz, n.d., Celina Biniaz Papers.

35. See Jeanne Bonnici, telephone conversation; and Anita Roll, telephone conversation.

36. See Saundra Tufel to Mr. W. Seuss, 15 June 1972, Celina Biniaz Papers; Celina Biniaz, telephone conversations, 17 August 2020; 5 May 2021; and Kerry Brennan, correspondence with author, 5 May 2021.

37. Kerry Brennan, telephone conversation with author, 24 April 2021.

38. Ibid.; and Celina Biniaz, telephone conversation, 5 May 2021.

39. Kerry Brennan to Mrs. Biniaz, 20 November 2012, Celina Biniaz Papers. See also Kerry Brennan, telephone conversation.

40. Celina Biniaz, telephone conversations, 17 August 2020; 5 May 2021.

41. First quote from Anita Roll, telephone conversation; second quote from Rob Biniaz, telephone conversation.

42. Celina Biniaz, telephone conversation, 17 August 2020.

43. Anita Roll, telephone conversation.

44. Rob Biniaz, telephone conversation; Celina Biniaz, correspondence, 23 May 2021.

45. Sue Biniaz, telephone conversation with author, 21 August 2021.

46. Celina Biniaz, telephone conversation, 17 August 2020; Rob Biniaz, telephone conversation; Sue Biniaz, telephone conversation; and https://www.belfercenter.org/sites/default/files/files/publication/sue-biniaz-podcast-transcript- 2020.pdf, accessed on 29 May 2021.

47. *Los Angeles Times*, 13 March 2001; and *New York Times*, 15 March 2001. For the complete story of the origin of the book and then the movie, see Thomas Keneally, *Searching for Schindler* (New York: Nan A. Talese, 2008).

48. Ibid.

49. For book review, see *New York Times*, 24 October 1982; and for Celina's reaction, see telephone conversation, 16 March 2021.

50. Rob Biniaz, telephone conversation.

51. Ibid.

52. Celina Biniaz, telephone conversation, 5 May 2021; and Jeanne Bonnici, telephone conversation.

53. Jeannne Bonnici, telephone conversation.

CHAPTER NINE

1. Quote from *Des Moines Register*, 26 December 1993.

2. See Peter Novick, *The Holocaust in American Life* (New York: Houghton Mifflin, 1999), 133. See also, https://encyclopedia.ushmm.org/content/en/article/eichmann-trial, accessed on 14 June 2021.

3. See *New York Times*, 23 February 1964; Novick, *Holocaust in American Life*, 142-43.

4. Novick, *Holocaust in American Life*, 158; http://content.time.com/time/subscriber/article/0,33009,941261,00.html; accessed on 12 June 2021; and https://timesmachine.ny-times.com/timesmachine/1968/03/03/90029738.pdf?pdf_redirect=true&ip=0, accessed on 12 June 2021.

5. Novick, *Holocaust in American Life*, 146-166; quote from 148.

6. Ibid., 209

7. *New York Times* 16 February 1982.

8. Irvin Karp, interview by Robert Mannheimer, Des Moines, Iowa, 12 May 1981, Des Moines Oral History Project, Iowa Jewish Historical Society, Waukee, Iowa; and Phyllis Karp, interview by Carol Stulberg, 25 January 1996, tape three, Camarillo, California, USC Shoah Foundation, Los Angeles, California.

9. Phyllis Karp, interview, 25 January 1996, tape three.

10. Ibid. See also *Des Moines Register*, 19 May 1968; 14 May, 8 October 1972; and 13 June 1995. On the Karps' condominium, see Celina Biniaz, correspondence with author, 8

March 2021; and *Des Moines Polk Directory 1982* (Kansas City: R. L. Polk and Company, 1982), 422.

11. Quote from Irvin Karp, Yom HaShoah interview, Rock Island, Illinois, 11 April 1983, Iowa Jewish Historical Society, Waukee, Iowa.

12. *Des Moines Register,* 22 January 1994. For story about Phyllis and the Sabbath luncheon, see Phyllis Cytron, Zoom video conference with author, 29 October 2020.

13. Irvin Karp, interview by Robert Mannheimer, Des Moines, Iowa, 19 May 1981, Des Moines Oral History Project, Iowa Jewish Historical Society, Waukee, Iowa.

14. Celina Biniaz, telephone conversation, 16 March 2021.

15. Story and quote from Celina Biniaz, Zoom video conference with author, 29 June 2021. See also Celina Biniaz, correspondence with author, 30 June 2021.

16. Ibid. See also, Celina Biniaz, telephone conversation, 16 March 2021.

17. See Celina Biniaz, Zoom video conference; and Celina Biniaz, correspondence, 1 May 2020.

18. Ibid.

19. Celina Biniaz, Zoom video conference. Oskar and Emilie Schindler were recognized as awarded the honor of Righteous Among the Nations by Yad Vashem in 1993, recognizing non-Jewish people who risked their lives to save Jews during the Holocaust, see https://www.yadvashem.org/righteous/stories/schindler.html, accessed on 1 July 2021.

20. https://www.washingtonpost.com/national/in-emotional-reunion-spielberg-re-visits-schindlers-list/2018/04/27/8912f406-49db-11e8-8082-105a446d19b8_story.html; accessed on 1 July 2021; https://www.independent.co.uk/arts-entertainment/films/news/steven-spielberg-schindlers-list-25th-anniversary-jurassic-park-martin-scorsese-a8655561.html, accessed on 1 July 2021; and https://catalog.afi.com/Catalog/movie-details/67172, accessed on 4 June 2021.

21. Novick, *The Holocaust in American Life,* 214.

22. See Richard Schickel review of 13 December 1993 at http://content.time.com/time/subscriber/article/0,33009,979812,00.html, accessed on 14 June 2021.

23. See *San Francisco Examiner,* 1 December 1993; and *Des Moines Register,* 2 December 1993.

24. *Los Angeles Times,* 12 December 1993. Celina's first quotes from Celina Biniaz, Zoom video conference; last quote from *Des Moines Register* 26 December 1993. See also tickets to the special Los Angeles premiere of *Schindler's List,* Celina Biniaz Papers, private collection held by Celina Biniaz, Camarillo, California.

25. Elinor Brecher, *Schindler's Legacy: True Stories of the List Survivors* (New York: Dutton, 1994), xvii-xviii. For profile piece, see *Miami Herald,* 2 January 1994.

26. Celina Biniaz, Zoom video conference. For quote, see Brecher, *Schindler's Legacy,* 122.

27. See *Des Moines Register,* 13 June 1995; Celina Biniaz, correspondence, 7 July 2021; and Celina Biniaz, telephone conversation, 7 March 2020. For quote, see Celina Biniaz, interview, 21 April 2020.

28. *Los Angeles Times,* 1 October 1994.

29. Celina Biniaz, Zoom video conference; and Celina Biniaz, correspondence, 7 July 2021. For interviews, see Phyllis Karp, interview by Carol Stulberg, 25 January 1996,

Camarillo, California, USC Shoah Foundation, Los Angeles, California; and Celina Biniaz, interview by Carol Stulberg, 25 January 1996, Camarillo, California, USC Shoah Foundation, Los Angeles, California.

30. *Des Moines Register*, 25 February 1997.

31. For quote, see http://www.thesandb.com/article/holocaust-survivor-celina-bini-az-52-spoke-to-students-about-resilience-survival.html?print=print, accessed on 2 July 2021.

32. Robbie Winick, correspondence with author, 6, 8 July 2021; Quote about cup is from *Des Moines Register*, 22 January 1994.

33. See *Star Tribune* (Minneapolis, Minn.), 12 October 1996; *Des Moines Register*, 17 May 1998; *Sioux City Journal*, 31 May 1998; Robbie Winick, correspondence, 6, 8 July 2021; Sandi Yoder, telephone conversation with author, 25 June 2021; and Jerome Thompson, correspondence with author, 9 July 2021.

34. Robbie Winick, correspondence, 8 July 2021; and *Des Moines Register*, 17 May 1998.

35. Robbie Winick, correspondence, 6, 8 July 2021.

36. Sue Biniaz, telephone conversation with author, 21 August 2021; and Celina Biniaz, correspondence, 17 December 2020. See also https://1997-2001.state.gov/publications/statemag/statemag_mar98/featxt3.html, accessed on 14 July 2021.

37. Celina Biniaz, Zoom video conference. On Emilie Schindler's house, see *David Crowe, Oskar Schindler: The Untold Account of His Life, Wartime Activities, and the True Story Behind The List* (Boulder: Westview Press, 2004), 496, and last page of photo gallery.

38. Celina Biniaz, correspondence, 17 December 2020.

39. Ibid; Celina Biniaz, Zoom video conference; and Linda Strachan to Sue Biniaz and Bob Harris, 17 December 2020, Celina Biniaz Papers.

40. See *Los Angeles Times*, 9 March 2004; *Santa Cruz* (California) *Sentinel*, 10 March 2004; and *The Scarlet & Black* (Grinnell College newspaper, Grinnell, Iowa), 24 April 2009.

41. Ibid. For quote, see Celina Biniaz, Zoom video conference, 29 June 2021.

42. Ibid. For quotes and Germain's story see, for example, *Santa Cruz* (California) *Sentinel* 10 March 2004.

CHAPTER TEN

1. Typescript of Celina's remarks at the Shoah Foundation's program, "Memory, Media, and Technology: Exploring the Trajectories of Schindler's List," 16-18 November 2014, Celina Biniaz Papers, private collection held by Celina Biniaz, Camarillo, California, hereafter cited as Celina Biniaz Papers.

2. First quote from Sue Biniaz, telephone conversation with author, 21 August 2021. For Celina's first quote, see https://www.vcstar.com/picturegallery/news/local/communities/camarillo/2018/04/05/camarillo-grandmother-shares-images-of-holocaust/33574459/, accessed on 2 September 2021; for second quote and more on starting to talk publicly, see Celina Biniaz, telephone conversation with author, 17 August 2021.

3. Jane Bohon to Celina Biniaz, 22 June 2004, Celina Biniaz Papers.

4. Celina Biniaz to Jane Bohon, 27 June 2004, Celina Biniaz Papers.

5. Kerry Brennan to Celina Biniaz, 20 November 2012, Celina Biniaz Papers.

6. Chris Daniggelis to Celina Biniaz, 4 January 2020, Celina Biniaz Papers.

7. Bernice Robles to Celina Biniaz, 18 May 2009. For helping students with history projects in general, see Celina Biniaz, correspondence with author, 19 August 2021.

8. Celina Biniaz, correspondence with author, 15 July 2021; and Shoah Foundation flier for *Voices for the List* program, 12 November 2016, Celina Biniaz Papers.

9. Celina Biniaz, telephone conversation, 17 August 2020. For more on event and quote, see Celina Biniaz, correspondence, 15 July 2021.

10. Celina Biniaz, Zoom video conference with author, 29 June 2021; Sue Biniaz, telephone conversation; Alex Biniaz-Harris, telephone conversation with author, 26 August 2021; and Nicholas Biniaz-Harris, telephone conversation with author, 6 November 2021. For Nicholas's quote, see https://www.grinnell.edu/news/defying-darkness, accessed on 25 August 2021.

11. Celina Biniaz, Zoom video conference, 29 June 2021; and Rob Biniaz, telephone conversation with author, 25 March 2021.

12. https://www.grinnell.edu/news/defying-darkness, accessed on 25 August 2021.

13. Rebecca Heller, correspondence with author, 21 October 2021. See also Rebecca Heller to Celina Biniaz, 9, 11, 24, February, 3, 16 March 2009; and Celina Biniaz to Rebecca Heller, 10, 19, 26 February, 5, 7, 18 March 2009, Rebecca Heller Papers, private collection held by Rebecca Heller, Astoria, New York. See also Celina Biniaz, Zoom video conference, 29 June 2021; Celina Biniaz, correspondence, 19 August 2021; *Grinnell Herald-Register*, 13 April 2009; and http://www.thesandb.com/news/holocaust-survivor-and-grinnell-alumna-speaks-at-grinnell.html, accessed on 25 August 2021.

14. Celina Biniaz, Zoom video conference, 29 June 2021. For quote, see Daveen Litwin to Celina Biniaz, 7 May 2009, Celina Biniaz Papers.

15. Celina Biniaz, correspondence, 18 August 2021. Quote is from Norma Maidel to Celina Biniaz, 7 July 2009, Celina Biniaz Papers.

16. Celina Biniaz, telephone conversation, 17 August 2021; and Rita Post, telephone conversation with author, 2 July 2020. For quotes, see Anita Roll, telephone conversation with author, 8 July 2020; Rob Biniaz, telephone conversation with author; Celina Biniaz, telephone conversation, 17 August 2021; and *Des Moines Register*, 31 March 2019.

17. Celina Biniaz, telephone conversation, 17 August 2021. Quote from https://jewishjournal.com/culture/survivor/217308/survivor-celina-biniaz-youngest-schindlers-jews/, accessed on 3 September 2021.

18. Alex Biniaz-Harris, telephone conversation with author, 26 August 2021. For quotation, see https://www.mainlinemedianews.com/mainlinetimes/news/holocaust-survivors-at-barrack-hebrew-oskar-schindler-saved-my-life/article_e55cad72-768c-5cc3-9213-f530a831c7f2.html, accessed on 20 August 2021.

19. Jayne Perilstein, correspondence with author, 26, 27 August 2021.

20. Ibid; see also Celina Biniaz, Zoom video conference; and Alex Biniaz-Harris, telephone conversation.

21. https://www.mainlinemedianews.com/mainlinetimes/news/holocaust-survivors-at-barrack-hebrew-oskar-schindler-saved-my-life/article_e55cad72-768c-5cc3-9213-f530a831c7f2.html, accessed on 20 August 2021; and https://www.yumpu.com/en/document/read/33748591/april-2013-vol-76-no-8-har-zion-temple, accessed on 30 August 2021.

22. https://www.hollywoodreporter.com/news/politics-news/president-obama-at-tends-steven-spielbergs-702223/, accessed on 4 September 2021; Alex Biniaz-Harris, telephone conversation; and Celina Biniaz, Zoom video conference.

23. Quotation is from https://www.pbs.org/newshour/arts/obama-guest-honor-star-studded-benefit-video-testimonials-genocide-survivors, 21 June 2021. See also https://www.pbs.org/newshour/arts/obama-guest-honor-star-studded-benefit-video-testimonials-genocide-survivors, accessed on 25 June 2021.

24. First quote from https://news.usc.edu/62416/obama-honored-with-usc-shoah-foundations-ambassador-for-humanity-award/, accessed on 18 August 2021; longer second quotation from https://www.latimes.com/nation/politics/politicsnow/la-pn-conan-obrien-la-traffic-obama-20140507-story.html, accessed on 18 August 2021.

25. https://www.pbs.org/newshour/arts/obama-guest-honor-star-studded-benefit-video-testimonials-genocide-survivors, accessed on 25 June 2021.

26. Ibid.; and Celina Biniaz, Zoom video conference; Alex Biniaz-Harris, telephone conversation; Rob Biniaz, telephone conversation; and Sue Biniaz, telephone conversation.

27. Rob Biniaz, telephone conversation. For more on this and second quote, see Sue Biniaz, telephone conversation.

28. Stephen Smith and Robert Singer to Celina Biniaz, 19 November 2014, Celina Biniaz Papers; https://news.usc.edu/74321/100-auschwitz-survivors-spielberg-convene-in-historic-gathering/, accessed on 30 August 2021; Celina Biniaz, Zoom video conference; and Sue Biniaz, telephone conversation. See also https://sfi.usc.edu/news/2014/12/7826-auschwitz-past-present-announces-committee-members, accessed on 30 August 2021.

29. Alex Biniaz-Harris, telephone conversation; and https://music.usc.edu/usc-thornton-students-alex-biniaz-harris-and-ambrose-soehn-to-perform-at-auschwitz-ceremony/, accessed on 25 August 2021; and Los Angeles Times, 26 January 2015.

30. Ibid.

31. Alex Biniaz-Harris, telephone conversation.

32. Ibid; and Celina Biniaz, telephone conversation, 17 August 2021. For Alex's quote, see https://splinternews.com/i-went-to-auschwitz-with-my-grandmother-the-youngest-w-1793844634, accessed on 8 September 2021.

33. See https://www.npr.org/sections/thetwo-way/2015/01/27/381862479/holocaust-survivors-mark-70th-anniversary-of-auschwitzs-liberation, accessed on 30 August 2021; https://www.theguardian.com/world/2015/jan/27/auschwitz-memorial-ceremony-extermination-camp-liberation-1944, accessed on 30 August 2021; and https://www.bbc.com/news/world-europe-30996555, accessed on 30 August 2021.

34. https://www.theguardian.com/world/2015/jan/27/auschwitz-memorial-ceremony-extermination-camp-liberation-1944, accessed on 30 August 2021.

35. http://70.auschwitz.org/index.php?option=com_content&view=article&id=18&Itemid=134&lang=en, Accessed on 30 August 2021; and videotape of event, https://www.c-span.org/video/?324020-1/70th-anniversary-liberation-auschwitz, accessed on 30 August 2021.

36. Celina has referred to this "out of body experience" often. See Celina Biniaz, telephone conversations, 16 March 2020; 17 August 2021; and Celina Biniaz, correspondence, 13 September 2021. Second quote from https://www.radioiowa.com/2018/05/18/

holocaust-survivor-from-schindlers-list-is-grinnell-commencement-speaker/, accessed on 10 September 2021.

37. Celina Biniaz, telephone conversation, 16 March 2020. For course title, see course syllabus, Mary Kay Rummel Papers, private collection held by Mary Kay Rummel, Ventura, California.

38. Ibid.; see also Celina Biniaz, Zoom video conference.

39. For quote and general information about course, see Mary Kay Rummel, telephone conversation with author, 23 August 2021.

40. Anita Roll, telephone conversation; Mary Kay Rummel, telephone conversation.

41. To hear Celina read the poem, see https://www.youtube.com/watch?v=H9yfcs-gUeaI, accessed on 27 August 2021; and to see it and several other of her poems, see *Askew* 17 (Fall/Winter 2015), 68-73. For quotation, see Mary Kay Rummel, telephone conversation.

42. Mary Kay Rummel, telephone conversation; and https://www.youtube.com/watch?v=H9yfcsgUeaI, accessed on 27 August 2021.

43. Rummel quote from Mary Kay Rummel, telephone conversation; Roll quote from Anita Roll, telephone conversation; and Celina's quote from Celina Biniaz, Zoom video conference.

44. For first quote and on her writing poetry in general, see Celina Biniaz, correspondence, 15 September 2021; for Rummel quote, see Mary Kay Rummel, telephone conversation; and for Celina's last quote, see Celina Biniaz, telephone conversation, 17 August 2021.

45. See typescript of Celina's remarks at the Shoah Foundation's program, "Memory, Media, and Technology," 16-18 November 2014, Celina Biniaz Papers.

EPILOGUE

1. The original print version of the story was, Peter Flax and Wesley Mann, "The Last Survivors," *The Hollywood Reporter* 25 December 2015, 97-154. I had access to the EBSCOhost version from its film and television literature database with full text and using that pagination for citations. "The Last Survivors," *Hollywood Reporter*, EBSCO version, 2.

2. Ibid, 1-24.

3. Rob Biniaz, telephone conversation with author, 25 March 2021.

4. Ibid.; see also section of article on Celina, Flax and Mann, "The Last Survivors," EBSCOhost version, 11-12.

5. Sandi Yoder, telephone conversation with author, 25 June 2021.

6. Ibid. See also *Des Moines Register*, 9 September 2017; https://www.dmschools.org/2017/09/holocaust-survivor-north-high-alum-celina-karp-biniaz/, accessed on 12 August 2021; and http://www.thesandb.com/article/holocaust-survivor-celina-biniaz-52-spoke-to-students-about-resilience-survival.html, accessed on 12 August 2021.

7. Quote from http://www.thesandb.com/article/holocaust-survivor-celina-biniaz-52-spoke-to-students-about-resilience-survival.html, accessed on 12 August 2021.

8. First two quotes from https://www.jewishdesmoines.org/our-pillars/iowa-jewish-historical-society/our-collection/celina-karp-biniaz/, accessed on 23 September 2021; second quote from https://www.reviewjournal.com/local/local-las-vegas/holo-

caust-survivor-on-schindlers list shares-story-in-las-vegas-1572958/, accessed on 23 September 2021.

9. Sandi Yoder, telephone conversation; Celina Biniaz, telephone conversation with author, 17 August 2021.

10. Ibid.; and Sue Biniaz, telephone conversation with author, 21 August 2021.

11. Sandi Yoder, telephone conversation.

12. Ibid.

13. Ibid.

14. https://www.radioiowa.com/2018/05/18/holocaust-survivor-from-schindlers-list-is-grinnell-commencement-speaker/, accessed on 12 September 2021. For the commencement speech, see https://magazine.grinnell.edu/taxonomy/term/275?page=3, accessed on 12 September 2021.

15. For a videotape of the program, see https://www.jewishdesmoines.org/our-pillars/iowa-jewish-historical-society/our-collection/celina-karp-biniaz/, accessed on 20 August 2021.

16. Ibid. For the poem "Tree" in print, see *Askew* 17 (Fall/Winter 2015), 72-73. "SS *Marine Marlin*" was originally entitled "SS *Sea Marlin*."

17. See https://www.jewishdesmoines.org/our-pillars/ iowa-jewish-historical-society/our-collection/celina-karp-biniaz/, accessed on 20 August 2021.

18. https://baylegal.org/pro-bono-spotlight-rob-biniaz/, accessed on 10 October 2021; and https://www.nytimes.com/2014/04/07/business/lucy-hood-innovative-tv-executive-dies-at-56.html, accessed on 10 October 2021.

19. Celina Biniaz, telephone conversation, 3 April 2020; and Celina Biniaz correspondence with author, 10 November 2021. See also https://thesource.metro.net/2016/10/20/business-interruption-fund-spotlight-next-gen-games/, accessed on 9 November 2021; and Alex Biniaz-Harris, correspondence with author, 11 November 2021.

20. https://unfoundation.org/media/united-nations-foundation-welcomes-sue-biniaz-as-new-senior-fellow-for-climate-change/, accessed on 10 October 2021; https://www.newsecuritybeat.org/2021/03/sue-biniaz-u-s-track-climate-action/, accessed on 10 October 2021; and https://www.law.columbia.edu/faculty/robert-harris, accessed on 10 October 2021.

21. https://www.alexbh.com/about, accessed on 2 November 2021; and Nicholas Biniaz-Harris, telephone conversation with author, 6 November 2021.

22. Anita Roll, telephone conversation with author, 8 July 2020; and Celina Biniaz, conversation with author, Camarillo, California, 31 July 2021.

23. First quote from Anita Roll, telephone conversation; other quotes uotes from chat comments from Celina's DMU program, 9 April 2021, attached to Sandi Yoder, correspondence with author, 24 September 2021.

24. Quote from Sandi Yoder, correspondence with author, 24 September 2021.

INDEX

WILLIAM B. FRIEDRICKS is professor emeritus of history and former director of the Iowa History Center at Simpson College in Indianola, Iowa, where he taught for thirty-three years. His first book, *Henry E. Huntington and the Creation of Southern California,* won the Historical Society of Southern California's Donald Pflueger Award for the outstanding book on Southern California history. Since then, he has written eight books focusing on Iowa topics, including histories of the *Des Moines Register,* the Iowa State Fair's Blue Ribbon Foundation, and several biographies. He was the recipient of Humanities Iowa's Iowa History Prize. Friedricks lives with his wife Jackie in West Des Moines.

The Ice Cube Press began publishing in 1991 to focus on how to live with the natural world and to better understand how people can best live together in the communities they share and inhabit. Using the literary arts to explore life and experiences in the heartland of the United States we have been recognized by a number of well-known writers including: Bill Bradley, Gary Snyder, Gene Logsdon, Wes Jackson, Patricia Hampl, Greg Brown, Jim Harrison, Annie Dillard, Ken Burns, Roz Chast, Jane Hamilton, Daniel Menaker, Kathleen Norris, Janisse Ray, Craig Lesley, Alison Deming, Harriet Lerner, Richard Lynn Stegner, Richard Rhodes, Michael Pollan, David Abram, David Orr, Scott Russell Sanders, and Barry Lopez. We've published a number of well-known authors including: Mary Swander, Jim Heynen, Mary Pipher, Bill Holm, Connie Mutel, John T. Price, Carol Bly, Marvin Bell, Debra Marquart, Ted Kooser, Stephanie Mills, Bill McKibben, Craig Lesley, Elizabeth McCracken, Derrick Jensen, Dean Bakopoulos, Rick Bass, Linda Hogan, Pam Houston, Paul Gruchow, and Bill Moyers. Check out Ice Cube Press books on our web site, join our email list, Facebook group, or follow us on Twitter. Visit booksellers, museum shops, or any place you can find good books and support our truly honest-to-goodness independent publishing projects and discover why we continue striving to "hear the other side."

Ice Cube Press, LLC (Est. 1991)
North Liberty, Iowa, Midwest, USA

Resting above the Silurian and Jordan aquifers
steve@icecubepress.com
Check us out on Twitter and Facebook.
www.icecubepress.com

Celebrating Thirty-One Years of Independent Publishing

To Fenna Marie—
*You are a beautiful "survivor" in your own
ways, finding your voice, learning who you are,
& navigating your way so bravely!*